DISCARDED

*Power and Television
in
Latin America*

Power and Television in Latin America

The Dominican Case

Antonio V. Menéndez Alarcón

PRAEGER

Westport, Connecticut
London

Library of Congress Cataloging-in-Publication Data

Menéndez Alarcón, Antonio V., 1953–
    Power and television in Latin America : the Dominican case / Antonio V. Menéndez Alarcón.
      p. cm.
    Includes bibliographical references and index.
    ISBN 0–275–94275–9 (alk. paper)
    1. Television broadcasting—Social aspects—Dominican Republic.
    2. Television broadcasting—Political aspects—Dominican Republic.
    3. Television broadcasting—Social aspects—Latin America.
    4. Television broadcasting—Political aspects—Latin America.
    I. Title.
PN1992.3.D65M46   1992
302.23′45′097293—dc20   92–383

British Library Cataloguing in Publication Data is available.

Copyright © 1992 by Antonio V. Menéndez Alarcón

All rights reserved. No portion of this book may be reproduced, by any process or technique, without the express written consent of the publisher.

Library of Congress Catalog Card Number: 92–383
ISBN: 0–275–94275–9

First published in 1992

Praeger Publishers, 88 Post Road West, Westport, CT 06881
An imprint of Greenwood Publishing Group, Inc.

Printed in the United States of America

The paper used in this book complies with the Permanent Paper Standard issued by the National Information Standards Organization (Z39.48–1984).

10 9 8 7 6 5 4 3 2 1

Copyright Acknowledgments

Excerpts from interviews with Juan Bosch, Jose Francisco Pena Gomez, Narciso Isa Conde, Rafael Taveras, and Juan B. Mejia appear by permission of the interviewees.

To Rosario
and Laura

Contents

Tables and Figures	ix
Acknowledgments	xi
1. Introduction: The Power of Television	1
2. The Growth of Television and Power Elite Control	15
3. Television as a Medium of Production	35
4. The Cultural Space	57
5. Television in the Marketplace of Ideas: The News	81
6. Election Ritual and Television	119
7. Conclusion: Diversity and Pluralism	155
Appendix A: Procedure	167
Appendix B: Programming on Four Private Networks	171
Appendix C: Television Networks' Share of Audience	179
Appendix D: Typical Editorial of RTVD Newscast	181
Appendix E: International News on Dominican Television: Average of All Networks	183
Bibliography	185
Index	193

Tables and Figures

TABLES

2.1	Television Transmitters in the Americas, 1960–1974	18
2.2	Population of the Dominican Republic, 1935–1988	20
2.3	Television Sets and Radio Receivers in the Dominican Republic, 1955–1990	21
2.4	Cost of Living and Monthly Wages, 1942–1960	22
3.1	The Top Thirty Shows on Dominican Television	43
5.1	Percentage of Time Social Actors Are Present in National Broadcast News	94
5.2	Percentage of International News on Dominican Television, by Continent	114

FIGURES

3.1	Average Ratings, 6 A.M.–2 A.M.	40
3.2	Average Ratings During Prime Time, 6 P.M.–11 P.M.	41
3.3	Average Ratings by Socioeconomic Status, 6 A.M.–2 A.M.	41
6.1	Percentage of Television Political Spots, by Party	147
6.2	Percentage of Television Political Spots, by Political Ideology	147

Acknowledgments

The field work of this study was supported, in large part, by a grant from the Kellogg Institute for International Studies and by the Zahm Travel Grant of the University of Notre Dame.

I wish at this point to express my profound gratitude to the people working in the Dominican television networks who not only allowed me to be present in the networks in order to observe and analyze from the inside, but also agreed to discuss with me their interpretation of television industry. I am grateful also to the people who received the interviewer in their homes and enlarged on their opinion of television. I also owe particular thanks to the leaders of political parties who consented to expose their views on television. Listening to all of them has been enlightening and enjoyable and made writing this work possible.

Eugene Rochberg-Halton offered his careful criticism and made major contributions to my thinking through his suggestions and questions. Martin Murphy, Fabio Dasilva, and Andrew Weigert also made significant comments that contributed to the development of this work. Finally, I wish to thank Hilary Radney whose sharp remarks on earlier drafts helped improve this book. However, any remaining defects are solely the responsibility of the author.

*Power and Television
in
Latin America*

Chapter 1

Introduction: The Power of Television

It's inevitable that I should seem a rather remote figure to many of you—a successor to the kings and queens of history; someone whose face may be familiar in newspapers and films but who never touches your personal lives. But now, at least for a few minutes, I welcome you to the peace of my own home.
 Elizabeth II, first telecast of her annual Christmas address to British Commonwealth, December 25, 1957

As we approached the shanty, I noticed the large brace against the sidewall, which probably helped prevent the leaning building from falling over completely. The house was approximately twenty-four by fifteen feet. The walls were wood and the roof of *cana* (a kind of palm). To the left of the entrance, around nine feet from the house, was the typical fireplace in which Dominican peasants cook their food. The interior of the house was divided into two rooms by a heavy, dark red, frayed curtain, and had very little furniture. Two beds and a small, broken mirror were in what was apparently the bedroom; in the room by which we entered, which could be called the living room, there were four chairs around a small table immediately to the right of the door, two wood rocking chairs in the middle of the room, and a small bed in the far right corner, opposite the table and to the right of the only window.

We were doing research on the sociocultural school environment in the Dominican countryside. A woman, obviously pregnant, invited the other researcher and myself to sit in the rocking chairs and started to answer our questions. She explained that her children, aged nine and eleven, could not go to school because they had to help their father on the farm. "It is the only way we can survive, and especially now that we expect another child."

The first thing we saw when entering the room was a sixteen-inch color television set on a pedestal, facing the rest of the room. One would probably ask: Why do people obviously so poor have a television? Even though the percentage of television sets in the countryside is not as high as in the cities, this was not an exceptional case. During all the years I spent doing research in the Dominican Republic, I met people all over the country who, despite being extremely poor, somehow managed to have a television set; even in areas where there was no electricity, some peasants had television sets powered by batteries. Many peasants acquire television sets as presents from their relatives who have emigrated to the United States, and as many or more decide to buy one at the expense of needs such as food, clothes, and medicines. Whether they buy it or receive it as a gift, the possession of a television set is viewed by these people as a virtual necessity. Such is the importance of television. It was experiences such as this that led me to inquire into the television industry.

Of all the new techniques that have affected human beings today, television is probably the most imbued with sociological significance. Television produces social representations and is at the same time a sign of the social. Television is today considered by most individuals to be indispensable in their lives. It is an element that connects individuals with other people, although rather artificially. Given decreasing face-to-face social interaction in modern life, television increasingly constitutes the point of reference for individuals, and as such plays more and more the role of cultural mediator.

Nobody knows exactly how great the power of television is in shaping society, but it is clear to most scholars of mass media and other commentators that television to a large extent influences the ways people think and represent the world. Most students of mass communication, whether following the critical perspective, the behaviorist perspective, the structuralist-psychoanalytic approach, or the uses and gratifications approach, believe that television has important effects on people. A host of studies have substantiated that television has important long-term consequences. Sometimes it can have short-term consequences as well. For instance, although people apparently do not always believe unconditionally what they see on the screen, for many the pictures presented on television in an apparently objective form provide the only reference to what happens in the outside world; this is particularly true of news stories concerning other countries or facts that people have no way of verifying. The images tend to be more convincing than what is heard or read in other media. The images constitute important points of reference in discussions: "I saw it with my own eyes!"

This book has been written with the view that modern society cannot be totally understood without the study of television. The analysis of television developed here emphasizes the specific television practices that contain an interplay of ideological and economic elements. It is recognized that television content is contextual, and can vary in form and with time as much as any other meanings and human actions. Indeed, whether conceived as part of the superstructure of society or as a material object of production, television is not a separate domain. It does not stand apart from the many other activities and relationships that make up a society, particularly the organized forms of social domination and power relationships.

When we engage in concrete analysis of the machinery of cultural reproduction and domination, we are trying to deconstruct a system of representing the world, to demystify a mechanism. To say that television functions within the system as a whole is the first step in understanding how television works. My purpose goes further, however, and attempts to reveal the mechanisms by which television functions and produces a given cultural content.

However, no research can simultaneously consider all the elements that affect a particular social phenomenon: any research always produces fractional knowledge. The fraction of a larger phenomenon that this book presents concerns the factors and mechanisms that affect television content. This book is about analyzing the process through which television messages are elaborated and the circumstances and influences that mold these elaborations, as well as about analyzing the interests involved in establishing the content of programs. Television messages are not isolated from the context in which they are produced. This medium works in conjunction with other forces and derives, as I hope to show, much of its power from its sociopolitical context. In other words, I attempt to analyze how social relations of power and domination are inscribed within television programming, including the production of its content, which is often held to embody the ideal or normative conception of a society.

I have written this book with the conviction that television criticism will contribute to social criticism, to awakening some reflections, and to enlarging our understanding of the relationships of the communication media to society.

TELEVISION AND SOCIAL PROCESSES IN LATIN AMERICA

Television multiplied and diffused in the period of great production and technological expansion that followed World War II. Since then, this medium has been the object of numerous studies from several approaches. Most of the recent studies and discussions about television in the United States, Europe, and Latin America, although from different perspectives and far from being in agreement about the direct effects that television produces on audiences, acknowledge the relevance of television for social processes and suggest that it plays a fundamental role in modern political and socioeconomic activities. Television is seen as the mass medium par excellence of the modern era. McQuail (1979), for instance, notes that television has to a large degree become responsible for the formation of public opinion, for the rapidity and flow of information, and for the stimulation of consumption. And Cazeneuve (1972) asserts that television is a means of mass communication that by its omnipresence, the immediacy of its action, its intimate association with the individual, and its audiovisual form has a tremendous influence on the population. Elliot (1973), Mattelart (1979), and Pascuali (1977) state that in contemporary society, television has an enormous significance in the transmission of ideas.

Television was introduced into Latin America soon after the United States, and in some Latin American countries, even before some developed countries. Rather than being a result of socioeconomic development, television, in most of these countries, was stimulated largely by foreign broadcasting firms (basically from the United States) and by the political and economic elites' search for national and international prestige and recognition. Indeed, for most people in Latin America, this medium is probably the central symbol of modernity.

Latin America presents disparate characteristics: there are more or less "modernized"[1] sectors within each country; there is no integrated national system organizing the economy and ways of living but, rather, a division by social classes, economic sectors, geography, and so on. The Dominican Republic is no exception to this pattern. Television was established there before such basic elements of development as highways, factories, rural electrification, and water distribution systems.

The Dominican Republic presents several aspects of particular interest for research in mass communication. The electronic mass media had a speedy development there (television was introduced in 1952) and have increased enormously and continually since then. Today the basic flow of information is regulated by television and radio broadcasts: these media, especially television, occupy a large part of the population's leisure time. The presence of television makes a significant difference in the level of information, as it includes in its audience people with a high educational level as well as people who are unable to read. Television plays a very important role in everyday life as well as in political and socioeconomic activities.

PURPOSE OF THE BOOK

As one of society's cultural institutions, television is symbiotically tied to the system that structures and reproduces society. That is, as a cultural subsystem television depends for its functioning on other institutions and subsystems, and they also depend on television. In these interdependent relations power is present, and power implies influence and control. For this reason it is particularly relevant to study the organizations or groups that control television, how this control is exercised, and the consequences of this situation for society. By addressing the interrelations of television with the power elite it is possible to understand the relation between the dominant ideology and its realization through television.

Television's presentation of a particular problem is usually made within a given framework, the limitations of which are imposed by the technology of television, by the specific ideas and employment conditions of journalists (as workers dependent on a salary), by censorship of coverage involving controversial issues by the owners or managers of television stations, and so on. Scholars such as Epstein (1973) and Hirsch (1975) claim that in deciding what to cover, journalists, editors, and news anchors are influenced by the day-to-day job, in which organizational routines, internal power struggles, and commercial imperatives play a basic role in programming. However, even if the ideological consequences of message production are not always intentional, they are present. The work of Argumedo (1982) shows that television exerts a considerable influence on the orientation of democratic policy in Latin America. Likewise, confirming the views of Lippmann (1950), the empirical research of Iyengar, Peters, and Kinder (1984) reveals that what is emphasized by television news programs has important political consequences: "by ignoring some problems and attending to others, television news programs profoundly affect which problems viewers take seriously. . . . Problems prominently positioned in television broadcast loom large in evaluations of presidential performance" (1984, p. 58).

This book aims to reveal the nature of the interdependent relationships between television and the structures of power, and the effects of these relations on television content. The organization of television, its pattern of ownership, and the relations within the networks among the media workers and between them and the owners and sponsors provide us with insights that reveal the nature of television in Dominican society. This book also analyzes how television can contribute to the transformation or to the reproduction of society, and the way in which it specifically affects the political democracy of the Dominican Republic.

In other words, this book is an attempt to interpret the extent to which the structure and the organization in which the television industry is enmeshed (intraorganizational structures and the structures of ownership and control) affect content of entertainment and news programs, the television industry's long-range effects on culture and development, and the extent to which television contributes to the free marketplace of ideas. This book focuses, then, on (1) television's role as intermediary between production and consumption; (2) television as a means of production; (3) television as an apparatus for the diffusion of ideas; and (4) television as an instrument of political power.

The methodology adopted in this book tries to overcome the traditional opposition between the objectivist structuralist perspective represented in the classic works of Marx and Durkheim and the subjectivist perspective found in works of ethnomethodologists such as Garfinkel (1967) and phenomenologists such as Schutz (1962).[2] In my opinion, both approaches reflect a part of social reality; in fact, social structures and everyday human action are dialectically connected. The lifeworld is a compound of structures, representations, and interactions.

I believe that there is simultaneity and continuous linkage between individual action and structural phenomena. The meaning of structures is directly related to the relationships that exist between individuals, between groups, and between institutions. The structures are not independent of the individuals who compose them. As Giddens says, "Structures must not be conceptualized as simply placing constraint upon human agency but as enabling" (1976, p. 161).

My research constitutes, then, an attempt to interpret the television industry—specifically, to implement an institutional analysis—from a structural-phenomenological perspective. In this work the concept "structuralism" is considered not in the tradition of Lévi-Strauss but in a sense closer to the one that it has acquired in the Marxist tradition. In other words, within the social world there exist objective structures, historically produced independently of the consciousness and will of agents, that are able to shepherd the daily activity of these agents as well as their social and individual representations. The term "phenomenology" is based here on Schutz's (1962) interpretation: that social reality has a specific meaning and relevant structure for human beings living, acting, and thinking within it, and that it is therefore possible to discover meanings and explanations for social tendencies through our connection to the person who is part of the analyzed phenomenon.

I looked at this phenomenon within the concrete historical reality of the Dominican Republic. The exercise of the function of television is dependent on certain unique historical conditions, and the variation in its content can be explained in reference to these conditions. The objectives of my research, then, implied not only a definition and classification of television's formal content but also an investigation of the social origins and role of the resulting messages. In response to these concerns, this project concentrated on (1) trends in Dominican television (patterns of ownership, control, etc.); (2) the production of the television message; (3) its content; and (4) the purpose that it serves—in other words, who says what, how, under what conditions, and for what purpose.[3]

FRAMEWORK OF ANALYSIS

The study of television has been influenced by the Frankfurt School, particularly Adorno (1957, 1982), Horkheimer and Adorno (1972), and Marcuse (1964). Television, like other mass media, is seen in this perspective as manipulated by the ruling class in order to reproduce its hegemony over society. It is considered an important agent of persuasion, and the masses are conceptualized as relatively easily influenced by it. Later the works of Lazarsfeld and Menzel (1963), Klapper (1960), and Katz and Lazarsfeld (1955), emphasizing the effects of television on audiences, introduced the concepts of "two-step" and "multiple-step" flows of information. These studies form the basis of what is called the "minimal effects theory." Further studies on the impact of television (Blumler and Ewbank 1969; Belson 1967; Wilson and Gutiérrez 1985; Fiske 1987) have suggested that television does not have an ominous persuasive power but, instead, tends to reinforce prior dispositions and is capable of satisfying a diversity of "uses and gratifications." In this view, television promotes diversity and contributes to the democratization of culture rather than to its standardization.

Other analyses (McLuhan and Fiore 1967; Postman 1985) emphasize television more as a technological device, considering its technological aspects as the basic determinant of its content. In this viewpoint, because of its particular inherent characteristics, particularly its "visual imagery," television creates an environment in which all public discourse takes the form of entertainment. Thus it is a prime contributor to growing cultural inertia.

A different paradigm to evaluate television messages and their impact on audiences is proposed by Hall (1979) and Morley (1980). These scholars assume that a given event can be decoded by the audience in different ways. The message is essentially complex and contains more than one potential reading, although it proposes certain readings over others. In this paradigm the message is treated "neither as a unilateral sign, without ideological flux, nor as in 'uses and gratifications' approach as a disparate sign that can be read anyway" (Morley 1980, p. 10). The message is seen as a structured polysemy. There is an emphasis here on the "control exercised over meaning" by those who produce the message and on the "points of identification" within its communicative structure. Encoding occurs through mechanisms that are particular to a given economic, technical, and social organization of television and its relationships with other social institutions. Therefore, the selection of codes in television responds to the rationality of this particular framework.

Other studies focus more on the process of producing the message and the factors that shape it than on its direct effects on the audience. In this perspective the structure of television is emphasized, relating the medium's content to the cultural, economic, and political environment. Most of the works developed within this perspective have been inspired by the critical theory of the Frankfurt School. For instance, Winick (1959), studying the pressures toward censorship in television, concluded that television is a fairly accurate mirror of maintaining the values of our society. More recently Tuchman (1974) and Herman and Chomsky (1988) hold that the way television is structured in the United States transmits an ideology which contributes to a cultural hegemony of the ruling classes; Paletz and Entman (1984) show the medium's cohesive directing of the socialization of the individual toward approved forms of behavior. Likewise, in a study on the impact of television in a secondary school in Mexico, Martín del Campo and Rebeil Corella state:

Television plays a major role in the day to day recreation of hegemony through its various forms of messages. It educates the dominated classes by communicating beliefs, understandings of social reality, and values. These ideas and feelings about the world and life create acquiescence on the part of the oppressed by the structural system of domination. (1986, p. 146)

Similar conclusions are reached by Pascuali (1977) and Kellner (1988). These authors, analyzing different national realities, found that because television is used as a means of production of benefits, it submits people to a process of massive cultural standardization. In a comparable critical interpretation Debord (1977), studying French television, stated that the ways this medium is used not only modify people's relationship with reality but also contribute to banalizing politics and to limiting the expression of real choices in the electoral process.

Other important works are the analysis of transnational media in Latin America by Mattelart (1979) and Schiller (1971). For these scholars television, as part of the mass communication system, has a transcendental character in the society because the ruling class uses it for perpetuation of power, and the First World countries use it for cultural domination of Third World countries—for instance, U.S. mass media's cultural influence on Latin America.

It is within these latter critical studies (which emphasize the structure and organization of the television industry) that my research is grounded. Most particularly, my research was inspired by a plurality of views within critical theory, such as the political economy of mass media advanced by Murdock and Golding (1987), and by Bourdieu's (1979) and Williams's (1974) thesis that in today's society the cultural and informative content of television is directly related to the nature and context of the production and control of media technologies. This view is further specified by Altheide's (1985) insights on television news formats; by Hall's (1979) explanation of the message interpretation by the audience and of the process by which television discourse becomes "inflected by dominant ideologies"; and by C. Wright Mills's (1956) conceptualization of the power elite. Gerbner's description of the circumstances of message creation in mass media has been particularly pertinent for my research:

This includes such things as external outlook and the internal dynamics of the producing industry; its relationship to competitors; its control over resources, facilities of production, and distribution; the position of its decision makers in the industrial structure, their relationships to audiences, markets, advertising sponsors. The social determinants of cultural industry thus find their way into the consequential meaning of the material. They are expressed not so much in conventional forms and "messages" as through patterns of selection, omission, juxtaposition, through just the way things are "looked at." (1968, p. 482)

Although these critical studies examine different factors of the television industry, when brought together, they present a comprehensive view of the ways in which television messages are created and shaped. Together, these conceptualizations, produced in different countries, offer effective insights for a sociological study of television in a developing country of Latin America, such as the Dominican Republic, and constitute important elements with which to contrast and compare some of the findings of this research. Some of these theories are more or less universal, and I expect the results of this study to be. However, there are aspects inherent in the Dominican Republic that cannot be totally explained by these theories. It is the aim of this book to contribute not only to the general theory of mass communications but also to start developing a sociological theory of television in the Dominican Republic. Indeed, except for a survey of television programming (Straubhaar and Viscasillas 1991), most studies have concerned the mass media in general. The most relevant of these works were published in *Revista Ciencia* by the Universidad Autónoma de Santo Domingo in 1975.[4]

The organization of the Dominican television system is largely based on the U.S. television system; it also has similarities with systems of other Latin American countries, which follow the U.S. model. This is a result of the internalization of production and of cultural merchandise that goes with the adaptation of a given television system. Thus, the fact that this analysis concerns the Dominican Republic does not isolate it from the television system in most American countries or in other parts of the world. Particularly, since the basic structure of Dominican television is similar to that of other Latin American countries, much of what was learned is generalizable to other developing countries of the Americas.[5] This study made it possible, then, to interpret the characteristics and consequences of a television-reliant society in a nation where modernization and stagnation are opposite sides of the same coin.[6]

Dominican television started and was shaped at its beginnings under the dictatorship of Trujillo, adopting a form close to Orwell's *1984*. In its subsequent development, television most closely followed the U.S. model, which bears a closer resemblance to Huxley's *Brave New World*, in which people willingly accept the mechanisms that oppress them.

ORGANIZATION OF THE BOOK

Chapter 2 is a historical overview of the growth of television in the Dominican Republic. It attempts to show the relationship between the development of television and specific political and economic processes. It is demonstrated that the constitution and functioning of the national broadcasting system have been shaped by internal as well as international influences. This chapter examines the process of control of television by the nation's power elite, beginning in 1952 under the dictatorship of Trujillo, through the transition to electoral democracy, and on to the present. It shows how it was used by the politically powerful under the dictatorship of Rafael L. Trujillo and exposes the mechanisms used by the dictator to control broadcast content. The start of privately owned television and its evolution under electoral democracy is also explained, showing particularly the process of concentration of ownership.

Chapter 3 is an analysis of the structure and organization of the television industry in the Dominican Republic and the factors that influence program content. After a descriptive analysis of the networks' organization and their relations with sponsors and advertising agencies, the type of programming that predominates in Dominican television is examined, and the causes of a tendency toward the same type of program in all the networks are assessed. Next, the logic of ratings and the traditional ways of classifying audience tastes within the television industry are discussed and questioned; it is suggested that the audience's desires concerning television entertainment change from day to day. Finally, the importance of the economic structure in the shaping of television programming and the value of television as a cultural commodity are addressed.

The cultural aspects of the television industry are emphasized in Chapter 4. This chapter attempts to outline the specific role that television plays for the Dominican audience and its importance as a conveyer of cultural values and representations, showing the impact of U.S. transnational companies on local advertising. It is revealed that television is perceived differently by people belonging to different socioeconomic strata. Furthermore, it is suggested that television's role as a social agent is affected by the economic requirements of the structure in which it is enmeshed, and is largely determined by the industry's perception of mass culture. The fundamental cultural message of television is a consequence of its transforming the audience into consumers and promoting consumption of particular merchandise and the symbols of that merchandise.

The role of television in the circulation of ideas and opinions is analyzed in Chapter 5. This chapter examines the production of television news in the Dominican Republic, including the international flow of news, and particularly the effects of the free market economy on television. The informative role of television is affected both by its own economic dependency and by the structure of power in which it is enmeshed. By analyzing how effectively different social and political groups in Dominican society are represented on television, it is revealed that even though some voices of dissent are allowed—presenting a facade of pluralism more extensive than in other countries of Latin America and even in the United States—the information diffused by Dominican television as a whole corresponds essentially to the basic elements and interests of a business-oriented society. Not only is the fundamental message of television newscasts largely biased toward the status quo, but the assumption of the right to hear different opinions is subverted by the commercial role of television.

Chapter 6 studies the use of television in Dominican politics, analyzing the electoral campaign of 1990. The relationship between the use of television and the availability of money is asserted, along with the interrelationship of television, the economic elite, and the conservative political sectors. The mechanisms by which television contributes to the stability and legitimation of the proponents of the status quo are described. Instances of interactions between television networks and politics are recorded. It is also shown that television has affected the structure and functioning of political campaigns. This chapter deals with the ways television handles political events, and the extent to which democracy is truly served by this medium. As a result of the growing reach and importance of television in political campaigns, politicians are more and more dependent on television for gaining political power and for survival as public figures. Therefore, the control of television by the economic elite, which predominantly pushes for the reproduction of the reigning system, limits the ability to carry out changes. The connections between television's economic objectives and political parties are shown, demonstrating that television professionals have considerable limitations imposed upon them by those who control the economics of the industry (owners, sponsors, and government). The relationship between economic power and political power through television is discussed.

This book concludes with an assertion of the overall effects of the commercial television system that predominates in the Dominican Republic on the diversity of programming and the informative pluralism of television, relating the possibilities for diversity and pluralism to the economic function that television fulfills of constantly stimulating the creation of new markets and promoting new items of consumption among audiences, as well as its structural relationship with the power elite.

NOTES

1. Understanding by "modern" the ways of life and organization of economy that characterize the urban sectors of industrial and postindustrial societies.

2. Durkheim wrote: "Social life must be explained, not by the conception of those who participate in it, but by deep causes which lie outside of consciousness" (1970, p. 250). Schutz holds the opposite view: "The thought objects constructed by the social scientists in order to grasp... social reality have to be founded upon the thought objects constructed by the common-sense thinking of men, living their daily life within their social world. Thus the constructs of the social sciences are, so to speak, constructs of the second degree, that is, constructs of the constructs made by the actors on the social scene" (1962, p. 59).

3. "Who" refers to the stations' owners and to those shaping broadcast messages (mainly management staff and journalists), their characteristics (principally political and economic), and perceptions of reality. "What" refers to the messages' content (basically ideas broadcast). "How" concerns the techniques of elaboration and broadcasting of the message (images, stereotypes, key words, camera angle, etc.). "Under what conditions" relates to the structure of television stations, their functioning, economic situation, and so on. "For what purpose" refers to the objective of the message: the reaction the broadcasting agency expects to evoke in the listener.

4. Volume 2, no. 2 (April-June 1975) of this journal was a special issue on the mass media in the Dominican Republic. It included "La Ideología en los Medios de Comunicación de Masas," by José del Castillo et al.; "Usos de Comunicación Colectiva en Santo Domingo," by Rafael Villalba; "Una Semana de Prensa en la República Dominicana: Análisis Cuantitativo y Estudio de Prensa Comparado," by Manuel Quiterio Cedeño; "La Investigación de la Comunicación Social," by Alberto Villaverde; and "Análisis de la Programación Diaria de Radio Guarachita," by Ramonina Brea.

5. According to the descriptions of the characteristics of television in other countries of Latin America made by Roncagliolo (1988), Ecuador, Venezuela, Bolivia, and Peru currently present similar situations. Typically, in Central and South America, governments own one network, but in general the television system is very commercial, fashioned on the U.S. model. The government's networks sell a large share of their airtime to individual producers or companies. Free enterprise is encouraged to a large extent, except in situations of crisis. Another feature of broadcasting similarities between the above-mentioned Latin American countries and the Dominican Republic is that the networks are controlled by a few companies, which are generally owned by rich and powerful families.

The transfer of broadcasting in the form of systems and institutions has meant that the financial structure of the most technologically advanced countries has to be adopted. This explains why in Africa most countries have a broadcasting system with important state participation, following the model of European powers such as France and Great Britain, and why in Latin America the broadcasting system was established on the U.S. model.

6. Furthermore, the Dominican Republic offered the author the possibility of performing empirical research because of the access he had to the networks and to other institutions of the society. Therefore, he was able to develop an empirically grounded theoretical model of interpretation.

Chapter 2

The Growth of Television and Power Elite Control

The history of television in the Dominican Republic can be divided into two periods: the first from its beginning in 1952 until the fall of Trujillo in 1961, and the second from 1961 to the present. From 1930 to 1961 the country was under the virtual dictatorship of U.S.-backed Rafael Leonidas Trujillo y Molina, even though he was not always the formal head of the government. He was officially president of the republic from 1930 to 1938 and from 1942 to 1952. Trujillo came to power after a campaign of terror against his political opposition, a few years after the first intervention of the United States in the Dominican Republic. It is difficult to say whether he was put into power with the active support of the U.S. government, but he was certainly helped considerably in the early years. What is clear, as Wiarda points out, is that "United States money, arms and moral support, during almost all the span of the Trujillo era, helped maintain the regime, and "the United States is still held accountable by many Dominicans for the atrocities, terrorism, and corruption of all kinds that marked his lengthy tenure"[1] (1968, pp. 137–138).

Trujillo was assassinated in 1961 by a group of high officers of the armed forces, according to several authors, with the collaboration of the Central Intelligence Agency.[2] He had enjoyed the confidence of the U.S. government for almost thirty years, during which he implemented an extremely brutal dictatorship. Torture and assassination of supposed political opponents were part of everyday life. He used the resources of the Dominican state for his enrichment, and committed such abuses of human rights as a new interpretation of the *jus primae noctis* of the Middle Ages (a custom that gave the lord the right to sleep with the vassal's wife the first night of marriage): according to several authors and people I interviewed, the dictator allowed himself the right to have any woman he wanted, regardless of her matrimonial situation.

Only at the beginning of the 1960s, when economic disputes with Trujillo's government arose, did the U.S. government withdraw its support and become his enemy. The fear that communism could gain support in the country—particularly considering the success of the Cuban uprising against Fulgencio Batista in 1959— and the growth of opposition to Trujillo in all sectors of society, including large groups within the Catholic Church (long Trujillo's most valuable ally), also played an important role in the U.S. attitude toward the Trujillo government.

THE FIRST EPOCH: THE YEARS OF THE DICTATORSHIP

Television in the Dominican Republic, as in most nations, arose from an existing radio network. This new enterprise inherited the name and the structure of the radio station La Voz Dominicana (The Dominican Voice). This radio station was a continuation of La Voz del Yuna, which was owned and run by José Aristides Trujillo (popularly called Petán), brother of the dictator. La Voz del Yuna, which originally was a regional station, had moved to the capital in 1942, with the objective of becoming a national station.[3] Several relays were installed around the country. La Voz del Yuna broadcast in shortwave and in AM, and had very good and modern equipment.

Radio developed rapidly in the Dominican Republic, especially in the late 1940s and early 1950s. By 1955 there were 31 radio stations broadcasting to 15,000 radio receivers (United Nations 1960). Trujillo allotted several private licenses for radio stations to some of his cronies, among them people who knew nothing about radio broadcasting. People in the broadcasting industry state that Trujillo granted these licenses with the intention of filling the dial in order to prevent the broadcast of information adverse to his administration. He had enemies among the governments of Latin American countries, in particular those of Colombia, Venezuela under Rómulo Betancourt, Costa Rica under José Figueres, and Cuba under Carlos Prío Socarrás. For a time, Trujillo used a well-equipped and efficient system of communication provided by U.S. companies to jam broadcasting from foreign stations. This system produced a noise in the receivers that the Dominicans called *el abejón* (The hornet) because it resembled the sound of a hornet in flight. Eventually, however, Trujillo decided that it was more effective to fill the radio dial. In this way the population of the Dominican Republic was almost completely alienated from the rest of the world. Only the ideas censored and authorized by Trujillo were allowed.

Eager to project the country as one of the most advanced in America, Trujillo soon converted the radio station La Voz Dominicana to a radio-television enterprise.[4] The first television network was inaugurated in the capital of the country, Ciudad Trujillo, in August 1952.[5] The Dominican Republic was among the pioneers of television in Latin America. Indeed, television was still in the process of development in the industrialized countries. It had started only eleven years before in the United States.[6] The next countries to inaugurate television broadcasting in America were Cuba, Brazil, and Mexico, in 1950. Argentina followed in 1951, as did Canada and Venezuela in 1952 (See Table 2.1).

Also in 1952 the first Dominican commercial FM system was established, along with several relay stations and a more powerful broadcasting system for the radio division. The radio broadcast of the FM and AM station was powerful enough to reach all of the country as well as other countries in America and even in Europe. This determination to reach other countries was inspired by Trujillo's desire for grandeur and by a desire to compete in the international broadcasting arena so as to dispel the negative image of his regime.

In the inauguration speech given by the president of the company, José Aristides Trujillo, we can see the role that was assigned to this television network: "The debt owed to Excellency President Trujillo by La Voz Dominicana is profound. President Trujillo is the archetype of the statesman, whom . . . future generations will contemplate as we contemplate, ourselves, the sun of midday"[7] (*La Nación* 1952, p. 8).

Later José Trujillo constructed a modern building to house the radio-television company La Voz Dominicana-TV (LVD-TV). This station still occupies the same building. LVD-TV reached the whole country except a small part in the east and is still the most powerful network in the country in terms of coverage.

LVD-TV, officially a private enterprise, was largely at the service of the government. In fact, Trujillo used the state resources as he wished. There was no real difference between what belonged to him and his family and what belonged to the state. He appropriated everything he wanted, even what belonged to others.[8] Not only was the state apparatus under his control, but so were most of the best land and biggest enterprises of the country.[9] Bosch (1961) asserts, "The government was only a public organ of a capitalist enterprise"—Trujillo's enterprise. The grand capitalists who could survive and develop their enterprises were people close to him, or who accepted his directives.

LVD-TV was an ideological apparatus in the service of Trujillo's regime. Social, political, and military events at which the dictator or his relatives were present dominated the programming. The news was dull propaganda,[10] and the entertainment shows served three functions: they offered the popular entertainment needed to balance authoritarianism of the regime, they were an important source of revenue for Trujillo and his family,[11] and they carried a great deal of pro-Trujillo propaganda. Enter-

Table 2.1
Television Transmitters in the Americas, 1960–1974

Country	Date of First Regular Broadcast	1960	1965	1970	1974
Antigua	1965		1	1	–
Argentina	1951	4	16	55	82
Barbados	1964	–	1	1	2
Bermuda	1958	1	2	2	2
Bolivia	1969	–	–	1	2
Brazil	1950	42	42	50	78
Canada	1952	98	262	360	661
Chile	1959	–	3	4	76
Colombia	1954	13	15	15	74
Costa Rica	1960	2	3	8	12
Cuba	1950	27	25	–	–
Dominican Republic	1952	4	4	6	10
Ecuador	1959	1	4	14	19
El Salvador	1956	3	3	3	7
Guatemala	1956	2	3	3	12
Guyana	1965	–	4	–	–
Haiti	1959	1	1	1	2
Honduras	1959	1	3	5	6
Jamaica	1963	–	7	12	13
Mexico	1950	29	33	78	83
Netherlands Antilles	1960	–	2	3	–
Nicaragua	1956	–	2	7	7
Panama	1959	1	10	13	13
Paraguay	1965	5	16	18	52
Peru	1958	5	16	18	52
Puerto Rico	1954	–	10	17	17
St. Pierre and Miquelon	1967	–	1	3	3
St. Vincent	1974	–	–	–	2
Suriname	1968	–	1	3	6
Trinidad and Tobago	1962	–	2	2	3
United States	1941	579	2555	2703	3695
Uruguay	1956	1	4	17	17
Venezuela	1952	14	27	30	49

Source: UNESCO, 1976a, 1976b; UCLA, 1960–1975.

tainers, even those from other countries of Latin America, had to praise Trujillo in their appearances on television.

The first program broadcast by LVD-TV gives eloquent evidence of the entertainment shows' propagandist character during that period. The first image that appeared on the air was the Dominican flag, a symbol used to strengthen the rhetoric of nationalism that the dictator used extensively (the flag traditionally is so used by the most conservative political forces around the world). The program was a live comedy show set in a rural environment.[12] Several references to the "civilizing enterprise" of Trujillo were made. To close the show, a popular Dominican singer presented a merengue[13] praising the dictator, "La Voluntad de Trujillo" (The Will of Trujillo).

Most of the news telecast by LVD-TV was based on information from the newspapers *El Caribe* and *La Nación*, both owned by Trujillo. Therefore, television news programs were merely a reproduction of the official voice that had previously appeared in the newspapers. The news from international agencies (received by Teletype) was carefully filtered according to government interests. The editorials were dedicated to nurturing the megalomania of Trujillo and to exerting psychological terror on the Dominican people. In fact, LVD-TV, like other media, was to a great extent an instrument for terrorizing the Dominican people.

In the early period, LVD-TV had limited programming. It started every day at 5 P.M. and ended at 10 P.M. In the 1950s the Dominican population, who numbered just over 2 million, was still very rural. The two most populous urban centers in 1950 were Santo Domingo (then called Ciudad Trujillo), with 181,553 inhabitants, and Santiago, with 56,558 inhabitants (see Table 2.2). People did not stay up late at night except on the weekends. Furthermore, in the 1950s, the Dominican Republic was one of the poorest countries of Latin America. Therefore, few homes in the countryside or even in the urban centers had a television set. According to data from the United Nations (1960) there were only 2,000 television sets (see Table 2.3). A set cost almost a year's income for a worker or small farmer (see Table 2.4). Moreover, most of the country lacked electricity. The majority of sets were in Santo Domingo (then Ciudad Trujillo), and a few were in other urban centers (Santiago, San Francisco, La Romana) where people had enough economic resources (cash income) to afford the price of a television set. Those who could afford an expensive item were the commercial and industrial classes, big landowners (*latifundistas*), high government officials, and successful urban professionals. The first television sets were imported by the owner of the only television network (LVD-TV), the dictator's brother, to be sold and to be distributed in public places of the capital and other cities. People rushed to watch it.

In January 1959, LVD-TV extended its programming with thirty-five new shows of various types. Some were educational,[14] but the bulk were entertainment shows—comedies, movies, game shows, musical shows—and reporting of government activities. In fact, every event in which the dictator participated was subject matter for a special broadcast, and for preempting the scheduled programming. Special broadcasts were also produced to launch campaigns in support of Trujillo against any local or foreign adversary. Furthermore, government repression of political opponents was telecast in order to instill fear into the population and discourage any hint of political opposition.

Table 2.2
Population of the Dominican Republic, 1935–1988

Year	1935	1950	1960	1970	1980	1988
Total Population	1,479,417	2,135,872	3,047,070	4,006,000	5,431,000	6,600,000

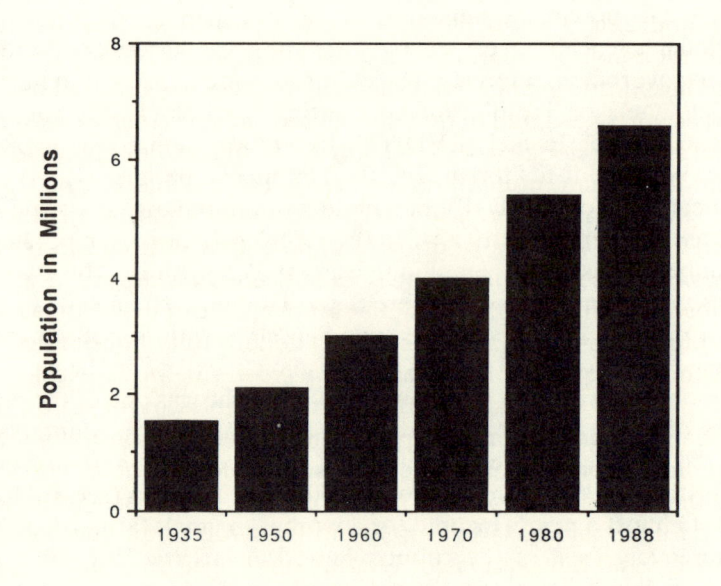

Population of Major Cities, 1935–1960

Year	1935	1950	1960
Santo Domingo	71,091	181,553	369,980
Santiago	34,175	56,558	85,640

Sources: Oficina Nacional de Estadísticas, Secretariado Técnico de la Presidencia, several volumes; UNESCO 1976a, 1976b; *Europa World Year Book* 1990.

Throughout the Trujillo regime LVD-TV modernized its equipment. It also attached particular importance to the education of personnel (artists as well as technicians). The company had a school for the training of anchormen, dancers, actors, and singers. Furthermore, it hired foreign technicians (most of them from the United States) to train its Dominican employees in television production. Despite the few technicians with extensive knowledge of that medium, Dominican television in the first years of its existence was not very different in quality from what was produced

Table 2.3
Television Sets and Radio Receivers in the Dominican Republic, 1955–1990

	1955	1960	1965	1970	1975	1980	1985	1990
TV Sets								
Number	6,000	15,000	55,000	110,000	190,000	400,000	550,000	670,000
Per 1,000 Inhabs.	2.50	4.90	14.20	25.00	33.60	71.40	85.90	98.50

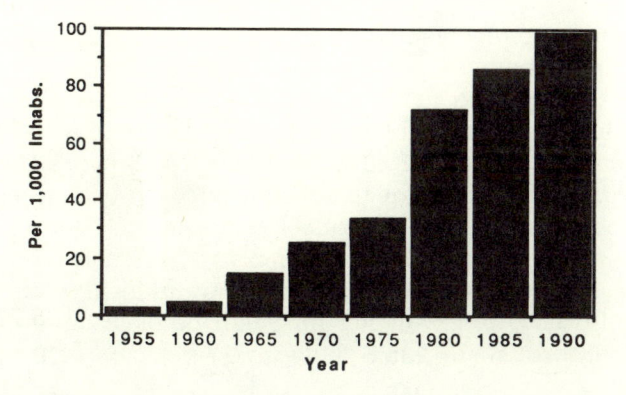

Sources: UNESCO 1959, 1983–1987; CEPAL 1983, *Anuario Estadístico de América Latina*; *Europa World Yearbook* 1990.

in the few countries of Latin America that had television, and even from the United States.[15]

The organization of LVD-TV was very similar to that of the military. According to Luis Lora Medrano (1984), who was for a long time anchorman and producer, there was a rigorous discipline; uniformity in dressing was mandatory, and the "most absolute devotion to the fulfillment of duties" was required. There was also a group called "radial observers" who watched everything broadcast. Their official function was checking the quality of work, but also, and probably more important for the regime, they prevented the transmission of information, however subtly, unfavorable to Trujillo. Each day the observers handed in a report to the director of the TV station that included anything they judged unacceptable. At the art school, the discipline and the order were so rigorous that in each studio, during the students' rehearsals, there was a uniformed inspector who reported any irregularity to the general administration of the station.

Table 2.4
Cost of Living and Monthly Wages, 1942–1960

Year	Cost of Living (1940=100)	Monthly Wages (Indexed)
1942	120.4	16.41
1943	150.0	19.00
1944	170.0	20.14
1945	181.0	23.22
1946	201.7	29.11
1947	226.7	34.83
1948	228.9	38.9
1949	220.1	35.83
1950	219.7	32.65
1951	238.3	33.43
1952	240.6	39.18
1953	237.2	38.41
1954	232.4	36.03
1955	232.4	35.77
1956	235.5	36.14
1957	246.9	36.32
1958	242.1	38.90
1959	241.8	36.34
1960	233.00	–

Source: Gómez 1979.

LVD-TV was portrayed as an independent enterprise, but nobody believed this. For the Dominican people, the independence of this network was only a sophism. It was owned by Trujillo's brother, and thus it was completely at the service of the regime. Trujillo had extensively utilized this means of communication to propagate his ideas, to condition the people to share his interests, and particularly to fight against political opponents. Opinion groups did not have access to the mass media.[16] No medium could be established and survive if it did not submit to Trujillo or did not take an obviously friendly attitude toward his government.

On March 1, 1959, a second television network was inaugurated: Rahintel, an enterprise that also operated an AM-FM radio station. The Dominican Republic, with two television networks, was then at the forefront of America with regard to the electronic media. The inauguration address delivered by the president of the company, Pedro P. Bonilla, was a clear testimony that this new television station would be at the service of the bourgeoisie:

> Rahintel came as a new contribution to the policy of cultural diffusion initiated by this government. This enterprise has been no more than a will and an aspiration to serve the cultivated Dominican people, to bring them the happiness and spiritual joy that they deserve, and to serve the business and industrial classes as an efficient and effective means to divulge their claims.

Rahintel was on the air from 6:05 P.M. to 10:05 P.M. Monday through Saturday, and from 12:05 P.M. to 2:05 P.M. on Sundays. Its programming consisted of shows with some cultural and religious content, but above all it offered traditional commercial television programming: game shows, animated cartoons, and U.S. movies, which were preferred by Dominican youngsters to those of Mexican and Spanish origin aired by LVD-TV. Rahintel reached only the capital and its suburbs, but this was not really a handicap; at that time most television sets were concentrated in Ciudad Trujillo. Although LVD-TV had a more extended schedule and covered most of the country, the competition was significant, since Rahintel offered more diverse programming and, most important, it gave less time than LVD-TV to the reporting of government acts and Trujillo's political meetings that had saturated the Dominican people.[17] But it does not appear that this television network had any political importance during its short time of operation under the Trujillo regime. It would not be allowed any content criticizing the government in any way.

THE SECOND EPOCH

The Trujillo regime fell as a result of the dictator's assassination on May 30, 1961. LVD-TV became the property of the Dominican state, as did most of the other holdings of the Trujillo family (land, factories, business, etc.). It was renamed Radio Televisión Dominicana. Theoretically, this network was to fulfill a cultural and educational role; however, it has presented mainly entertainment programming and frequently has been used as the government's political instrument, although in a more subtle way than during Trujillo's dictatorship.

With the fall of Trujillo, the country started to live a kind of political democracy (at least until 1965 and again after 1978)[18] that tolerated some freedom of speech and allowed the bourgeoisie to exert more influence on society. Trujillo's death made possible the beginning of privately owned television. Furthermore, the country experienced economic improvement; between 1965 and 1980 the annual increase in the Dominican Republic's gross domestic product averaged 7.3 percent in real terms, one of the highest growth rates in the world.

In this period, television coverage and the programming were extended (from morning until late at night), and new networks were founded. In 1969 the first network to transmit in color, Colorvisión, appeared.[19] The principal owner of this enterprise is the Bermúdez family, the biggest rum producers in the country. Colorvisión usually achieved the highest ratings of prime time programming in the period 1985–1990.

The next network to arise was Teleinde (independent television) in 1973. According to its owner, José Semonile, this network was conceived as the first cultural television network in the country, but this project could not be realized because of economic limitations. Mr. Semonile was neither a big capitalist nor tied to any important economic group; furthermore, the idea of a cultural network was very far from the interests of those who had the financial resources to support the project. At that time Teleinde was not even a network, since it covered only the capital city. In the mid-1980s it was placed on the market, and Jacinto Peynado, a businessman from an old and powerful family (import-export is among his most important businesses) and a politician linked to the conservative Social Christian Reformist Party (he is presently a senator), became Teleinde's major stockholder. This network is also owned by the Hazoury family, who are, after Peynado, its largest stockholders.

Currently Teleinde is more often identified as TV13. Its new format appeared in 1986, after the elections of May 16. Though it was ready to start broadcasting at the end of 1985, the government (under the presidency of Salvador Jorge Blanco, of the Dominican Revolutionary Party), citing problems of wave interference between stations operating on the same channel, denied the network the right to start broadcasting. Actually, the government feared it would be used as a political instrument of the Social Christian Reformist Party during the political campaign. Teleinde reaches only half of the country. Its programming tends to follow that of the other networks, although it allows more time to interview programs with special emphasis on politics and economics.

In the same period Rahintel changed ownership. In 1983 this network became the property of Grupo Financiero Universal, whose principal stockholder is Leonel Almonte, a businessman who in a few years built an economic empire during the Blanco administration.[20]

Telesistema Dominicano, inaugurated in 1978, is owned by Pepín Corripio, one of the most important capitalists of the country. Besides this network, he also presently owns and manages a second television network, Teleantillas; two national newspapers; a weekly magazine; import-export firms; and industrial concerns. He also has large participation in banking. This network did not have a special impact. Its programming was composed of traditional commercial programs, relying heavily on soap operas and U.S. serials.

A year later Teleantillas appeared, revolutionizing Dominican television by its modern technological resources. Teleantillas was situated in a very modern and comfortable building. The network had all the modern requirements of a television studio, and at that time it was the biggest and best television network from the technological point of view. It offered a brighter picture, better color, and very well decorated stages. It aired several new serials that drew a large audience. Its programming consisted of many U.S. serials and of musical spectacles, some of them produced in the Dominican Republic.

Teleantillas arose as part of the rebirth of the publishing company El Caribe, which publishes the newspaper of the same name. This company, which belonged to Trujillo, had been transferred (for a not yet elucidated reason)[21] to the Ornes family, who had always been linked to journalism and who had high social prestige in the country. They were the managers of the newspaper *El Caribe* under Trujillo's rule. This newspaper has always presented an ultra right-wing editorial line. However, the television network went on the air with a more centrist editorial line. Like the competing networks, it devoted some time to diverse opinions and even social claims. In other words, it adapted to the market in order to enter the homes of the very politicized Dominican people. Teleantillas covers all the country except parts of the southwest and east.

Later this network, which had first place in the ratings during the late 1970s, lost popularity and started to suffer from economic problems. José Luis (Pepín) Corripio, the owner of Telesistema, became the major stockholder. Today Teleantillas has a large group of stockholders who include the wealthiest families of the country; the most important after Corripio are the Bonetti family, which has investments in most economic sectors, especially the agroindustry; the Vicini-Cabrals, the largest private producers of sugarcane; E. León Jiménez, the largest producer of tobacco; and Villeya-San Miguel, whose major businesses are agrochemicals and finance.

In 1987 the network Independencia was established, but until May 1990 (when I ended my field research), it only telecast movies. The largest stockholder of this network is the Gómez Díaz family, importers of appliances.

By 1990, these networks were on the air for more than 780 hours a week altogether. It was estimated that there were 85.9 television sets per thousand inhabitants (see Table 2.3) in the country in 1988. In my opinion, there were probably more.[22] Thus, today, though the country has little industry and the general economy is continually declining, and most of its 7 million inhabitants live in poverty, there are seven television networks (six private and one state-owned), nineteen relay stations, three cable TV companies that together broadcast more than thirty channels (most from the United States and a few from Mexico),[23] and some forty radio stations. More than 95 percent of homes have a radio and more than 65 percent have a television set.[24] Thus, in respect to the mass media and their use, the Dominican Republic is quite advanced for a Third World country.[25] Today the flow of information is regulated by television and radio; these media, especially television, occupy a large part of the population's leisure time.

With the development of television a certain awareness of public life has developed throughout the Dominican Republic. People receive opinions on subjects they would not know about without television, especially given the high illiteracy rate among the adult population.[26] Furthermore, interpersonal relations involving direct contact, especially in the urban areas, have eroded; people experience a more fragmented life than in the past. As a result, television has increasingly taken on a role of social control and of cultural institution—that is, television is an apparatus through which people learn the culture of their society. As with family, school, and other factors, television constitutes an agent of socialization. Television is more and more responsible for providing the cultural basis on which Dominican people construct a meaning for their lives.

As in most countries of the Third World with a dominant capitalist system, Dominican society presents a complex and hierarchical patchwork in which precapitalist modes of production exist within the predominant system. The economy of the country depends basically on the exportation of primary products (sugar, tobacco, gold, and silver) and on the tourism industry. The most important enterprises are more or less organized according to the modern capitalist model (some are controlled by only one family, and others by small groups of stockholders). The state plays a large role in the economy, as direct producer or investor, especially in the sugar industry and in tourism (a good number of enterprises are state property),[27] and indirectly through exemptions and other incentives to encourage private investments and production. Around 70 percent of the exports go to the United States (O.N.E. 1987, 1988). The production of manufactured goods is limited to middle-sized enterprises. The Dominican Republic is a major importer of electric, electronic, and automotive products. Its current external debt exceeds $5 billion, and production is in continual decline. Even the financial sector, which had continued to progress considerably until the mid–1980s, is now experiencing serious difficulties.[28]

Television has added a substantial burden to the foreign-exchange resources that the Dominican Republic has to raise, and it has made it more dependent on nations capable of supplying the technology required for broadcasting. The basic structure of the networks requires large investments, and the production equipment that needs to be replaced is particularly expensive; for instance, according to a network administrator, a color television camera costs between $120,000 and $160,000; a videotape recorder for recording color television programs on magnetic tape costs between $80,000 and $110,000; and a telecine (device used for showing films on television) costs between $45,000 and $80,000. Almost all production and distribution equipment of the Dominican television networks comes from the United States, and most television sets are provided by Asian countries (Japan, Taiwan, South Korea). The value of imports of these goods has increased since 1980 because of the devaluation of the Dominican peso in relation to the dollar.[29]

The power elite in the Dominican Republic has always stated the importance of television for socioeconomic development and for national culture. The Dominican ruling class, whether under dictatorship or in an electoral democracy, presents itself as the defender of Dominican interests and of the well-being of the nation, equating the pursuit of class interests with the pursuit of the national interest. The reality is that the concern for the country that the ruling class proclaims is not reflected in its actions. Narrow and immediate political interests, and the search for personal prestige and profits, have overwhelmed any other goal in the constitution and development of television.

The economic groups which own the networks are the same groups that control the largest part of the country's economy. They have investments in most areas of the economy (finance, industry, tourism, agriculture, etc.). These groups, which constitute the ruling class, have the highest concentration of wealth and occupy the most important positions in the economic and political power system.

The boom in television since 1970 reflects four basic factors: (1) a need of businesses to attract consumers (television growth is directly related to the growth of advertising agencies); (2) considerable capital available for corporate groups; (3) television's seeming to be a relatively stable investment and to offer the possibility of very good profits; and (4) the possibility of its serving as an instrument to defend the owners' interests.

The predominant system in the Dominican Republic, taken as a whole, tends to create a system of mass communication that can be analyzed in the context of Gramsci's theory of cultural hegemony. Dominican society is composed of social and ethnic groups and subcultures that are held together in a network of relations in which the most sharply differentiated factor is the unequal distribution of power and wealth. As Gramsci writes: "Power relations in societies with high and structural levels of inequality are maintained through physical and symbolic violence and through the creation of acquiescence, even consent, by subaltern social classes to an exploitative social order" (1979, p. 204).

But how does this kind of social control and cultural diffusion operate in a system of electoral democracy? Is the complex and multiform television industry in the Dominican Republic used by a particular party or political power to manipulate, control, or determine human behavior, as it was under Trujillo's rule? As Baudrillard (1974) suggests, the media, in the stage of mass consumption, are not unambiguous mechanisms outside the domain of values, models, symbols, and signs of capitalism. The media function within channels and mechanisms of communication that are determined by the position of the individuals and groups in the social structure and in a specific system of mass communication. In other words, the actions of the broadcaster and the viewer are in large part delimited by their situation in the socioeconomic system. Therefore, the ways in which television networks function can be comprehended only if they are related to their position as commercial enterprises in a capitalist economic system. As Garnham suggests, television displays a close interweaving within its concrete commodity form of the economic, the ideological, and the political. Indeed, television, as ordained within commodity production in general, performs an ideological function and operates within politics (1986, p. 16).

Furthermore, the internationalization of culture has produced new arrangements that fundamentally question the traditional national limits. In the Dominican Republic, as in other developing countries, the styles of consumption, and the organization of the economy and institutions, follow in large part the model of the richest postindustrial societies. In most countries of Latin America the model that the economic elites try to follow is the United States.

Generally speaking, the dominant classes as well as some people from the urban middle class in Latin American developing countries have ways of living similar (in life-style as well as in standard of living) to those same groups in developed countries of the western hemisphere. In any case, their desires and ideas of a good life are strongly related to the representations of life in the urban areas of the United States or Europe. There are several aspects of urban culture that have clearly crossed borders. In fact, people from urban areas in Latin America frequently have more direct contact with the characteristics of postindustrial societies than have people of rural areas in the same postindustrial societies.

The external influences on the culture as well as on the economic organization of these Latin American countries are the result of a variety of factors: direct imposition (violence or economic sanctions);[30] the requirements of international financial agencies (International Monetary Fund, World Bank, etc.); the penetration of transnational corporations; the personal contacts of citizens (most of them members of the privileged strata) with the richest countries (study abroad, doing business, vacations, etc.); contacts with tourists; emigrants who return (for vacations or to stay); and the mass media, particularly television, which is probably the most important factor, since it reaches most of the population directly.

And the messages that television transmits are not a cultural stimulus to development—rather, they are the contrary. As Beltrán and Fox de Cardona (1980) claim, referring to Latin America in general, the manner in which television is used can constitute an obstacle to development.

Indeed, the economic programs of the Dominican government, like those of most Latin American governments, since 1970 have been oriented toward reducing consumption of luxury goods and creating savings for investment in productive projects (at least in their official plans).[31] The same tendency is observed in small-scale community projects (at the level of villages, production groups, grass-roots organizations, etc.). Television's advertising and programming systematically erode these efforts because they propose and diffuse ideas contrary to this model of development through stimulating consumption. Television presents life-styles focused on consumerism as the driving force in life. Of the different aspects of the culture of developed countries, what is most easily transferred is the consumption style. As a matter of fact, it is what is more encouraged by the transnational and exporting firms (the role of television as cultural agent is basic here); in Latin America since 1970, the transnational firms have tended to produce consumers rather than producers.

Television in the Dominican Republic is characterized by a commercial system whose private networks[32] compete not only among themselves but also, to a certain extent, with the state-owned network for the same resources (both are competing for advertising money). The state-owned network, Radio Televisión Dominicana (RTVD), behaves in many ways like a commercial network. It functions both inside and outside direct commodity production.

In this chapter we have seen that the rise of television in the Dominican Republic is directly related to the will and interest of Rafael Leonidas Trujillo, who governed the country from 1930 to 1961. Trujillo systematically exploited the opportunities that the development of television made possible. It has also been shown that after the death of Trujillo in 1961, there was a multiplication of private television networks which are controlled by the same groups that control most of the economy of the country. Today, as with most industries and businesses in the country, television ownership appears to be substantially concentrated among a few people, some of whom are involved in other media (although not always as major stockholders). That is, with the exception of the fairly recent and still underdeveloped network Independencia, television networks are controlled by the same people who own the most important firms of the country.[33] In sum, basically because of the capital necessary for equipment and for covering the cost of production, television networks are developed by and under the control of financially strong companies or by the government, and such organizations inexorably have special interests to serve. As has been the rule in most countries, the nature of the predominant system in the Dominican Republic, taken as a whole, tends to create a pattern of mass communication that concentrates absolute control of the television industry in the power elite.

In Chapter 3 the specific organization of Dominican television will be analyzed, along with the relationships of this organization and its goals to the programming content.

NOTES

1. The U.S. government, on the pretext of constraining the Dominican state to organize its economy and to pay its debts, invaded the Dominican Republic and remained there from 1916 to 1924. In fact, during the twentieth century, citing reasons of political unrest, financial instability, or violation of U.S. rights, the United States has undertaken major military interventions twice in the Dominican Republic (1916, 1965), as well as in Nicaragua, Grenada, Honduras, Haiti, Mexico, and Panama; it also has maintained forces in Cuba and Panama. The U.S. Marines created a National Guard in which Trujillo was enrolled, and he received formal training in the U.S.-created military academy. In contrast with most Dominicans, who opposed the U.S. forces, he served as an informer and as a guide for the invaders. When the Marines left the country, Trujillo was a major in the pro-United States National Guard, or National Police, as the United States preferred to call it. In a few years he became head of the army. This rapid promotion was also due to the fact that the traditional elite of the Dominican Republic was in general patriotic and therefore could not serve in local army forces trained by the United States to enforce U.S. policy in Latin America.

2. See, e.g., Espaillat (1963), Beals (1961), Szulc (1968), Wiarda (1968).

3. The most important newspaper of that time, *La Nación*, praised that event as follows: "La Voz del Yuna has transformed itself into La Voz Dominicana because, rather than aiming to gather the echo of the Northwest region, it wanted to erect itself an interpreter of every vibration and every thought of the motherland" (*La Nación* 1942, p. 3). Translated from the Spanish by the author.

4. The introduction of television on a caprice of the president or for political reasons is not infrequent in the developing countries of Latin America. President Rojas of Colombia mandated the establishment of a television system in time to celebrate the first anniversary of his dictatorship (Fox de Cardona 1975).

5. The equipment, supplied by RCA Victor, was among the most modern at that time. It was installed under the direction and supervision of George Graham, an engineer from the National Broadcasting Company. There were a good number of U.S. citizens among the team of technicians (the Dominicans were not technically prepared for the task).

For the U.S. companies the development of radio and television in Latin America was good business because of the supplies needed by radio and television stations. For the Latin American countries, the introduction of television accentuated their dependency on U.S. companies (after World War II the influence of the United States on Latin American broadcasting was almost total) for equipment and expertise, not only for the construction of the stations but also for rural electrification and for capital investment and expenditure that the installation of a broadcasting system requires. This influence was also very important in determining the character of Latin American television. The U.S. involvement in broadcast activities began with radio and continued with television.

6. Television was first developed in Europe in the 1920s and 1930s (especially in England, the Soviet Union, and Germany). Experimental telecasts and closed-circuit connections had been in use throughout the 1930s, in Europe as well as the United States; but regularly scheduled programs began in England and in the Soviet Union just before World War II (as these countries entered World War II, broadcasting ceased and the television factories were closed). On the American continent television began in 1939 in the United States. The Federal Communications Commission approved commercial television in 1941; a New York station aired several hours of commercial entertainment on July 1, 1941 (Wheen 1985; Bogart 1972).

7. All citations from documents or declarations originally in Spanish or French have been translated by myself, unless otherwise noted.

8. He commonly forced farmers to sell him their property at a very low price, especially when the farm was productive—even when the owners were members of the bourgeoisie.

9. The goods and investments that Trujillo had in his name and the name of his wife in 1961 were worth U.S. $148,811,029.75 (Rivera 1986)—and the amount was probably larger.

10. Every person I interviewed agreed on this point.

11. He had no problem finding advertisers (both foreign and national) who were willing to pay for entertainment and for other programs.

12. The show starred the team Macario y Felipa, who originally acted in radio comedies. The program was directed by Rafael Western, and the master control engineer was George Graham.

13. The merengue is a very popular Dominican dance form.

14. There were shows such as "La Escuela en Televisión" (School on TV), which offered basic lessons in history, geography, Spanish grammar, and English, and "El Médico en Su Hogar" (The Physician in Your Home), which gave practical health advice.

15. That was not the case later on. The skills levels did not follow the multiplication of networks; today most managers do not have a clear idea of communication technology, and the production staff—producers, directors, floor managers, cameramen, script editors, lighting experts, and sound technicians—do not have formal training. They learn by practice. Furthermore, in general (with the exception of the four biggest producers: Veras Goico, Corporán, Televisa, and Núñez del Risco), there is very little investment in the improvement of the shows (by independent producers as well as by the networks). This results in shows of very poor technical quality.

16. Even during the three years after World War II when he tried to give an appearance of democracy, the use of the media by the opposition parties, such as the Partido Socialista Popular, and the trade unions was highly controlled. By the time television appeared, even this token opposition was forbidden; any opposition was subject to rigorous persecution.

17. The RTVD, from the day a competitive network was established, has had a comparatively low popularity. Its overall programming shows little creativity, and government activities still occupy a considerable share of the programming. Only in areas not reached by the other networks does the state television network draw big audiences.

18. In 1965 the U.S. Army intervened, with the complicity of the Organization

of American States, in order to control a revolt that was trying to return power to the elected president, Juan Bosch, who was ousted from power by a coup d'état encouraged by the U.S. government in 1963. The intervention was successful and, after almost two years of rule by a civilian junta, allowed the return to power of one of the most important figures of the Trujillo regime, Joaquín Balaguer, through rigged elections. From 1966 to 1978 the Balaguer government imposed a semidictatorship, although it held elections every four years (political opponents were subject to persecution, and some of them were assassinated). With the victory of the social-democrat party, the Partido Revolucionario Dominicano (Dominican Revolutionary Party), in 1978, the nation returned to at least a semblance of democracy.

19. This network had its principal broadcasting station in the second city of the country, Santiago, but in the late 1970s moved to the capital.

20. Jorge Blanco was elected president of the republic in 1982, on the slate of the Partido Revolucionario Dominicano (PRD), a centrist social-democrat party that belonged to the Socialist International. He governed with a group of close followers within the party. (The party was at that time divided into two strong and opposite groups.) Later during the Blanco government the traditional leader of the PRD, José Francisco Peña Gómez, created a third group.

21. After the fall of the dictatorship, all the belongings of Trujillo's family were considered property of the state.

22. The statistics on television and radio receivers in the Dominican Republic do not reflect reality; according to my observations and opinions I have gathered from people involved in the broadcasting industry, there are many more television sets in the country than the statistics show, probably over 110 sets per 1,000 inhabitants. However, I use the data from these agencies as proxy, since I do not have better general data available.

23. However, the regular networks control about 90 percent of the television market.

24. There are nine newspapers with national circulation, five regional newspapers, ninety movie theaters, a dozen academic and scientific journals, some literary reviews, one national weekly magazine, and around fifteen general-interest international magazines. Estimates are based on interviews with top executives of the broadcasting industry, on previous empirical studies by the author (Menéndez 1984), and on the data of *Europa World Year Book* (1990). Television is very common even in families with low income, and in some of the very poor neighborhoods, the people who possess a television set frequently allow neighbors or friends to watch programs. Thus, television reaches significantly more people than the number that would correspond to the estimate of 65 percent of homes.

25. Scholars such as Schramm (1964) and McQuail (1979) consider the high average use of the mass media and the subjective concern for this use of leisure time to be two pertinent facts in determining the relationship between the mass media and the development of advanced industrial societies.

26. In most countries of Latin America, as in the Dominican Republic, more than 40 percent of the adult population is illiterate.

27. Around 65 percent of the sugar production is under government ownership and management; most of the largest tourism enterprises are joint ventures, gen-

erally with foreign enterprises; and most services (electricity, water, mail, etc.) are controlled by the government.

28. The number of banks and other financial enterprises increased dramatically from 1976 to 1986. But then this sector has also been affected by the crisis.

The foreign debt of the Dominican Republic has increased dramatically since 1970, and the conditions of living for most wage workers, even for high-level professionals, have been worsening (especially in the second part of the 1980s). But this crisis did not affect all the capitalists; for some of them it was profitable.

29. In 1980, U.S. $1 = 1.8 Dominican pesos; in 1990, U.S. $1 = 10 pesos. This devaluation brought sharp increases in the prices of goods without corresponding wage and salary rises.

30. The Dominican Republic has been invaded twice by the United States (1916, 1965). In the first invasion the United States governed the country for eight years, organizing the Dominican army, the customs, and other aspects of the state apparatus.

31. Of course, there have been different interpretations of what are productive projects, depending on the party or individual who occupies the presidency. For example, in the Dominican Republic, the current president, Joaquin Balaguer, tends to favor government investment in construction of infrastructure over investment in direct production. However, at the same time there is a tendency to reduce consumption of luxury imported goods.

32. A network has been described as "a group of radio or TV stations that broadcast the same programs. The stations can be owned by a headquarters company—the network—that is the source of the programs or can be independent—a network affiliate" (Weiner 1990, pp. 309–10). The U.S. Federal Communications Commission classifies as "network" any group of stations broadcasting over fifteen hours a week in twenty-five cities and ten states simultaneously. In the Dominican Republic most television stations reach more than one region, have more than a single relay station, and broadcast over fifteen hours a week. There are no local television stations, however, only relay stations. In any case, given the similarity of the Dominican television organizations to what are generally called networks in the United States and according to the classification used by the *Europa World Year Book* (1989) and UNESCO (1976), I consider it appropriate to refer to the Dominican television companies as "television networks."

33. As far as I know, since it has been extremely difficult to learn the names of all the stockholders of the television networks. This kind of information is not officially available, even from government agencies. Therefore, I could confirm only the most important stockholders in each network.

Chapter 3

Television as a Medium of Production

Broadcasting in the Dominican Republic is treated today like any other service industry. As is the case in most Latin American countries, the television system is entirely commercial, following the pattern of the United States.[1] Entrepreneurs are free, subject to minimal restrictions, to establish and manage broadcasting networks in accordance with demand and supply. Officially, as long as they observe the basic laws of the industry, they are free to broadcast what they like.[2]

Owners consider television to be one product among many, and thus they aim to make it as profitable as possible. Dominican television networks and independent producers, like any commercial television, need to appeal to advertisers to support their broadcasting. The greater the audience the television network can reach, the more advertising, and thus the more revenue it can attract.[3] Therefore, the basic role of the networks' executives is to seek the largest audience in order to attract advertising. Even the state-owned network competes for audience and advertising income (although unsuccessfuly).

Programmers are not subject to a particular network's official internal regulations concerning the content of the programs. However, they are subject to commercial pressures. All the networks have a similar formal structure. For example, the network Teleantillas has a board of directors headed by the most important stockholder. On the next level there are general administrators (finance, accounting, personnel) and several divisions (programming, news, sales, and technical).[4]

The board of directors is not concerned with specific programs; they only see results. Their major concern is whether a given program has benefits. They make decisions only on that basis, rarely analyzing the reason why a given program is not drawing well or does not have the expected audience size. This happens because (1) most stockholders and people in high management are interested in money, in the bottom line, and (2) because they do not understand the problems of television production.

Normally the director of programming is responsible for the programming of the network, although at some networks the owners make suggestions. This situation varies from one network to another, and seems to depend more on the personal characteristics of individuals (particularly the owners) than on other considerations. The entrepreneurs concentrate more on the short term than on the long term regarding general management as well as the ideological content of their programming. They do not seek to impart a particular political ideology[5] (except the one implicit in doing business). The driving force of the programming is to make as much money as possible as fast as possible. Any television show is viewed as a commodity that should produce an audience which can be sold to advertisers.

There are three ways for the networks (both state and private owned) to earn income:

1. The regular programming of the network. The sales team sells commercial time to advertising companies or directly to clients. Occasionally the advertising agency agrees to buy an entire program. The portion of programming produced by the network itself varies; on the average it represents between 25 percent and 45 percent of the programming other than news. News is always produced entirely by the networks.
2. Participatory advertising. The time is offered to independent producers. Sometimes the sale of time to advertisers is done entirely by the producer, sometimes by the network, and sometimes both the producer and the network sell commercial time. The network receives between 40 percent and 50 percent of the advertising income that the show produces, depending on the agreement.
3. Time "rented" to independent producers for a fixed rate each month (which varies substantially according to the show and the time of the day at which it is broadcast).

The programming of any network is determined, in large part, by the sale of time to independent producers (between 40 percent and 70 percent of the total time is covered by this system).[6] The independent programs have brought large profits to the networks. For a producer, the choice of participatory advertising or "rented" time will depend on negotiations and the characteristics of the show. For shows that are not expected to draw big audiences, "rented" time is generally preferred. The network considers it a good solution to "rent" the times of day when few homes have television sets turned on.

In order to allow time to independent producers, a network committee assesses the quality of the program, its content, the possibilities of scheduling it, and the curriculum vitae of the producer(s). The deciding factor, however, is whether a particular show will be good for the network. Sometimes personal relations between the producer and an important stockholder or a person of influence within the network help to determine acceptance of a show independently of its success (it will seldom be accepted, however, if it does not at least pay back its costs). This practice is more common in the state-owned television network. For example, the time allotted to an independent producer can be affected by his relations with the director general of the network or with the president of the country or with other important members of the party in power (these relationships can be personal, economic, or political). Special relations also help the independent producer by allowing remissions of payment and lower "rents" for time. Programs with special arrangements are rarely found in prime time, unless they draw a large audience.

SPONSORS' DEPENDENCY

Television networks in the Dominican Republic, as around the world, aim to reach the largest possible audience in order to attract advertising money. The basic indicators of success or failure of a programming are the ratings and the share.[7] Therefore, they try to broadcast programs that will be pleasing to the greatest number of people. In their competition to attract an audience, television networks have developed several strategies; copying the basic elements of a program that is successful on another network is the most frequent, but they also use counterprogramming and create new programs. The network rivalry is especially strong in the forty-seven hours of prime time each week.[8] It is very important to have the leadership in order to get more advertising income.[9] For the sponsors, television advertising is a means of selling more products; thus they will prefer to place commercials on networks or stations that reach the largest audiences. For this reason, the period in which most people watch television is the most important for the ratings.

To reach the audiences that advertisers want, television broadcasters focus their programs on the maximum number of available viewers who, in their view, are potential buyers of the advertised products. They look for the largest subset of viewers, demographically defined, for every part of the day. Usually the ratings firms define the audience in terms of age, sex, and socioeconomic status. For example, the principal target of the soap operas (*telenovelas*) is women; the target of the news is both men and women.

Frequently the programming plans are formulated according to the suggestions of the advertising companies.[10] As a director of a network sales department said, "Advertising clearly establishes paths in the programming of this network. We should always think who will be willing to sponsor a given program." Usually the sales department is in contact with the advertising companies; it transmits their opinions to the network's director of programming and sometimes also to the administrator. In other words, although the sales department is not officially in charge of programming, its opinions are always considered in the formulation of the overall programming of the network or before airing a new show. In fact, as Head and Sterling point out, "The stars of commercial broadcasting may seem to be the performers the public sees and hears, but in the broadcasting business the real stars are the sales people" (1987, p. 234). Indeed, the salespeople typically receive the highest pay among television employees in the Dominican Republic and in most countries of Latin America.

The programming of the networks is highly dependent on the major sponsors, who are basically the manufacturers of spirits (there are sixteen different national brands of rum and two of beer), the tobacco industry, the lottery, and manufacturers of soft drinks (Coca-Cola, Pepsi, etc.), laundry products, cosmetics, and drugs—products of mass consumption.

The content of most shows reflects what it is supposed that the masses who consume this merchandise want. The greatest consumers of rum, beer, and cigarettes, for example, are considered to be people of middle and low socioeconomic status.[11] These people, especially those with a low educational level, are the majority in the country and are the heaviest viewers of television. As an advertiser commented, "The audience is composed in the majority by a mass of illiterates that agglomerate around the cities." Indeed, my study of the audience shows that the more people are educated, the less time they spend watching TV, a tendency consistent with observed behavior in most of the world. About 80 percent of low-education people interviewed spend more than four hours a day watching television; the proportion decreases to 55 percent of those with a moderate education and to 30 percent of persons with a high education.[12] Women spend an average of 20 percent more time than men in front of the TV set.[13] The average length of time television sets are on in the Dominican Republic is around six hours and thirty minutes per day,[14] almost as much as in the United States, which, according to the Roper Organization (1988), is seven hours. In the United States a large number of both husbands and wives work outside the home, while in the Dominican Republic fewer wives work outside the home. Also, numerous maids in the middle- and upper-class homes turn on the television while they are doing their tasks.

It is possible to say that television has only one public: those who watch it. Based on the ratings companies' data and on my own data, we can estimate that heavy television users account for 70 percent of the total volume of television watching. Thus, they are very important in the ratings; since the measurements for the ratings are done by show, those who watch television four hours a day will give their opinion more often than those who watch only one hour. And, of course, those who watch more are the people who have more free time. The audience is, then, in great part composed of those who do not work or are maids, that is, people who have few economic resources, and are less educated. Because of the logic of rating—to seek the common denominator of the audience's taste—the programming of television will be above all oriented to these people.

Furthermore, when making decisions about the broadcasting of a new show, television producers and administrators are strongly influenced by what they see as cultural symbols that will work, and tend to select them and reformulate them through television, giving special consideration to the kinds of shows that have worked in the past: "We know that most dramatic-oriented shows such as *telenovelas* will work, and when we buy U.S. serials and movies, we try to choose as much as we can those with action adventure, which are the ones that always drew largest audiences." They choose shows that they expect will be accepted by a mass audience almost immediately. The time required in the Dominican Republic for a national production to be successful rarely exceeds two months.[15]

THE RESULTING PROGRAMMING

The programming of all the Dominican networks follows the same agenda: imported shows, such as serials and movies (mostly from the United States),[16] and soap operas called *telenovelas* (imported from other countries of Latin America); local entertainment productions, such as marathon variety shows, comedies, and musical shows; and locally produced news and interview and debate shows (see Appendix B).

Dominican television programming at first based its format on a kind of Hollywood style that was successful with audiences, and has since then followed more or less the same tendency, without departing radically from what has been accepted. There is no great difference from one network to another. All the networks are full of the *telenovelas*' dramatic and glamorous representation of love, the same expressions of hosts and anchormen/women, the same game shows and the applause on command of the audience (when it is not prerecorded), and the same car chases and shooting of the U.S. serials and movies.

"The programs that draw the largest audiences are those of popular music and those with a general content that appeals to the entertainment taste of the lower classes. Television is in this aspect very democratic," said a producer. Indeed, most people we interviewed who had a low education were primarily interested in variety musical shows, *telenovelas*, game shows, and U.S. serials.[17] They also indicate Colorvisión as their preferred network—and it is unequivocally first in the ratings. (Figures 3.1–3.3 indicate the average ratings of the networks that have been most directly the object of this research. Appendix C presents the audience

Figure 3.1
Average Ratings, 6 A.M.–2 A.M.

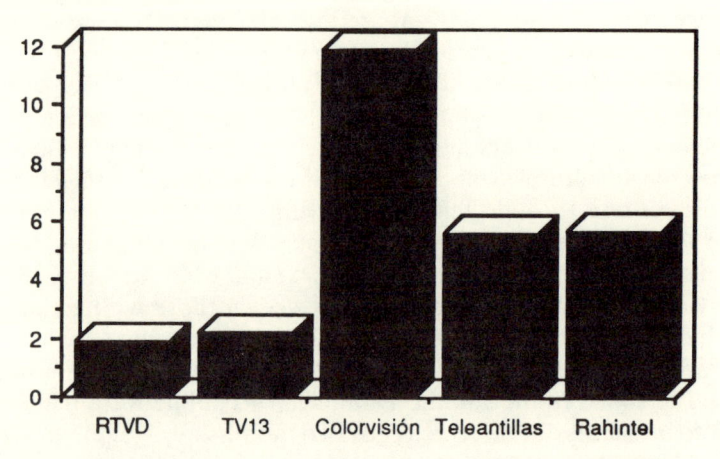

[Bar chart showing: RTVD ~2, TV13 ~2, Colorvisión ~12, Teleantillas ~5.5, Rahintel ~5.5]

These ratings were established by using the "coincidental/recall" procedure.
Source: Asesores Asociados C.A., Santo Domingo, March 1990.

share of all the networks.) Colorvisión broadcasts the most popular game shows, variety-musical shows, and *telenovelas*.

For instance, with three hours of soap operas a day—the most successful networks in the ratings broadcast a minimum of three hours of *telenovelas* a day, from Monday through Friday (that is, between 15 percent and 25 percent of daily programming)—the network can make U.S. $320,000 a month (more than 2 million Dominican pesos).[18] According to the television staff members interviewed, this income alone is enough to cover the cost of running the entire network. The U.S. serials yield around the same amount of profit, though their cost, on the average, is slightly higher. The nationally produced shows of Veras Goico, Corporán, and Televisa[19] yield even more than the soap operas and serials.

The prices of commercials depend on the audience of a given program and on the overall position of the network in relation to the other networks. The prices are established by time: the basic thirty-second ad on prime time normally varies between U.S. $130 on the lowest-ranked network and U.S. $200 on the highest-ranked.[20] The price increases in proportion to the length of the ad. Colorvisión, the number-one-ranked network, charges around U.S. $200 in prime time,[21] although discounts and rebates are very common in Dominican television.

The time structure is as follows: three minutes of show, two minutes of advertising. That means twelve minutes of advertising per thirty-minute segment, or seventy-two minutes of advertising for three hours of show.

Figure 3.2
Average Ratings During Prime Time, 6 P.M.–11 P.M.

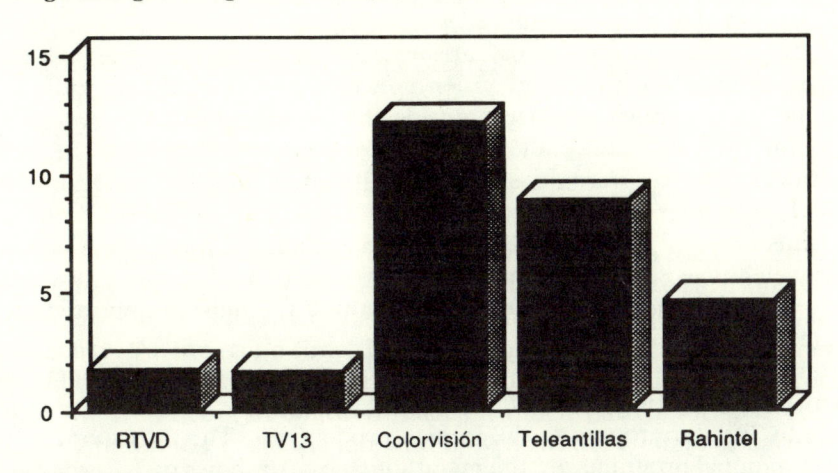

RTVD	~2
TV13	~2
Colorvisión	~12
Teleantillas	~9
Rahintel	~5

These ratings were established by using the "coincidental/recall" procedure.
Source: Asesores Asociados C.A., Santo Domingo, March 1990.

Figure 3.3
Average Ratings by Socioeconomic Status, 6 A.M.–2 A.M.

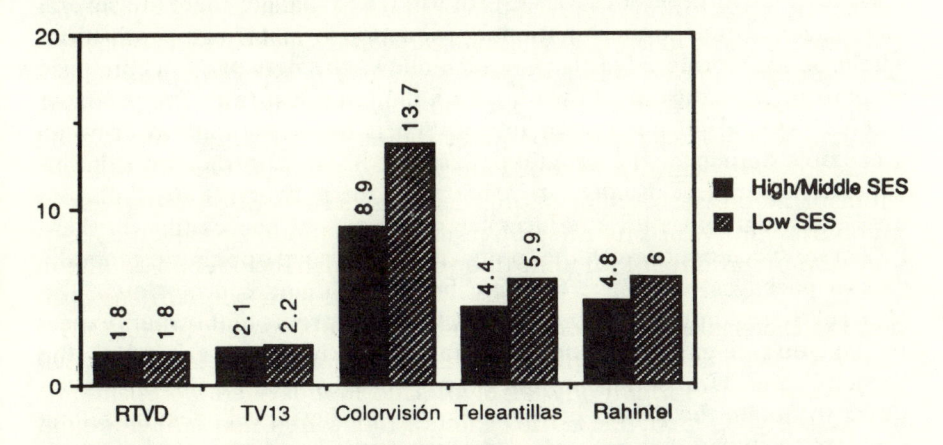

Station	High/Middle SES	Low SES
RTVD	1.8	1.8
TV13	2.1	2.2
Colorvisión	8.9	13.7
Teleantillas	4.4	5.9
Rahintel	4.8	6

These ratings were established by using the "coincidental/recall" procedure.
Source: Asesores Asociados C.A., Santo Domingo, March 1990.

This implies that people get more than one hour of advertising and less than two hours of show for every three hours they spend watching television. The length of an ad can vary enormously, and some are quite long, but we estimate an average of 35 seconds. That gives around 20–21 ads during a 30-minute soap opera (some are an hour long) and a total of 120–126 ads per day in the 3 hours of soap operas.

Lately, economic constraints, arising from the scarcity and the high cost of the dollar, have forced television networks to reduce dramatically the number of programs produced outside the country; the Latin American soap operas[22] and, above all, the U.S. serials are seen less often on some networks. "It has become extremely difficult to develop programming based on foreign products with such an unstable money market," said an administrator.[23] For example, in 1987 the percentage of foreign productions was well above 40 percent on all the networks. In 1991 it was between 25 percent and 35 percent. *Telenovelas* constitute the bulk of imported programs.[24]

Musical shows and comedies, most of them produced by independent individuals and companies, are the core of the Dominican productions that little by little are replacing the foreign productions. The most popular of these national programs are the marathon one-man shows on Saturday and Sunday afternoons (in which some basic educational material is mixed with popular music, talk, and games) and the musical shows, especially the ones between noon and 2 P.M. (some start at 11:30 A.M.) every weekday.[25] This is evidenced in the interviews I conducted and in the rankings established by the rating firms (see Table 3.1).

For the network, besides the costs of foreign exchange, there are several advantages of independent national production over foreign production. The producers bring advertising, which allows the network to economize on personnel because it can work with a limited sales staff. The producer receives around 40 percent of the profits; if the show fails to draw an acceptable audience, the program is canceled. The contract with the independent producer usually can be ended by the network at any time (not until the program or the producer has proved to be successful will there be a more specific contract); the foreign movies or soap operas are generally sold in packages, and once they are bought, nothing can be done. The terms of these contracts no longer allow the great profits that owners expect to make on foreign productions, especially the movies and serials from the United States. U.S. serials are bought in packages because this allows the buyer to obtain the lowest prices; however, in these packages the selling company includes, for example, one high-ranked and two or three low-ranked serials. The same thing happens with the movies: out of 120 movies bought, 20 are successful, 30 are more or less acceptable, and 70 will draw a very small audience. This also limits the decisions made by the network

Table 3.1
The Top Thirty Shows on Dominican Television

Rank	Show	Rating	Network	Day	Time
1	Sábado de Corporán (marathon one-man show)	20.0	Rahintel	Sat.	noon–6 P.M.
2	El Gordo de la Semana (marathon one-man show)	19.4	Colorv.	Sun.	noon–8 P.M.
3	El Show del Mediodía (variety show)	19.1	Colorv.	M.–F.	11:30 A.M.–2 P.M.
4	El Chavo (Mexican comedy show, mostly directed to children and teenagers)	18.4	Colorv.	M. W. F.	2 P.M.–2:30 P.M.
5	Nuria en el 9 (variety show)	17.7	Colorv.	Sat.	9 P.M.–10 P.M.
6	El Chapulín (Mexican comedy show, mostly directed to children and teenagers)	17.5	Colorv.	Tu.–Th.	2 P.M.–2:30 P.M.
7	Luisito y Anthony (comedy show)	17.4	Colorv.	Sun.	8 P.M.–9 P.M.
8	Telenovela: Rubi Rebelde (soap opera)	15.1	Teleant.	M.–F.	6:30 P.M.–7 P.M.
9	Telenovela: Carrusel (soap opera)	14.9	Colorv.	M.–F.	6:30 P.M.–7 P.M.
10	Cine Continuo (U.S. movie)	14.2	Colorv.	Sun.	8 P.M.–9 P.M.
11	Punto Final (comedy)	14.0	Colorv.	M. to F.	9:30 P.M.–12 P.M.
12	Telenovela: Amigail (soap opera)	13.9	Teleant.	M.–F.	5:30 P.M.–6 P.M.
13	Noticiario 2da Emisión (evening newscast)	13.8	Colorv.	M.–F.	9 P.M.–9:30 P.M.
14	Noticiario 1ra Emisión (afternoon newscast)	13.4	Colorv.	M.–F.	2:30 P.M.–3 P.M.
15	Esta Misma Semana (variety and information)	13.2	Colorv.	Sat.	10 P.M.–11 P.M.
16	Alf (U.S. sitcom)	13.1	Teleant.	M. W. F.	7:30 P.M.–8 P.M.
17	Super Tarde (variety show, mostly directed to children and teenagers)	12.0	Colorv.	M.–F.	3 P.M.–5:30 P.M.
18	Telenovela: Amanda Sabater (soap opera)	11.8	Telesist.	M.–F.	8 P.M.–9 P.M.
19	Telenovela: Vale Todo (soap opera)	11.7	Teleant.	M.–F.	7 P.M.–8 P.M.
20	Cine Continuo (U.S. movie)	11.5	Colorv.	Sun.	11 P.M.–1 A.M.
21	Telenovela: Lo Blanco y lo Negro (soap opera)	11.3	Colorv.	M.–F.	8:30 P.M.–9 P.M.
22	TV Todo (variety show)	11.3	Colorv.	Sat.	1:30 P.M.–7 P.M.

Table 3.1 (continued)

Rank	Show	Rating	Network	Day	Time
23	La Bella y la Bestia (U.S. serial)	11.1	Teleant.	M.	8:30 P.M.–9:30 P.M.
24	Merengue Show (variety show)	10.7	Colorv.	Sat.	7 P.M.–7:30 P.M.
25	Telenovela: Simplemente Maria (soap opera)	10.6	Telesist.	M.–F.	12:30 P.M.–1 P.M.
26	Película Americana (U.S. movie)	10.4	Independ.	Sat.	11:30 P.M.–1:30 A.M.
27	Porta-Aviones (U.S. serial)	10.1	Teleant.	Fr.	8:30 P.M.–9:30 P.M.
28	Telenovela: La Dama de Rosa (soap opera)	10.0	Teleant.	M.–F.	5 P.M.–5:30 P.M.
29	El show de Charytin (variety show)	9.7	Colorv.	Sat.	8 P.M.–9 P.M.
30	Misión en Houston (U.S. serial)	9.6	Teleant.	Wed.	8 P.M.–9 P.M.

Source: Elaborated from data from Asesores Asociados C.A., Santo Domingo, February 1990.

executives about programming, since they must use what they have, even if it will not draw big audiences.

An effective way of meeting the public interest that some network executives and other people assign to television is to broadcast documentaries and other cultural and educational programs,[26] but it is usually hard to find advertisers willing to sponsor them. All the programs with an educational content, such as educational shows for children, have little advertising support. There are fewer and fewer of these shows. As a matter of fact, in 1990 there were very few high culture or educational shows on a regular basis in all of Dominican television, including the state-owned network (see Appendix B). The advertising companies do not want to sponsor what is categorized in the industry as "cultural" programs. A director of programming said, "The most important thing in this business, as in any other business, is to make money, and the cultural programs have never worked. When you say the word 'culture,' potential clients do not want to get involved."

For example, a documentary about Dali broadcast during the summer of 1989 on the Rahintel network could hardly find enough advertising money to cover its cost. The very few programs considered important for their educational and cultural content are financed in part by the surplus that the network generates from other shows, such as *telenovelas* and variety musicals. Actually, most of the time these shows are presented when the networks have nothing else to broadcast at a particular time.

The public network follows more or less the same path: "The state-owned network is supposed to play a role of cultural orientation for the population. But as soon as it acquires that role, it loses audience,"[27] stated a producer of the state network. Thus, though recognized by most people in the television industry, politicians, and popular leaders as highly important for the public interest, documentaries and educational shows are almost totally absent from Dominican television. A director of programming explained it thus: "Given the market structure in which we are enmeshed, it is not wise to broadcast materials that can be rejected by the majority of the audience. And believe me, the audience is far from being sophisticated."

The networks' directors of programming believe that their programming responds to the taste of the public, even if some of them do not like it. Indeed, several producers and directors of programming have experienced personal conflicts between what they are expected and compelled to do, given the constraints of the market, and what they would like to do. A director of programming stated:

I will even turn off the television in order to avoid watching what I have... scheduled, but we should understand that television is an enterprise whose basic purpose is to make money. If not, I would not be here. A good programming [plan] would be to... convert this medium into an instrument that really serves the best interest of the television audience. However, if the only motive is to earn money, then it is not possible to reach that objective, because we have a mass . . . television audience that by the education that they have, are asking for a specific content. If we do not give them that, we simply do not earn money.[28]

However, whether the networks really follow the taste of the audience is subject to debate; on the one hand, it depends how the audience is interpreted, and on the other hand, the economic requirements are such that television programming does not always follow the taste of the public. Most of all, there is the search for the easiest way of making money. It has been shown that the reason network executives try to limit the importation of foreign productions has little to do with the audience's wishes. No Dominican capitalist takes a big risk in the television industry,[29] especially if the risk will not produce immediate profits. For example, some *telenovelas* from Brazil draw the largest audiences. They are watched by large numbers in all social groups. These *telenovelas*, everyone in the television business agrees, are better done in all respects. But they are more expensive than *telenovelas* from Venezuela, Colombia, and other Latin American countries. Therefore, because the market does not permit a large increase in the price of advertising, networks (and private companies) import few of these *telenovelas*. And sometimes programs that are a disaster from the point of view of quality, and from the point of view of drawing audiences, continue on the air because the producer is paying for the airtime. The general image of the network is sacrificed in order to obtain immediate profits.

Economic imperatives of profit result in the broadcasting of very few shows of social and innovative value, and the replacing of some foreign productions has opened the market still more to producers of low-cost interviews and game shows of little substance and low technical quality. The commercial television system of the Dominican Republic attracts both people able to create a different program and persons of questionable skills and integrity who use the medium for personal profit. The management is chosen and retained not for effective management, ability to develop imaginative programming, and work for society's cultural good, but for their ability to make money.

The programming is, then, a result of interrelations within the television industry: (1) between the network and the advertisers (direct client or advertising agency), (2) between the advertising agencies and their clients, and (3) within the networks themselves (between network owners and network executives, and between the services within the network, especially between sales and programming). Joined with this is the fundamental question that underlies the television business: What is the best way to get money out of an audience, which is viewed simply as a market for products?

REMOVING DIVERSITY

Diversity lies in the specific content of television that reflects the different trends within society (tastes, life-styles, opinions, etc.).[30] Research reveals that behind an appearance of diversity based on titles of the shows and individuals who perform on them, there is actually little variety in the television networks of the Dominican Republic, in prime time as well as in other periods of the day.[31] Frequently all the networks offer almost the same thing at the same time (see Appendix B). Even the programs specifically called entertainment (actually, all the programs on television seem to be oriented to entertainment) tend to be very similar, be they nationally produced or imported.[32] What is labeled "new" most of the time reproduces the same traditional format.[33] When one of the networks or stations decides to make real changes in some aspect of programming (which rarely happens) and is successful, the other networks and stations make the necessary readjustments in order to be in the race. This corresponds to the logic of seeking maximum benefits with minimum risks. For example, until 1988 the time after 11 P.M. was traditionally considered not commercial (prime time was basically from 7:30 P.M. to 10 P.M.). Then a variety talk show, "El Show de la Noche," was very successful on Teleantillas. Immediately Colorvisión followed suit with the variety talk show "Punto Final." Prime time on these two networks was then extended to midnight.

In other words, the programming is adapted to what the competition is doing, generally by imitating the successful programs of the other networks.[34] As a consequence, there is a considerable likelihood of finding the same thing on all the networks at the same time because usually they are competing for the same subset of the audience. Frequently the products advertised are the same.

There is also repetition through time. Programming is established with the ratings in mind; in this way of thinking, previous shows play a very important role. Therefore, the network executives will look for programs that are similar to ones that were successful in the past. This produces a repetitive, standardized programming that changes little through time or from one network to another.

This lack of diversity is not entirely due to the fact that networks are responding to the desires of the audience. It is due more to the industry assumptions and representations of the audience. In other words, the tendency toward standardization of the message broadcast does not occur because the audience is uniform but because television networks and ratings companies try to find aspects that are common to the average taste. Their goals involve a classification of the audience, based on market considerations, that unifies different groups and artificially assembles the multiple diversities of the social reality. Audiences are differentiated by social class, level of knowledge, political opinion, taste, level of academic education, and so on, but also by moods, desires, and ways of interpreting the world. The television industry overemphasizes means, percentages, and numbers, thereby creating uniform categories of people they target. And these uniformities, these standard visions of the world, will be applied to the format and content of the programs. Through the use of statistics[35] the executives of the television industry create a specific world to which they will address a message. This message will be what they think responds to the real demand of people, a situation that has been constructed through assumptions and the use of statistical data from audience research. For television, and above all for the advertisers, the real world is what the ratings say it is.

The idea of a common denominator is also present in the specific content of movies and serials. There is always, in the fiction presented, an average or normal world, with average people and "others." This observation is valid for most foreign as well as for Dominican productions. In fact, the "average person," as some anchors like to say, is also a creation of a statistical-business way of representing the world: It is another assumption that has been accepted as reality by most people. Television companies find a differentiated audience that little by little is led to accept at face value the metaphors of life diffused in television's programming.

Furthermore, it is not absolutely certain that these classifications of the audience and the uniformity that they create in television programming are really effective in selling a product. There is no way the networks or the advertising companies can estimate how many among those who are watching a given show are potential buyers of the product that they are trying to sell. The fact that a certain number of people are watching television does not automatically imply that more of the advertised products will be sold. The manner in which the ratings are compiled does not allow the establishment of a qualitative classification of the audience in terms of buyers/nonbuyers.[36] They start from the premise that most people targeted will watch the programming and more advertised products will be sold.

In fact, all these mechanisms constitute more a kind of agreement within the broadcasting industry, in order to have some "objective" rules of the game, than a real assessment of the efficiency of television advertising. As Gitlin asserts, referring to the United States, "The presumed rationality of audience measurement and scheduling works just well enough to satisfy advertisers that they are getting their money's worth" (1983, p. 62). In this context, the numbers are a currency for transaction. These assumptions allow the system to work (and to grant network owners and sponsors the power to control the industry). That is what counts for the broadcasting industry and, basically, that is what shapes the general programming of Dominican television.[37]

From our interviews we can infer several other ways of understanding the audience. On the one hand, there is a clear tendency among the public of low socioeconomic status[38] (and less educated) to prefer musical shows, *telenovelas*, marathon variety shows, and game shows. They will rarely watch another type of program (a documentary, for example) if they have the choice. On the other hand, numerous people of high and middle socioeconomic status have less strongly determined preferences in general; they can very easily watch a cultural or educational program one day and a soap opera the next. They do not have an absolute and fixed desire for the same kind of show every day.[39] In other words, on a given evening, if there is a real choice of programming, one part of these social groups will be watching a cultural program, another part will be watching a movie, and another part will be watching a soap opera. There is not, among those of middle or high socioeconomic status, a different, fixed, and isolated audience with a specific demand that television should satisfy (with the exception of the intellectuals, who are more interested in programs of high quality and cultural content); instead, among these groups television should satisfy several desires—desires that can change from one day to another— and not different groups of people with established and invariable demands.

In other words, among those of high or middle socioeconomic status, there are not three or four different publics but different groups of one public who want to watch, on a given evening, a cultural program, a soap opera, and a movie. However, to say that there is not a clear and specific public within those of higher socioeconomic status does not mean that there is not a categorization that could be made among them according to time of day.

In any case, the predominant logic of market considerations in the television industry produces a tendency toward uniformity in programming. Daniel Boorstin's (1978) appraisal of the role of television in the culture is valid for the characteristics of television in the Dominican Republic; television makes apparent something that was never before shown so clearly: "the common denominator of popular taste."[40] Indeed, as Boorstin points out, the television industry is not the only producer of sensationalism or soap serialism that characterizes the popular taste.[41] However, it is indisputable that television is a fundamental reproducer of these values and tendencies. Culture is a dynamic process; thus, even if at a specific moment of modern history the mass culture were expressed in what Boorstin calls "subliterature," we can not ignore that television as a cultural institution has played a very important role in its propagation. As Elliot rightly argues, television consumption and preferences are

more a matter of availability than of selection. . . . [In this sense] availability depends on familiarity. . . . The audience has easier access to familiar genres partly because they understand the language and conventions and also because they already know the social meaning of this type of output with some certainty. (1973, p. 21)

The structure of the television industry encourages one type of content over another, which implies that Dominican television, rather than contributing to improvement of education and general knowledge, is reproducing and expanding the most negative aspects of popular culture. (This will be further developed in Chapter 4.)

Good or bad, this situation is defended by some network executives as being democratic because television programming responds to the taste of the majority. It is argued that television broadcasts what the mass audience wants. But it is too simplistic to say that the audience gets what it desires. In this view, the ever-present dynamic interaction between television and audience is forgotten. In reality there is a vicious cycle: Television programming is supposed to respond to the mass audience's desire for entertainment, and the mass audience in turn likes what has been presented to it over a long period of time. The audience will respond to a specific fabric of symbols that it has learned to recognize within the images and discourses that the medium has been transmitting for decades. Dominican audiences in the 1990s expect from television the kind of content that they have learned to desire through the messages which television has been broadcasting since the 1950s. As Postman wrote, "Our media-metaphors classify the world for us, sequence it, frame it, enlarge it, color it, argue a case for what the world is like" (1985, p. 10). In other words, television has created ways of interpreting its own message and environment; it has conditioned what people expect to find in it. In fact, the industrial structure defines the audience; networks' and especially sponsors' perceptions largely determine television content.

Economic dependency can affect the content of programming in another way. The enterprises whose advertising is broadcast by television can choose the station or network with which they associate. This implies that if, for example, a television program is considered too controversial by the advertising company or does not fulfill its commercial requirements, or if the advertising company does not like it for any reason, this company will probably shift its business to another station or network, especially since in the Dominican Republic there is rarely an enduring contract between advertisers and networks. The same situation could occur if any television network or show favors a political candidate who does not please the advertiser. Television networks and independent producers have to take this into account in their programming. This is an invisible but very effective censorship. These economic imperatives bring about a private censorship. Network officials can cut, retouch, and mutilate programs without violating any law. Network executives are running profit-making operations, and thus they work in the interest of business.

In sum, diversity in programming cannot be evaluated in terms of state/private ownership, but rather by the basic goals and organization of the television industry as a whole. Television programming in the Dominican Republic is, with some exceptions, a reflection of the business culture, of a society founded on the circulation of consumer goods. The uniformity of Dominican television does not arise from the will or ignorance of television staff. Private television networks are all basic agents for profit. Their goal is to produce images in such a way as to ensure a market in which to sell their audience to advertising agencies. In this context, it is the search for maximum profit that will structure the programming, for shows that will hold an audience. For television network owners and for those who advertise their products, what counts is not culture or social values; they are interested in how much profit they will derive.

The state-owned network is also interested in drawing large audiences. To a certain extent, this network is looking for advertising money, but it also seeks to extend government influence on the populace. Therefore, this network does not offer an alternative that could contribute to producing more diversity in television programming. Chapter 4 constitutes an analysis of the cultural content of Dominican television programming as a whole.

NOTES

1. Most developing countries followed the pattern of the powerful nation under whose influence they are. Former French colonies tend to adopt the French pattern; British colonies follow the pattern practiced in the United Kingdom; and so on.

2. However, as we will see in this chapter and the other chapters of this book, what is officially established is one thing and the reality of everyday television production is another. Indeed, the government sometimes pressures any network that broadcasts information which could affect government interests.

3. The basic factor that affects the prices advertisers pay for broadcast time is market size. The standard measurement of the cost of commercial time is CPM (cost per thousand). The formula for this calculation is commercial cost/audience delivered/1,000.

4. However, I found a variety of situations concerning everyday functioning within the Dominican television industry. In some networks there is a substantial direct collaboration between the directors of the different services, and in others there is little coordination between the directors of programming, the sales office, and the producers. The communication between different services more often than not passes through the administrators. In the opinion of a director of programming, some programs fail because they have not been adequately promoted by the sales department.

5. Ideology is conceptualized here in the sense proposed by Althusser (1984). It is not an abstract, stable set of ideas that we unconsciously adopt, but a practice. While a person is watching television, interpreting the messages received, he or she is constituted as a subject in ideology; there is a simultaneous and joint practice of making sense of what is being watched.

6. This procedure is very common in Latin America. In Colombia, where the networks are state owned, the sale of airtime to independent producers constitutes the bulk of the programming.

7. The ratings are a representation of the percentage of sets in use in a given sampled area at a given time; the share is the percentage of the audience a particular program is drawing in relation to other programs broadcast at the same time.

8. Thirty-five hours of prime time on weekdays (two hours between noon and 2 P.M. and five hours between 6 P.M. and 11 P.M. each day), and six hours on Saturdays and on Sunday afternoons (between 2 P.M. and 8 P.M.). This is a general average of all the networks. In reality there are slight differences from one network

to another; for instance, Teleantillas and Colorvisión have established the hour from 11 P.M. to midnight as prime time.

9. There are four audience-research firms in the Dominican Republic. The best-known are Asesores Asociados and Orientación Mercadológica S.A. Several television staff members interviewed think that this measurement is not always reliable. A journalist asserted, "If we totaled all the audience represented by the ranking companies, there would be more than 10 million inhabitants in the Dominican Republic."

10. In general, there is planning for one year, but many changes are made along the way. In fact, the planning is more a set of ideas and general goals than specific items.

11. This is what was expressed by most people I interviewed who were working in advertising and TV broadcasting. As a result of these considerations, there is some general tendency to distribute the advertising according to the targeted audience. For example, rum, soft drinks, laundry products, cigarettes, cosmetics, and the companies themselves are advertised more specifically in the shows directed to the people of lower socioeconomic status. Cars, banks, and some perfumes are advertised in serials, movies, news, and other programs that are supposed to draw more of their audience from a higher socioeconomic status. This is only a very general tendency; actually, in Dominican television there is no great rationality in the distribution of commercials within the programming.

12. "Low education" means those people who did not finish primary school; "moderate education" means those who completed at least the highest grade of primary school; and "high education" means those who have at least a secondary school diploma. These data and percentages are given only as approximations developed from the in-depth interviews.

13. However, there is no real difference between men and women during the two late hours of prime time, 10 P.M. to midnight.

14. This average is not valid for the entire year. Especially in 1990 and 1991, several sectors of the country, including Santo Domingo, experienced long electricity outages that the government caused in order to save fuel.

15. This does not apply to all the foreign productions, particularly from the United States. These shows are bought as packages in order to obtain good prices; therefore, once the network buys the package of serials, sitcoms, and movies, it has no choice but to broadcast them, even with low audience ratings.

16. According to Varis (1985), the three U.S. networks—ABC, NBC, and CBS—had one-third of their sales in Latin America. Bisbal's (1988) data indicate that three-fourths of imported television programs in Latin America are from the United States; in the Dominican Republic it was around 40 percent in 1988, with only 3 percent from Europe.

17. People interviewed were asked to indicate their primary choice in television programming and to describe what would be, for them, the best programming on a television network. Low education: variety musical shows, 24 percent; marathon one-man shows, 21 percent; *telenovelas*, 21 percent; comedy shows, 10 percent; U.S. serials, 9 percent; game shows, 8 percent; movies, 7 percent. Moderate education: programs of information (including news and informative talk shows, round tables, etc.), 19 percent; movies, 16 percent; marathon one-man shows, 14 percent; *telenovelas*, 14 percent; variety musical shows, 12 percent; U.S. serials, 12 percent; comedy shows, 8 percent; game shows, 5 percent. High education: programs of information, 32 percent; movies, 23 percent; U.S. serials, 12 percent;

marathon one-man shows, 12 percent; documentaries, 10 percent; variety musical shows, 8 percent; comedy shows, 3 percent.

18. Each episode of the soap opera yields between U.S. $1,500 and U.S. $2,500 profit. The cost of an episode varies from U.S. $300 to U.S. $700. A complete soap opera costs around U.S. $50,000. The U.S. serials cost around U.S. $600 per episode, and in some cases the price is higher; for example, when "Miami Vice" was in its heyday, it was U.S. $1,000 per episode. Considering that the average price of an ad is U.S. $140, that means more than U.S. $16,000 a day, U.S. $80,000 a week, and U.S. $320,000 a month in ad revenues. These figures are based on prices during the summer of 1989. The conversion to U.S. dollars has been done according to the official exchange rate at that time: 1 U.S. dollar = 6.35 Dominican pesos.

19. There is a very important Mexican television company also called Televisa, but there is no relation between these enterprises.

20. There are also special arrangements. For example, a Brugal ad (second most important rum producer company of the country) each hour yields 16,000 pesos (around U.S. $2,100) per month.

21. These figures correspond to September 1989. If we consider the prices in the United States, these rates appear very low; however, the average salary per month of engineers, university professors, and so on, was around U.S. $250.

22. The soap operas traditionally broadcast by the Dominican networks are produced in Mexico, Brazil, Argentina, Colombia, Venezuela, Puerto Rico, and Peru.

23. Dominican currency has experienced a devaluation (with respect to the U.S. dollar) of more than 15 percent each year since 1985. Although officially a dollar is worth 6.35 Dominican pesos, it is extremely difficult to find all the dollars the television industry needs at that price. A considerable part of imports are bought with dollars acquired in the black market, which fluctuates considerably. The price of a dollar in the black market was 7 pesos in September 1989 and 8.5 pesos in November 1989. In 1991, 1 U.S. dollar = 12 Dominican pesos.

24. Unless the network decides, as the network Independencia did, to show old and low-rated U.S. and Mexican movies, which are usually very cheap and can draw enough audience to pay for themselves.

25. These musical shows produced in the Dominican Republic, such as "El Show del Mediodía" (The Midday Show), draw a large audience in New York as well, where around 800,000 Dominicans live.

26. In this context, "cultural and educational programs" refers to those shows which present classical music, documentaries, talk shows about philosophy, art, or social problems, language courses, or any other aspect of life that is not presented under what has traditionally been considered as entertainment.

27. A high official of the state network, who has been involved with television for a long time, explained: "There has been an intent to create an educational television since the 1960s. In 1964 we brought several specialists from Puerto Rico and Boston in order to create a mixed programming in RTVD of commercial and educational television, but this never was really put in practice. In fact, in this country, culture does not pay."

28. As Cantor (1980) asserts, commercial television is rooted in business interests. Consequently the programs must be produced by people who are in agreement with the system or are willing to suppress dissident values. Work in Dominican television is particularly scarce; there are far more people with the desire to work in

television than there is work for them. In fact, directors of programming and network producers have only a small degree of freedom if they want to stay in the business. Within the networks there are frequent differences between the administrators and the directors of programming. The administrators accept as valuable only the programs that make money, and do not consider that some shows could give the network a good image and, in the long run, attract more advertising money. If a show does not produce immediate profits, the administrators tend to exert pressure to drop it.

29. For the purpose of this book, "television industry" refers basically to the networks, advertising agencies, independent producers, and importers of foreign productions. I did not include the importers of television sets.

30. Here television content is most particularly concerned with diversity in programming. The specific aspects of ideological and political pluralism are developed in chapters 5 and 6.

31. In the United States cable television allows for more choice. In the Dominican Republic the use of cable television that broadcasts the programs of the most important U.S. cable networks is limited to the urban upper-income groups.

32. For example, the movies produced in the United States, although different in theme, are often almost the same in format and in the structure of the story. Movies never lack a car chase, two or three fistfights, shouting battles, and the inevitable love scene; in comedy movies, the same jokes are reproduced continually.

33. Sometimes we can find a program that is really innovative, but that is rare if we analyze television programming as a whole.

34. There is competition not only between the networks but also between the big production companies.

35. This does not imply that statistics are useless; what is a mistake is to limit the explanation of human interaction to statistical measurement, as is the case in the television industry.

36. Not to mention the possible inaccuracies of the sampling system as well as the statistical margin of error, which is generally higher in the Dominican Republic than it is in the United States.

37. I am not stating here that television advertising does not stimulate consumption; rather, I am saying that its specific ways of reaching and influencing the audience are not really known. Therefore, the logic of the television industry today could be wrong, even for the purpose of selling products to the audience.

38. In order to approach and better describe the complexity of the social world, I use two conceptualizations for distributing people within social space: the concept of dominating (or ruling) and dominated classes and the classification by socioeconomic status. I have stratified the audience into three socioeconomic strata. The upper stratum consists in the main of those who control the most important means of production—the dominant class or bourgeoisie. The middle socioeconomic stratum is composed of the wage-earning middle class, the owners of small means of production and commercial enterprises, and the professionals. The low socioeconomic stratum is made up of urban workers, peasants, and peddlers. Members of the middle and the low socioeconomic strata have little power; they are dominated classes (although the expression of domination is experienced in different ways). See Appendix A, for more details.

39. Most people interviewed from middle and high strata (62 percent) look for

educational programs less often than for entertainment, but they like to have the opportunity to watch different kinds of programs.

40. What is represented by what Boorstin calls the popular taste can also be conceptualized as the taste inherent in mass culture.

41. This excerpt from his book expresses Boorstin's assertion very well:

Much of what we hear complained of as the "vulgarity," the emptiness, the sensationalism, the soapserialism, of television is not a peculiar product of television at all. It is simply the translation of the subliterature onto the television screen. . . . Never before were the vulgar tastes so conspicuous and so accessible to the prophets of our high culture. Subculture—which is of course the dominant culture of a democratic society—is now probably no worse, and certainly no better, than it has ever been. But it is emphatically more visible. (1978, p. 19)

Chapter 4

The Cultural Space

Culture is both an expression of a group or society and a result of external influences through time. For example, Spanish, African, and U.S. contributions have affected the culture of the Dominican Republic. Culture is a continuous and dialectical process, determined by traditions as well as by the continuous renewing of expressions of life within a given society. In earlier days the interaction of individuals, groups, and institutions such as the school and religion was the chief mode of cultural transmission; in contemporary society, however, the electronic media, particularly television, also play a powerful role in this process.

Through television, meanings, social representations, and desires are circulated; thus it is a generator of culture as well as the bearer of a particular vision of the world. Television is a fundamental arena of exchange of ideas and values.[1] The cultural and ideological content of television may be more or less influential, depending on multiple social psychological factors, but it is always there and it should be analyzed in terms of its impact on society as a whole.

In the Dominican Republic, television has become a crucial part of the social dynamics by which the culture maintains itself in a constant process of production and reproduction. This medium, because of its technological possibilities, plays a very important role in the collective imagination and, therefore, in the formation of a national culture. The fact that television does not require a literate audience makes it the mass medium par excellence in the Dominican Republic, where nearly 50 percent of the population is illiterate.

In this chapter I attempt to outline the role that television plays for the

Dominicans and its importance as a conveyer of cultural values and representations.

TELEVISION'S SIGNIFICANCE

This section of the chapter presents an analysis based on the audience's perception of television. One obvious deduction from my interviews is that the Dominican people (especially from the middle and low strata) enjoy television, and watching it is a major source of pleasure in their lives.

Television offers a daily dose of emotion, entertainment, and information to most Dominicans. As the political leader Rafael Taveras said, "Television is present in the quotidian needs that people must satisfy." The people sit in front of the television set every day even if they do not have any specific program to watch. The interviewees spend an average of four hours a day watching television. The members of the middle and lower classes particularly need daily contact with television. They see it as the least expensive way of spending their leisure, and it is also conveniently at hand: "With the television we do not have to go out for having fun," said a respondent. However, the higher the individuals in terms of social class and, above all, the more educated they are, the more negative is their attitude toward TV.

Television as Sign-Object

Television is a producer of culture and symbols, but it is also itself a symbol, a sign. As a cultural commodity it has a value in itself. In the Dominican Republic, especially among the lower socioeconomic strata, possession of a television set constitutes a status symbol.

Generally, within the domestic space of the lower social class, the television set is located in the corner of the living room on a pedestal, the other furniture being arranged in the room more or less within its scope of vision. The television set constitutes an eccentric pole to the traditional center of the room.

In the middle class home, the television set is in the bedroom (60 percent show a preference for this location) or in the living room (40 percent prefer this), on the coffee table or in a storage unit. Generally the apartments or houses of the middle class do not have a family room. In this social class television is viewed as a basic necessity but it is not as polarizing as in the lower class. It is less preeminent.

In general those of high socioeconomic status have a minimum of two television sets. Seventy-five percent of our interviewees locate the first set in the master bedroom. The second set is placed in the family room (50 percent) or in the children's playroom (20 percent). Only 10 percent of the members of the upper social class locate the television set primarily in the living room, and only 5 percent in the dining room. If they have more than two sets, the others are in the bedrooms. In most of these high status homes the television set is integrated with the other pieces of furniture or with the wall. Here the television set as object-furniture is eclipsed; it does not exist as a status symbol and is not an explicit object of ritual.

Television's Contribution to Education

There is a sharp difference between socioeconomic strata in the perceived importance of television as a learning resource. According to those of middle and high socioeconomic status, TV contributes poorly to education. People of low socioeconomic status, on the contrary, think that television is very useful for "learning things."[2] This could be explained by the differences in level of education and of comprehension of the world. Most of those of high and middle socioeconomic status have at least a secondary school education. Also, professionally, they occupy positions where they learn through means other than television. People of low social class in general have very little formal education, and they live and work in an environment that reinforces the limitations of their knowledge. Therefore, any information or orientation that is transmitted by television, even if it is mixed with entertaining programs, is viewed by the lower social class as an educational message. For example, they consider that they learn a lot from game and quiz shows, and from the very popular marathon comedy one-man shows like "El Gordo de la Semana" and "Sábado Grande." In such shows there are short "cultural capsules" stemming from a philosophy accepted by many Dominican television producers: *cultura con sabrosura* (culture with fun).

In addition, concerning a more general role of television as transmitter of knowledge and ideology, I found that people tend to believe that television generally portrays the "normal" way of living. Indeed, although there are diverse ways of interpreting a program, overall television transmits a particular way of life with which people compare their own, even if they do not agree. I could observe in the in-depth interviews that in several aspects people are quite influenced by what they see on TV.

For instance, they gain their knowledge of national and international events basically through television. And their opinion about those events is clearly determined by the telecast. They establish a set of values as a result of the images and messages they receive through their television sets. In events explicitly related to political parties, they tend to agree with the position closer to their beliefs, yet they look for orientation in the television shows. Likewise, the consumerist messages of television attract the viewers' attention. People, particularly of low socioeconomic status, see consumerism as the kind of life they should have in order to live "*como dios manda*" (as God requires), as a respondent expressed it. The basic and immediate dream of Dominican people of low socioeconomic status is to get money to buy material goods (a new TV, music systems, beauty products, clothes, etc.). Thus, it seems that television contributes not only to the creation of patterns of consumption among the poor that perpetuate their impoverished condition but also, since most of their desires for consumer goods cannot be satisfied, to reinforcement of their sense of economic frustration.

In terms of judging the ideology carried by television, people interviewed consider that a given network or program is more on the left or on the right in the political spectrum, more or less conservative or more or less liberal; rarely do they see a television network as working to transform the dominant social system. As one respondent said, "The shows on television indicate the normal way of living in the present society." This brings us to the problem of television's role as a cultural agent.

TELEVISION AS A CULTURAL AGENT

The institutionalized mass culture reproduced and diffused through television perhaps is not an exact expression of the culture of the masses, but it has become more and more its mirage, its representation. Cultural content is present in all television productions: in the news programs, in the entertainment shows, and in the commercials. The cultural message, of course, varies depending on whether the shows are U.S. serials and movies, *telenovelas* produced in Latin America, or talk shows produced in the Dominican Republic. In the following pages I analyze the cultural content of entertainment programs that are most popular among Dominican audiences. These programs include the one-man marathon shows, *telenovelas*, and U.S. productions (basically serials and movies). I also analyze the content of television advertising.

Marathon Shows

These shows are eight hours long and present a little of everything. Games and contests in which the studio audience participates and popular music are mixed with talk segments and short documentaries (sometimes with educational content) as well as discussions of current social problems that affect people's everyday lives (for example, lack of electricity or water, problems with gangs in a given sector of the capital city, etc.). Moreover, these shows are full of commercials. They present an enormous number of previously filmed advertisements, and the host (who is also the producer) also advertises products and businesses live during the show. The two most important of these shows are "El Sábado Grande" (The Big Saturday) and "El Gordo de la Semana" (The Week's Fat), which are on the air Saturday and Sunday afternoons, respectively.

Marathon shows secure the spectators' participation. They create a collective festivity with exciting music and lively action. These shows have a very informal format, and offer direct contact and immediate participation to the audience, allowing members of the studio audience to become performers by participating in games, singing with the stars, or telling jokes. This induces the viewers in their homes to identify with the action.

Furthermore, the antics depicted are inspired by everyday situations. The plain speaking and hearty laughter of the producer-host is liberating because it overturns conventions and proprieties. People present on stage refer to the hosts with familiarity, calling them by their first names without any formality, as if they were talking to their close friends. These marathon shows create comedy situations that offer direct and immediate satisfaction to spectators. They reproduce various aspects of the lower social stratum subculture (which is frequently classified as popular culture) that the program hosts often ridicule through their jokes.

In these shows some segments address problems of Dominican society, although their overall message focuses on the fact that these problems are created by the negative actions of a few ("the bad guys"). There is no real critique of the organization of the economy and the society.

The producers of the two most important marathon shows, Rafael Corporán de los Santos and Freddy Veras Goico, are so popular and enjoy such status that they are even playing political roles. Corporán de los Santos ran for mayor of Santo Domingo on the ticket of the conservative Partido Reformista Social-Cristiano in 1986 and 1990. In 1986 he lost by a slim margin, and in 1990 he became mayor. Veras Goico was seriously considered as a candidate for vice president by the centrist Partido Revolucionario Dominicano (PRD) in the 1986 election, although this did not materialize. In the 1990 elections, the PRD candidate for mayor of Santo Domingo was Johnny Ventura, a television producer and popular singer of merengues (a very popular Dominican music and dance form), who had been a member of Congress from 1982 to 1986.

Telenovelas

Most *telenovelas* are based on familiar themes, sometimes mixed with new ideas.[3] Romance is the central theme, most of the time a crazy or impossible love. Frequently the *telenovelas* depict the story of a poor girl who, after experiencing numerous adversities, ends up marrying a handsome, rich man. There is also the representation of a naive and good person who is a victim for most of the episodes, but at the end finds the way to liberate herself and become successful in life. Most of the time, this success is equated with becoming rich. *Telenovelas* also depict the experiences of people migrating to the big city from rural areas. Sometimes the conflicts between old and young, tradition and modernity, are presented.

Social climbing, the desire for economic security, and financial ambition are constant elements in most *telenovelas* broadcast on Dominican television. Moreover, the impulse behind these shows is usually not to gain social equality by fighting injustice and exploitation, but to suggest the possibility of rising to a higher class by marriage, social relations, or other individual means. With some exceptions (for example, the Brazilian *telenovela* "Malu Mulher"),[4] *telenovelas* project the idea that women can best achieve success through marriage. Value is attributed to developing social skills (for women and for men) in order to have access to the superior class. Progress and social change in these shows are limited to individual access to economic power and social position. Conflicts between social classes and generations are presented as interpersonal affairs. Indeed, there is usually social mobility, in particular among the main characters. The central characters have lower-status occupations only as a point of departure in life. The central characters, chiefly the men, are most often successful professionals (businessmen, physicians, lawyers, etc.) in a wealthy setting. As a matter of fact, a luxurious environment is never absent from the *telenovelas*, even when the setting is rural.

Most stories in *telenovelas* revolve around the family. There is an extended family (which includes parents, grandparents, aunts, uncles, sisters, brothers, cousins, etc.), and there is constant reference to the unity of the family against outsiders. Representations of marriage and the family in these shows contain several contradictions. There are always stable unions counterbalanced by precarious relationships continually in crisis and threatened by disturbances largely due to the desires or faults of individuals. The adversities experienced by marriage and the family in managing people's desires is not a negation of their importance. Rather, there is constantly an ideal of a good and happy marriage and a secure family.

Telenovelas feature a multiplicity of characters and plots. In some the numbers of characters exceeds twenty, and a variety of topics are introduced and explored from diverse positions. This multiplicity of characters and plots constitutes a "paradigmatic complexity" (Allen 1985) that enlarges the possibilities of interpretation. Thorburn suggests that this "multiplicity" opens up the text and, therefore, "familiar characters-types and situations become more suggestive and less imprisoning" (1982, p. 539). These characters are perceived both as individuals offering opportunities for identification and as bearers of social and moral values. Every social group has its presence, though the rich and famous and the middle and high socioeconomic groups are depicted as the model. In other words, this diversity of plots allows the *telenovelas* to offer a variety of fantasies and potential identifications to viewers. They can choose the situations and the characters they like.

Indeed, *telenovelas*, particularly those of the 1980s, offer some latitude concerning sexuality, class, and race. Homosexuality, interracial marriage, and union actions are presented through experiences of a number of characters. However, some perspectives, such as the traditional idea of what constitutes a happy family life and normal middle- and upper-class consumer life, are generally given higher priority. The traditional view is usually held by the principal characters. The most controversial social issues are usually brought into question by characters who play a secondary role, rarely by the hero or the heroine. The absence of a definite closure during most of the episodes allows the juxtaposition of traditional values with new ones, although at the end the apparent contradictions are generally resolved by compromises acceptable to the mainstream.

The viewer of *telenovelas* is required to adapt to a different focus and to several characters' reactions to an event. Therefore, to help the viewer accommodate to the story, particularly to follow the relational network of characters, and as a means of bringing up to date viewers who missed an episode, *telenovelas* use repetitive conversations about the same events or relationships by several characters under different circumstances. That is, *telenovelas* not only activate meanings and pleasures in their viewers, but also provide the textual space for those meanings and pleasures to be articulated within the viewers' perception of the lifeworld. Moreover, these shows offer individuals—in particular from the lower social groups—the opportunity to dream of escaping their everyday life of economic limitations and frustrations by giving them possibilities to identify with the powerful and the elite, and with the poor persons who become rich on screen. It is common for people who comment on *telenovelas* to identify themselves with particular characters or specific events. The *telenovelas* are a subject of conversation at home as well as between neighbors (especially between women).

As a matter of fact, much of the pleasure of the Dominican viewers of *telenovelas* lies in playing with the boundary between the representation and the real. Viewers of *telenovelas* talk about what they see on the screen and refer to it in their lives. They give the stars of the *telenovelas* almost a real life. For example, while watching the *telenovela*, there are very often comments such as "This makes me think of my sister's relations with her husband" or "This man is as unfaithful as my husband." Or a viewer may comment to a neighbor about a particular story: "You know, life is hard, but there is always some possibility to improve. Look at Maria [a *telenovela* character]; she finally found happiness."

Telenovelas viewers experience pleasure through the ease with which they accommodate themselves to the shows' produced meanings and subject positions. *Telenovelas* offer them the possibility of making meanings significant to themselves. These shows are related in many ways (although idealized) to the life of the people as well as to their dreams, and the codes used are within any viewer's psychological and verbal skills. These elements, along with their dramatic content, their emotional images, and glamorous settings, enable *telenovelas* to pervade large sectors of the Dominican society.

U.S. Productions

Two forms of collective representations determine the popularity of serials and movies in the Dominican Republic: (1) the conventions of the genre (adventure, action, etc.) and (2) the oral tradition of the Dominican audience. For business reasons the U.S. television industry tries to project images that tap into the oral tradition of a large part of the population, primarily in the United States but also in other parts of the world.

This is facilitated because the cinematic experience of Hollywood movies has engrossed viewers in Latin America and all over the world for a long period. As a consequence, a taste for U.S. productions has developed. Those who were born after the creation of television have also been influenced by its particular frame of reference. Furthermore, in the context of the Dominican market, U.S. productions, compared with most competitors from Europe, provide a more escapist and fantasy type of entertainment that Dominican mass audiences prefer. They also offer the networks the possibility of new material each year.

U.S. serials and movies depict a society related to the mainstream culture of the United States. "Miami Vice" and "Dallas," for example, are cultural forms of a postindustrial capitalist, consumerist, pleasure-centered society, with plenty of sex, sensuality, leisure, music, and fashion. The attractiveness of characters is a result of the way they are encoded as a result of the blend of sophisticated technical codes (camera work, lighting, setting, casting, etc.) and cultural codes. These shows have large audiences in the Dominican Republic because they represent the power of money and make extensive use of sexual symbols. In these shows, there are numerous representations of the female body as an object for the masculine eye and as a source of voyeuristic pleasure. The actresses who provide much of the backdrop in shows like "Miami Vice" and "Dallas" are clear evidence of this voyeuristic pleasure at work. These shows offer a great deal of escapism and are considered to be a personal flight into action and sexual fantasy.

The portrayal of the family is here very similar to that in *telenovelas*. Contradictions are shown, but at the end the idea that a good marriage is the best alternative and ultimate objective is upheld. However, values such as community life, equality, dignity, solidarity, and sharing are less emphasized in the U.S. productions than in *telenovelas*. In *telenovelas*, the world is more complex than in the serials. Actually, since U.S. serials and movies are basically centered on Americans of middle and low socioeconomic status, the world depicted in the bulk of these productions tends to be less complex and diversified. The few elements of social criticism in defense of the poorest that from time to time appear in the *telenovelas* are even more scarce in the U.S. serials and movies.

The U.S. serials have elements that differ from one program to another (for example, different characters or stories), in order to give an appearance of novelty. This is necessary to ensure their profitability, but the diversity they present is quite limited. They reproduce a group of ideas and approaches using the same basic structures and framing, and therefore the resulting message is more or less standardized. In other words, when considering the cultural content, diversity exists only within the limits of certain fundamental ideas, which are no more than variations on standard themes. When a show differs considerably from the standard, it does not last long.

In fact, the U.S. serials and movies allow a smaller margin of interpretation than the *telenovelas* do. This is because *telenovelas* are addressed to a broad audience (women, of course, but also men) in different countries and less integrated subcultures, while the serials need to draw big audiences in the United States first in order to become profitable.[5] Therefore, the content of the latter is more accommodated to the way the television industry views the cultural structure.

Gerbner's research on violence in television (1970) is still relevant for explaining most of the cultural and ideological content of U.S. fiction shows. Despite some sophistication and a little more subtlety in today's U.S. productions, the basic trends in the representations of the world in the most popular U.S. serials have been consistent through time. Gerbner's findings suggest that heroes are socially central types who embody the dominant ideology, whereas villains and victims are members of deviant or subordinate subcultures who represent the dominant ideology less intensively and frequently embody ideologies that oppose it (for example, atheism or communism). Some ideological codes are more explicit than others—for instance, representations of heroism, villainy, attractiveness, aesthetics, and political ideology are used fairly openly and amply. But there are other codes—such as class, morality, and race—that are not so evident although always present. As Fiske asserts, "It is in the aggregate of apparently insignificant encoding that ideology works most effectively" (1987, p. 13).

Gerbner also demonstrates that both heroes and villains use violence, but heroes are always successful in their violent enterprise, whereas villains are not. He establishes several categories of killers and their victims by age, sex, race, and class. The killers are both heroes and villains; the killed are mostly villains. He found that a character who was white, male, middle class, and young was very likely to be alive at the end of the show. On the other hand, those characters who were not, were usually killed during the show. Furthermore, the villains rarely correspond to the stereotype of the middle-class U.S. citizen. The opposition between heroes and villains, and the ways in which it is dramatized, is an expression of power relationships in society, and thus a process through which the dominant ideology is furthered.

Similar trends are present in cartoons and Disney movies. Dorfman and Mattelart (1975), in their study of Donald Duck cartoons, described how Walt Disney consistently expresses villainy through working-class appearance and manners. And Real (1977), analyzing Disneyland's representation of the world, finds an ethnocentric insensitivity to the Third World and an idealization of the U.S. past, as well as a reinforcement of a U.S. business worldview and motivational structure.

In other words, the "normal and good people" in U.S. serials and television movies belong most of the time to the middle class, which upholds the family, patriotism, consumerism, individualism, winner/loser paradigms, and other ideological patterns that characterize the "American way of life." This is an ideal that is a reality only in the television world and in other U.S. media productions. But this idea works very well as the collective imagination in the Dominican Republic, and it is reproduced through television as a notion of what most people of the United States stand for. That is, these images of the world presented in television drama are not exactly reality but a dominant perception of reality. As Fiske (1987, p. 21) remarks, television "has a great ability to carry a socially convincing sense of the real."

Some shows are more sophisticated than others, but in general what is conceived of as the dominant ideology in U.S. society is still reproduced in television fiction shows, through the heroes and heroines. Even if, as Cantor (1980) remarks, there have been some changes in "moral teachings" since the 1960s, it is unthinkable that a central character of a TV serial could be an atheist, a homosexual, a leftist political activist, or even someone who fights against the business society. Gitlin's observations on this issue are particularly enlightening:

Television's world is relentlessly upbeat, clean, and materialistic. Even more sweepingly, with few exceptions prime time gives us people preoccupied with personal ambition. If not utterly consumed by ambition and the fear of ending up as losers, these characters take both the ambition and the fear for granted. If not surrounded by middle-class arrays of consumer goods, they themselves are glamorous incarnations of desire. The happiness they long for is private, not public; they make few demands on society as a whole, and even when troubled they seem content with the existing institutional order. Personal ambition and consumerism are the driving forces in their lives.

... The sumptuous and brightly lit setting of most series amounts to advertisements for a consumption-centered version of the good life, and this does not even take into consideration the incessant commercials, which convey the idea that human aspirations for liberty, pleasure, accomplishment, and status can be fulfilled in the realm of consumption. The relentless background hum of prime time is this packaged good life. (1983, pp. 268–69)

The desire for material comfort and for consumption, which is so ingrained in most people in the Dominican Republic, is not a result solely of the U.S. productions, but the messages broadcast by television do disseminate these ideas and contribute considerably to their reinforcement.

The content of the U.S. productions is inevitably ethnocentric (as are, although perhaps to a lesser extent, the *telenovelas* produced in Argentina or Brazil, or any production from Europe). The reason for this is that the U.S. serials and movies have been created in a system which requires gaining the highest viewer ratings in U.S. society. Therefore, the way of life they promote is in various aspects alien to the constitution and formulation of a Dominican national culture.[6]

These programs play a very important role in the promotion of the business ideology that pervades the United States. They project the customs and habits of a greedy, competitive society that intensifies desires for consumer goods and luxuries, and in which success is achieved through aggressive and sometimes violent behavior. The heroes of these productions basically portray the happy side of consumerism (luxury and sports cars, swimming pools, sumptuous homes, etc.). Social problems such as crime, violence, the difficulties of urban life, and social insecurity are represented, but they are rarely linked with the organization of the society. There is little critical questioning of the business society. Crime and violence are explained as the result of individual deficiencies. As Gallo put it, "In the kingdom of the hamburger the vegetarian does not speak out. He or she will perhaps discuss the style of cooking the meat, but no more than that" (1989, p. 34). In these productions even the process of political democratization is equated with capitalism and consumerism.

People who control television in the Dominican Republic contribute enormously to the dissemination of these cultural influences and thus also to the hegemony of the business-oriented society, in which only money is important (which is not astounding, since those who control this medium are businessmen).

The imports of U.S. television productions started at the beginning of the 1950s, with the establishment of the first Dominican network, Radio-Television Dominicana, increased with the appearance of the network Rahintel, and developed dramatically after the fall of Trujillo. Most of these programs have been concentrated during prime time, and so their effect on Dominican society has been proportionately even higher if it is calculated in terms of audience impact.

Furthermore, many programs that are not directly imported are derived from an imported model that has been translated into local terms. A good number of national programs follow U.S. formats, such as talk shows, game shows, and variety shows. This is not strange, since salesmen for the international television market frequently offer catalogs of ideas for local production together with the packages of films and serials. Thus, the form is followed, if not always the content.

Television Advertising

Stephen Leacock, a British humorist, described advertising as "the science of arresting the human intelligence long enough to get money from it" (quoted in Green, 1982, p. 400). Advertising is indeed a stimulus to consumption, but it also has an important influence in the constitution of culture. This is so even if its impact is not immediate and cannot be interpreted as a pattern in terms of cause and effect.

As a matter of fact, it is still difficult to know how effective television advertising is in making people buy a specific product. People's personal tastes are not completely predictable and manipulable in the short term, and probably not in a specific and mechanistic cause-and-effect manner.[7] The reception of a commercial message is subject to many variables that are difficult to measure either individually or socially. The audience may create a meaning different from the one intended by the producers of the advertising, and so may not react to a commercial as hoped. Besides, it is extremely difficult to evaluate the direct impact of television advertising on the consumer through survey techniques (as some marketing research firms do), or even through in-depth interviews. People are not always honest when asked why they buy a given product.[8] If asked directly why they buy a specific product—for example, a laundry product—they may answer that it is cheaper or that it is a good product. If asked about a specific brand of clothes, they will reply that the quality is good (among the higher stratum) or the price is good (among lower strata). If asked about a car, they will say that it is reliable. They try to give a rational answer and do not want to appear to be influenced by television advertising. People, particularly adults,[9] rarely say that consuming a specific product makes them feel that their life-style matches the one depicted in the commercial.

In other words, the impact of television advertising is not only in its most immediate purpose—to create a desire for certain products in the population (in order to sell them)—but also in the changes that it produces in consumer habits and in the extent of its influence to impose models of living. The effect of advertising on culture is not a result of the television commercials only; it works in connection with the content of the fiction shows (serials and movies) and other television productions. In fact, the most pervasive aspect of advertising is its effect on the culture as a whole rather than its ability to sell a given product.

Since the 1980s the tendency in advertising has been not to emphasize rational aspects—for instance, how good a given product is—but to relate the product to specific situations of joy and pleasure, appealing more to the emotional aspect of the individual than to rationality. "Making consumers feel something is much more important than convincing them that a product is better," says Esther Thorson, advertising researcher at the University of Wisconsin (quoted in Allman 1989, p. 60).

In general, television viewers in the Dominican Republic have a negative attitude toward television advertising. They criticize the overabundance of advertisements as well as their content. There is also concern about the fact that more than 50 percent of the commercials advertise alcohol and cigarettes. Indeed, a large part of television production is supported by the advertising of national as well as international firms (mostly from the United States) that produce alcoholic beverages and cigarettes. The advertising of hard liquor and tobacco, forbidden on U.S. television, is extensive in the Dominican Republic as well as in the rest of Latin America.[10]

All interviewees stated that television advertising does not cause them to buy more of a specific product or to choose to buy a product. Nevertheless, some people from the lower stratum said that if they needed it, they would perhaps choose to buy a specific product over another that was not advertised, as long as there was not a large difference in price.

However, I found that the interviewees' familiarity with most brands of products they knew was a result of television advertising.[11] Knowing a product does not imply that it will be chosen, but it is an indication that television commercials fulfill at least part of their purpose.[12] I also perceived a direct relation between what viewers considered to be a good product and the advertising of this product on television.

It is necessary to distinguish between two means of promoting consumption. The first is the traditional direct advertisement, presented specifically and clearly as what it is: commercial advertising. The second may be more pervasive but is more difficult to evaluate because it is very subtle: the influence that movies and serials have on consumerism and on the culture in general.[13]

Therefore, the cultural influence of television occurs as a result of the general marketing campaign (explicit as well as implicit) that includes the content of movies, serials, and other programs as well as direct advertising. The movies and serials constitute an ideal setting for advertising because fiction shows promote a way of living. They promote furniture, cars, clothes, drinks, and so on without being commercial advertisements, even if there is seldom a reference to a specific brand. Several products may be advertised in a single serial or movie.

Advertising works not only by directing people to consume a specific brand of a given product but also, and above all, by stimulating people to consume that product in the long run. For example, if there is an advertising campaign for Johnny Walker whiskey, people may not buy that brand but they may consume whiskey.

As was stated earlier, advertising does not necessarily have an immediate effect on the population, but it does influence in some ways how people perceive life. As far as I can ascertain from the interviews and observations, the messages seem to be received and assimilated differently from one person to another, but it is also clear that if there were not television advertising, the level of consumption of a given product would not be as high as it is (chiefly of drinks, cigarettes, and beauty products).

Overall, in the Dominican Republic, advertising seems to affect the habits of consumption of people with a low level of education (workers, peasants, etc.) more directly. This appears to be a general tendency in the Third World countries, and sometimes it has dramatic consequences. One of the best-known examples was the campaign in favor of bottle-feeding babies in Africa in the 1960s. The misuse of the formula contributed to the deaths of thousands of babies. Since then the World Health Organization has elaborated an international code to control the commercialization of formula for babies, forbidding advertising it and any other form of promotion.[14] However, this international code has not been followed by all countries. The Dominican Republic, for example, still telecasts formula advertisements.

Television advertising promotes consumer ideology as part of the collective consciousness. Advertising agencies utilize the ideas, beliefs, and feelings common to the collective organism (Cathelat 1976) for promoting consumption. Advertising takes some elements, some ways of doing things, and some expressions that already exist among some groups, and amplifies them, giving them a kind of general legitimacy and thus playing the role of a reproducing and enhancing agent.

In the Dominican Republic, television advertising praises the goods possessed by rich urbanites of postindustrial societies and exalts the ways of life of these societies. Even when the advertisement promotes agricultural products, it presents very modern farms as models. For example, the ads of Ferquido (probably the most important fertilizer company in the country) depict peasants working in an ideal modern environment with machinery and lush crops.

A triple mirage in the advertising process is continually developed in order to capture the imagination of the population for the profits of the advertising agencies and their clients. It presents an idealized urban life as the model to the rural inhabitants; the mirage of the consumption of the elite is offered to the middle class and the urban poor; and the mirage of distinctiveness and a model of rich countries' (like the United States) way of life is presented to all. In most advertisements, the same cultural stereotypes, with some variations, pass from the urban centers of the United States to the television screens of the Dominican Republic.[15]

The drive to create a global life-style in the advertising content is the product of the interaction between the growth of global communication systems, the international expansion of advertising agencies, and conceptions about consumer psychology.[16] The global advertising campaign involves the creation in one country of a common theme or message that is applied in all countries where a particular product is made or distributed (the best-known examples of this are the advertising campaigns of Marlboro, Winston, Coca-Cola, Pepsi, and Revlon). An advertiser explained: "This mechanism assures the transnational advertiser of increased efficiency, quality control, a uniform company image in all markets, and a substantial reduction in agency fees." In this view, it is supposed that there are certain universal consumer characteristics. Arthur C. Fatt, the former head of a large U.S. advertising agency, claimed that despite obvious language and cultural differences, people of the world have the same basic needs and desires: "People everywhere from Argentina to Zanzibar want a better way of life for themselves and the desire to be beautiful, to be free of pain, to be healthy, etc., is universal" (quoted in Ryan 1969, p. 70).

For instance, the advertisements for the locally brewed brands of beer in the Dominican Republic (Presidente, Quisqueya, and Bohemia) consist of groups of attractive young people playing on the beach, in the sea, or in the mountains, or dancing the lambada or merengue. The screen is full of fun, of magnificent natural landscapes, and of young, tanned bodies in constant movement, emphasizing particularly the female body.

These scenes project a deep sensuality and give the impression of physical and spiritual liberation. There is no control or submission. The beer bottle is part of this moment: The scene is edited to make it a part of the bodies of the young. The way the bottle is opened and the manner of drinking the beer suggest sexual liberation and pleasure. The beach or the mountains represent a space of freedom far from the constraints of society. These ads are very similar to those used worldwide in the advertising of Coca-Cola, Pepsi, and other drinks, although the latter are less explicitly sexual.

The fragmentation of the female body into a sexual object is commonplace in Dominican television (as it is in the United States and in most parts of the world), especially in commercials. This is true not only for products directed toward men, but also for products directed toward women, such as underwear and cosmetics. It is clear, as Fiske remarks, that "The mobilization of masculine desire in the female viewer and the construction for her of a masculine reading position from which she can make sense of her own body through masculine eyes is an obvious business strategy of the industry" (1987, p. 226).

The representation of aesthetics in television advertising probably also contributes to produce an inferiority complex among most people in this country. The Marlboro cowboy and the fascinating blondes of beauty products present a clear model of northern cultural inspiration. These images are frequently imitated, even in the ads produced by Dominicans. In the Dominican Republic the existence of some racial prejudice is used by the advertisements in order to sell creams that are supposed to lighten the complexion as well as products for helping to make the hair straight. Therefore, although the advertising firms may not have created racial prejudice and the aesthetic taste of the public, they have contributed amply to reproduction of racial prejudice and reinforcement of a given idea of beauty.

The advertising firms, Dominican or international, follow the same pattern of advertising, which consists in reducing the cultural values to consumable signs and, in doing so, emptying them of their real content. Each time the myths of the traditional Dominican culture are taken as a reference point by the advertising companies, they actually serve as a means to a new acculturation. Indications of this are commercials based upon certain aspects of traditional life in the Dominican Republic. These commercials idealize expressions of popular culture, particularly those related to rural life (such as singing folk songs while farming, helping a neighbor to build a house or a stable, etc.), and empty these cultural expressions of their real value by portraying an idealized and superficial image of them. For example, an advertisement for Barceló rum represents a group of happy agriculturalists singing while working on a humble farm; but the extremely clean and idealized environment does not have any existence in the real world.

The fundamental message of advertising is that no society can escape becoming a society of consumption.[17] Advertising on television not only creates commercial products but also contributes to creating ways of living. As Cathelat (1976) remarked, it creates a particular civilization.

TELEVISION AS CONSUMERIST CULTURE

The logic of consumer capitalism aims at constantly stimulating the level of consumption through the production of signs and reproducing these signs materially.[18] In this context, television has become a primary apparatus for the mass production and circulation of self-imitating artifacts. This medium has perhaps accelerated the consumerist culture of Dominican society more than any other cultural institution.[19] In fact, the cultural values of the Dominican Republic are strongly characterized by a frenetic consumer life-style, inspired by the most superficial aspects of the life-style of a postindustrial society such as the United States, despite the disparity in the economic situations of these two societies.

The constant aim of the official economic programs of the Dominican Republic since the 1970s has been to stimulate savings and to reduce the consumption of luxury products. However, television, through advertising and entertainment shows, proposes and diffuses ways of life that undermine these goals by stimulating consumption of luxury products and, therefore, undercutting productive savings. In other words, the official economic positions are systematically eroded by one of the most important apparatuses of social information and learning that the Dominican society possesses.[20] And the concern of the advertising agencies and their clients will not in any way modify that tendency. As the following statement of one advertiser interviewed shows, their view is to a certain extent similar to that of drug dealers:

I think that our role consists in selling things, reaching the potential buyers, and thereby contributing to stimulate the economy. I do not think that there are superfluous needs. If people want, for example, a VCR or . . . a bottle of whiskey, it is a need for them, as important as food. I do not believe that the government should promote controls or impose taxes which would deprive people of what could be categorized as superfluous under the pretext that they lack the basic necessities.

The deleterious content of Dominican television programming has been recognized by the executive staffs of the networks, although they emphasize the content without criticizing the fundamental business role of television. In a document that they presented to the country on the very popular television marathon show "El Gordo de la Semana" (in June 1989), they stated that "the exploitation of passion, violence, and sex in order to stimulate consumption is a violation of individual human rights." They also declared that "some foreign programs bring with them transculturation, which affects the essence of Dominican values," and that "transculturation introduces elements of escape that could affect the young." They committed themselves to support the concern of Comisión Nacional de Espectáculos Públicos (National Commission of Public Spectacle—an institution similar to the U.S. Federal Communications Commission) to promote the defense of the essential values of the Dominican Republic. They also committed themselves "to use television to create a mentality of dialogue that would lead to the creation of a new language, which would in turn allow the development of a national identity." They further agreed that television would promote the basic human rights which are the basis for a just and free society.[21]

Two years after that declaration, no significant changes had been made, except for a slight reduction in the number of U.S. serials and movies on some networks. As a matter of fact, the reduction of U.S. productions was basically for economic reasons. This process started in the first half of 1989 in most networks. In any case, the question is not just one of imported programs versus national productions, since most of the shows and commercials produced in the Dominican Republic do not present a message that can be considered less alienating than that of imported programs. In fact, some are even worse. The bulk of popular Dominican shows have as much escapism and "exploitation of passion" in their content as the imported programs.

The problem lies in the nature of the television system in the country, in its dependence on commercial arrangements. In fact, the messages of television are very similar throughout Latin America, and in most countries with a commercially oriented television system.

Everybody Likes Milk

Dominican society, like most societies, is composed of a variety of groups and subcultures. It is marked by divisions of class, levels of education, age, political positions, and so on. Therefore, television messages will not always be received in exactly the same way by all audiences, a situation which causes the television industry to develop programs in such a way that they validate not the differences among the various groups but the cultural elements they have in common. Commercial television, because of the way it is organized, can succeed only by overcoming this diversity and finding the elements common to most groups: the largest common denominator.

Telenovelas and U.S. serials offer some possibilities for exploring diversity. But this openness does not imply that their content inspires people to negate the social structures of consumerism. As Hall argues, the openness of the message should not be overestimated:

Polysemy must not be confused with pluralism. Connotative codes are not equal among themselves. Any society/culture tends, with varying degrees of closure, to impose its segmentations... its classifications of the... world upon its members. There remains a dominant cultural order, though it is neither univocal nor uncontested. (1973, p. 13)

Television's need to draw large audiences in a society composed of groups with different and often conflicting interests requires its content to be more or less open to interpretation and to address aspects that are common to a majority of the population. But above all, television programs should present easily attainable meanings for a variety of viewers. A television program, in order to be a success, must be familiar, immediately understandable, and acceptable to most viewers. These are common elements of the most popular shows in the Dominican Republic.

The rules of the game in Dominican television do not allow it to produce programs for all specific subcultures and different minorities; television producers have to use elements of each subculture in almost every show. There is a trend to produce something neutral and common to everybody. As a movie director, referring to the success of his last production, said while he was interviewed on the U.S. network ABC: "This movie is like milk, and everybody likes milk." That is the basic cultural drive behind television entertainment programming in the Dominican Republic: to produce something that can be liked by almost everyone. Television producers try to find cultural symbols that will appeal to the largest part of the population. In particular, when a new program is created, they choose themes that will be accepted by a mass audience almost immediately (in the Dominican Republic, a new production is not allowed much time to draw audiences). And any individual show aims at being attractive to a variety of people. Even when a show is aimed mainly at a specific group, it also addresses matters of interest to other groups.

Consequently, the bulk of Dominican television programming makes use of mainstream ideas that overlap the different subcultures. Because those elements of the dominant culture which are shared by the different groups and subcultures are overemphasized, there is a tendency toward homogenization.

The Dilemma of Dominant Taste

Television organizes its content according to the taste of those who constitute the majority: the less educated people, most of whom are of low socioeconomic status. It is not unusual, though, to find a fair number of almost illiterate persons in high socioeconomic status, because political influence and corruption provide possibilities for the rapid accumulation of wealth.

The greater the audience the television networks aim to reach, the less controversial the content of their programming. There is, then, a limitation in the diversity of the programs. The extent of the influence of television programs on viewers is open to debate; I do not assume that television has a direct manipulative effect on an audience, and it is possible that viewing a program does not inevitably involve embracing its ideology. Studies of the processes involved in forming opinions or altering ideas show little evidence that a specific television program directly produces sudden or radical changes in people's views on important subjects. However, if we consider television programming as a whole, we can suppose that in some ways television does affect the view the audiences have of the world. There are enough elements (as Gerbner 1970, 1984; Gitlin 1980; Schlesinger 1987; Iyengar et al. 1984 and others reveal) to propose that generally, though frequently mediated, television has a basic importance in people's representation of the world.

This is further evidenced by the stereotypes formed of people in other countries. What image does the United States have abroad? In Europe and in Latin America the media, especially television and the cinema, identify the United States with sex, power, freedom, adventure, and money. This image is furthered by producers and distributors in their movies, serials, and video clips in order to provide audiences in the United States and abroad with vicarious fulfillment of their fantasies. The television and cinema industries make money with the selling of dreams. But the point is that most people around the world do not interpret the content of movies and television serials only as fiction. Even if they do not always watch television with naiveté, the only way they can have an idea of what the United States is like is through the serials and movies. And this happens in reverse as well. Most U.S. citizens take the depiction of other countries in the movies or on television as the basis for their perception of those countries. Few people have the possibility to travel extensively in other countries in order to formulate a more accurate idea of what they are like.

Furthermore, in order to understand and enjoy a given show on television, viewers are required to adopt the social position and the social identity that the content implies. In doing this on an almost daily basis, they construct a particular sense of themselves and their social relations, and also participate in the reproduction of the ideology being expressed. This does not mean that viewers identify absolutely with the content. The maintenance of a given content in television programming does not require an identification (although frequently there is identification), but only the passive approval implicit in the act of watching. In general, as long as a given program is watched by a large audience, it will continue to be on the air and its content will be imitated by shows on competing networks as well as by future programs of the same network or producer.

Without a doubt there is a potent, continuous influence of television on a level more fundamental than that of daily events and opinions. The hegemony of the business ideology is produced through the daily messages that work to validate and render acceptable the society of consumption. This change does not occur overnight; rather, it is a long process, even if cultural changes in the age of the electronic media are more rapid than ever before.

Dream Machine

As we saw in the analysis of *telenovelas* and U.S. productions, television entertainment offers the viewers a sort of daydreaming that allows them to fulfill their desires in a way impossible in the real world. Television entertainment constitutes, as Fiske points out, "a compensatory domain which results from and disguises their [the viewers'] lack of power" (1987, p. 317). It is also a way of escaping the everyday struggles of a competitive and difficult way of life, especially for those who occupy subordinate positions.

The fascination of Dominicans for the life-styles of the postindustrial countries, as they are presented by television and the movies, could be interpreted as a "normal" human dream. Everyone dreams about what is far away. This happens in the postindustrial countries as well as in the developing countries. However, there is a difference. In developed countries, people dream of a picturesque Third World. For the people of developing countries such as the Dominican Republic, the dream of consumption is not just a simple escape from their monotony. It is an escape to a way of existence considered superior. It represents what they desire to become. However, only some will occasionally experience the luxuries of consumption; most of the population will know only the luxury of identification.

In this chapter I have analyzed the role of television in the constitution and reproduction of culture in the Dominican Republic. We have seen that television is perceived differently by people belonging to different socioeconomic strata. Its role as a social agent is affected by the economic requirements of the structure in which it is enmeshed, and is largely determined by the industry's perception of mass culture. This view, in turn, influences the programming content of Dominican television as a whole, which overall tends to promote conspicuous consumption, cupidity, and individual ambition as cultural values.

I have suggested that the fundamental cultural message of television is a consequence of its function of transforming the audience into consumers, and promoting consumption of consumer goods and their symbols. Its ideological action fulfills in the first instance the economic function of constantly stimulating new markets, new items of consumption, and new consumers. Therefore, the culture diffused by Dominican television as a whole corresponds essentially to the basic elements of a business-oriented society, although it is not a direct portrayal of the subculture of the economic elite. It is expressed in terms of the factors and interconnections that constitute the dominant culture in society.

NOTES

1. Any televised event is already encoded by social codes. These social codes, following Fiske (1987, p. 5), can be categorized in three levels:

1. *Reality* (as represented by TV). There may be an objective, empiricist reality out there, but there is no universal, objective way of perceiving and making sense of it. What passes for reality in any culture is the product of that culture's codes, so "reality" is always already encoded; it is never "raw."
2. *Representation*. Appearance, dress, makeup, environment, behavior, speech, gestures, expression, sound, and so on are encoded electronically by photography, lighting, editing, music, and sound, which transmit the conventional codes that shape the representations of, for example, narrative, conflict, character, action, dialogue, setting, and casting.
3. *Ideology*. The codes of reality and representation are organized into coherence and social acceptability by ideological codes, such as those of individualism, patriarchy, race, class, materialism, and capitalism.

2. Only 20 percent of the people from high strata and 35 percent from the middle strata consider that television contributes to education, while 78 percent of the lower strata believe that television is educative.

3. These assertions are based on the analysis of several *telenovelas* of the 1980s,

particularly "Rubi Rebelde," "Carrusel," "Simplemente Maria," "Amigail," "Lo Blanco y lo Negro," "Amanda Sabater," and "Vale Todo." All of these shows were broadcast by the Dominican networks during 1989 and 1990.

4. Some *telenovelas* from Brazil depict elements of society from a critical point of view. In "Malu Mulher" the principal character is a divorced sociologist who lives with her daughter and mother. The everyday problems of a single mother and the issues of women, sexuality, and machismo are openly discussed. This *telenovela* has been very successful in the Dominican Republic among the middle class and intellectuals.

5. Although the international aim of the Latin American television industry and a more politicized population are major factors in *telenovelas*' relative cultural openness, the difference I found in that aspect between U.S. serials and *telenovelas* is also probably due to the genre itself. Indeed, if we compare the U.S. soap opera with U.S. serials, it will also be found that the soap operas present more multiplicity of plots than do the serials.

6. "National culture" in this work consists of the particular expressions that describe, justify, and explain the reasons and actions that give rise to a given group of people and through which they conserve their existence as autonomous and different from other groups. It does not exclude the influence of other countries in the constitution of a national culture. But in the particular economic and social conditions of the Dominican Republic, an ideological transfer of the ways of life carried by the U.S. productions tends more to prevent the development of a national culture than to contribute to its enhancement.

7. New research in the area of advertising is undermining the conventional ideas of what sells. After monitoring the commercials seen daily by a group of consumers and the purchases they made for a year, Gerard Tellis (1988) concludes that advertising has almost no effect on consumer buying habits. Other researchers using similar data have concluded that advertising does have an effect on sales when using emotional appeals. A study by Deighton, Henderson, and Neslin (1989) suggests that rather than attracting new customers, commercials for a particular brand serve a crucial role as cheerleader to those who already buy it. Furthermore, in the last few years, with the advent of remote control, it has become more and more difficult for advertisers to capture the attention of viewers (although some viewers do like to watch advertisements). At any rate, advertisers want their investment to be worthwhile; therefore, the advertising industry is trying to find the best way to influence people. Michael Rothschild is trying to pinpoint the most effective stimuli by monitoring consumers' brain waves as they watch television (Allman 1989).

8. Although I can infer from my interviews some of the viewers' interpretation of commercials, my purpose in interviewing a small sample of the audience was not to evaluate the specific effects of television on the behavior of these people but, rather, to gain a general sense of their perception of television content as a whole. I think it should be possible to establish at least some basic tendencies of the extent of the influence that advertising has on consumer habits by doing a relatively long participant observer research.

9. Children tend to be more spontaneous and to say more easily than adults that they like a given product because they saw it on television.

10. It is paradoxical that while the government of the United States exerts

pressure on the governments of several Latin American countries where drugs are produced to fight against the producers of narcotics, the U.S. manufacturers of alcohol and tobacco promote their use in Latin America through strong advertising campaigns.

11. People were asked to enumerate brands of products they could remember and where they heard about them. There was a clear relation between brands advertised on television and the interviewees' account.

12. There are so many aspects that influence the success of a given brand of a product, as well as so many ways that are used to promote it, that it is difficult to establish whether television promotion is decisive. For example, another factor could be the large community of Dominicans who live in the United States. When they go to the Dominican Republic to visit families and friends, they bring with them ideas and representations of which products are good or bad. Another possible element is the elite's contact with other countries, which also brings judgments about merchandise.

13. Western movies and detective stories, highly appreciated by Dominicans and other Latin Americans, may have played an important role in the promotion of whiskey consumption in Latin America. The heroes of these movies in the 1950s and 1960s drank whiskey. And children playing Indians and cowboys refer in their games to the situation—never absent from a movie in that period—of the cowboy entering a saloon and asking for whiskey. Thus, it is defensible to deduce that probably these movies contributed to promoting whiskey consumption among a generation of individuals. Today in the Dominican Republic whiskey is consumed by large sectors of the population. Those who can afford it on a regular base always have a bottle of whiskey for visitors, and others buy it for special occasions. Among the middle and high socioeconomic groups the consumption of whiskey is now very common.

14. A complete analysis of this problem has been developed by Buffle (1986).

15. Television sets in the homes of the middle and upper classes, which are connected to cable TV, receive the same programs and ads as in the United States.

16. The largest volume of advertising in this country is placed by international agencies: Young & Rubicam Damaris is in first place, with U.S. $8.2 million in billing; McCann-Ericson is second, with U.S. $5.9 million; Leo Burnett is third, with U.S. $4.0 million; and Foote, Cone, and Belding is fourth, with U.S. $3.6 million. These all are based in the United States. In fifth place is the United Kingdom-based Saatchi & Saatchi, with U.S. $1.8 million (*Advertising Age* 1990).

17. Most U.S. journalists usually presented the desire for change in eastern Europe during 1989 as exclusively a desire for freedom. That is probably true for some intellectuals, but most people were more concerned about another dream: the possibility of consumption they think they can find in Western society. During the author's visits to several of these countries in 1976, he observed that most people with whom he talked had an idealized image of the West. Most of their interpretations of western Europe and the United States were based in large part on what they saw in movies from the West, and on the contact they had with tourists. This phenomenon is also valid for the countries of Latin America. The image people in these countries have of the United States is a world of goods that are within easy reach, in prodigious abundance. They do not see that not everybody can afford to buy all things advertised and that what is presented in most movies

and serials corresponds more to a glamorous Hollywood representation of life than to reality.

18. The people themselves become the signs and the advertisers of a particular product. These brands are visible in jeans, T-shirts, jackets, and shoes. This also applies to other products, such as computers, cars, motorcycles, drinks, and so on.

19. Television, of course, is not the only influence. Personal contact plays a very important role as well. (There are almost a million Dominicans in the United States.) However, when describing life in the United States, most interviewees referred to what they saw on their television sets.

20. This is partly due to the imported programs and partly to imitation, but it is also due to the inherent nature of the television system in the country, which is basically business-oriented, in the same way that a manufacturer of tobacco or rum is.

21. The document was signed by the general directors of all seven networks (Luzón 1989). While this declaration is not without social psychological value, it remains on an abstract level. There are no concrete propositions, and it reflects two basic facts: (1) that the staffs of the networks do not have the power to make modifications in the overall program (those who do, the owners of the networks, did not sign the document) and (2) that this declaration reflects a popular tendency in the Dominican Republic to see the problems as the result of foreign influence. It avoids saying that foreign programs invade the networks because of the structure of the television industry. The owners of the television networks want benefits; thus the staff who signed the document should appeal to the producers of programs that attract large audiences, such as the U.S. productions and *telenovelas* from Brazil, Puerto Rico, Mexico, and Argentina.

Chapter 5

Television in the Marketplace of Ideas: The News

A journalist is the lookout on the bridge of the ship of state.... He peers through fog and storm to give warning of dangers ahead.... He is there to watch over the safety and welfare of the people who trust him.
                Joseph Pulitzer (quoted in Paletz and Entman 1981, p. 9)

The right of the people to know is part of the democratic model promoted in most societies of the western hemisphere. In order to judge and form opinions, citizens need to be able to listen to diverse voices in the marketplace of ideas, as well as to have the possibility of expression in the different media. This is an idea of long standing; indeed the French Declaration of Human Rights (1789) considered "the free circulation of ideas and opinions" in Article 2.

The fact that there are several media is considered evidence of democratic expression and pluralism (see, for example, the debate on the McBride report [1980] about international communication, especially the reactions of the media industry's owners).[1] These ideas are based on the traditional bourgeois identification of free expression with free enterprise, and of democracy with the possibility of unlimited benefits. In these views the concept of freedom of information is reduced to freedom of consumption, and the concept of pluralism to the choice between several channels or products.

The defenders of these conceptions seldom take into account that few people have effective control over the media. In reality, the supposition that people have access to the means of expressing ideas is only a metaphor. Not every person who wants to express ideas in the media has easy access to broadcasting stations or newspapers owned by others, and not every person or social group can own a broadcasting station or other medium. Entry into the mass marketplace of ideas as an owner is very expensive, particularly in television.[2]

This chapter examines the fundamental factors that determine information content, shows how effectively different social trends and social groups are represented in Dominican television newscasts, and asserts the ability of different social groups to influence the flow of information.

TELEVISION AS PRINCIPAL SOURCE OF INFORMATION

Despite the Dominican Republic's having nine newspapers, radio and television have a greater impact in disseminating information on a large scale. This is logical, given the high level of illiteracy in this country.[3] Furthermore, public education is very deficient. This implies that even those people from the lower social class (the majority of the population) who have attended primary school for three or four years still have problems reading fluently. In consequence, communication here is basically oral or pictorial. Even though the radio has traditionally been an important source of information, most people today find television more "interesting" than the radio and easier to understand than newspapers. Television is, then, a major source of information, particularly for people of lower socioeconomic status.

In fact, television in the Dominican Republic brings knowledge to more people than any other medium. Because it is audiovisual and it tends to address a large population (for commercial reasons, Dominican television newscasts distribute information in a form that will be familiar to a large audience), television has helped people to become more aware of events in the country and around the world. Indeed, at the time of the field research, almost all the persons interviewed knew at least superficially about most of the events reported by television.

This does not imply that everybody watches the newscasts. In particular, some people from the lower strata do not like to watch the newscasts; 20 percent of the people interviewed from this strata declared that though they watch most television programs, they usually avoid the newscasts because they consider them boring. However, they still see television as the basic source of information. A large percentage of the people from the lower strata (61 percent) consider themselves poorly informed, and when they were asked why they thought they were not well informed, they responded, "Because I do not watch the television newscasts very often."

As for the members of the middle class, 66 percent consider themselves adequately informed, 5 percent well informed, and 29 percent poorly informed. Their concept of being well informed is reading as many newspapers as possible and watching television newscasts regularly (two or three times a day).[4] But most of the people interviewed complained that they do not have enough free time to become as well informed as they wish by reading; therefore they rely mostly on television newscasts. Thus 45 percent of the members of the upper social class interviewed consider themselves well informed, 30 percent see themselves as "average" informed, and 25 percent as poorly informed. For the upper social class and for the professionals and intellectuals, economically part of the middle class, television newscasts are as important a source of information as the newspapers.

Although Dominican viewers do not always uncritically accept everything that is broadcast on television newscasts—only a small percentage of people (14 percent) considered the information broadcast on television to be true and objective most of the time—in practice they rely on it heavily for their judgment of events.

BASIC DETERMINANTS OF TELEVISION NEWSCASTS

Television newscasts not only transmit information but also define and limit what will be communicated about given events. The selection, treatment, or rejection of a story is based on its significance, the impact that it could have on society, and the consequences of its broadcast for the network and its staff. In more concrete terms, two interrelated sets of elements frame television broadcasting news: one that I call "technical" and a second, perhaps more important in the Dominican Republic, that I call "political-structural."[5] These sets are interwoven in the everyday news production and, depending on the circumstances as well as on the specific content of a given piece of information, they configure the way this information is presented. Sometimes political-structural considerations overshadow the other elements (especially when the information is sensitive), and sometimes the technical elements are favored, but there is never a sharp separation; there are no technical considerations totally free of political-structural elements, and vice versa.

From the strictly technical point of view, a news item is broadcast over the Dominican networks for the following reasons:[6] (1) its visual richness, (2) its novelty, (3) its possibility for dramatic debate, and (4) its saliency, which most often is a function of the personalities involved. These four are considered along with organization convenience factors, such as easy access, habitual coverage, and cost, which are always implied when determining which story to broadcast. And all of this with the ratings in mind.

From the political-structural point of view, news content is determined by (1) the frame of reference created by the bureaucratic structure of the television network, (2) the journalists' and editors' cultural and political considerations,[7] and (3) the economic and political requirements of those who control television networks.

In other words, television news producers ask three basic questions about their stories: Will this story interest all (or most) of the viewers? How can this story be shown? Will this story be acceptable to our owners or sponsors? The most sophisticated could also ask: How will this story fit in with other news events or with the pacing of the newscast? Most interviewed programmers profess to present newscasts by linking items thematically, "because of the psychological association that people need to understand the news," as a managing editor declared. In practice, however, this latter element is seldom considered in Dominican television newscasts. A single program moves freely between important news and trivialities, and between news about tragedies and news in a less serious vein.

Technical and political-structural considerations work together in the consciousness of those who produce the news on an everyday basis. These factors are not separate but overlapping. They are formulated here separately for clarity's sake. The basic technical aspects will be examined first.

Technical Considerations

Visuals. Television newscasts are to a large extent dominated by the need for visuals. More often than not, the visual aspects are privileged in Dominican television (as in the United States and most other countries). The laws of the spectacle value violent and explosive actions. For example, demonstrations (of students, political parties, unions, etc.) are very attractive events for newscasts, particularly if there are police charges, burning tires in the streets, wounded people, and so on. (Demonstrators conscious of this infatuation with spectacular visuals often perpetrate tumult in order to attract television interest.) As an editor alleged:

Sometimes a given story has such rich visual elements that we start with it, privileging it over a heavier story. For example, a demonstration at the Autonomous University of Santo Domingo, even when there are no wounded or dead people, is very attractive... with tear gas, fights between students and police, and so on.

However, despite the fact that good visuals are considered very important, the camera is not used in a sophisticated manner. Visuals are seen more as an essential accompaniment to the voice, and rarely are consciously used to distort or foster a particular image.[8] The basic concern of newscast producers concerning the image is to be able to film what they want with the few resources they have (in human ability as well as in equipment). Sometimes the film coverage does not entirely parallel the words spoken by correspondents.[9] As a result, what is said plays the more substantial role in expressing the ideas that the news team wants to convey.

Novelty. Besides action, a good spectacle calls for changes in content (though not in basic structures). A subject loses interest if there are no new elements. "The public constantly wants new stories," said a reporter.

Dramatic Potential. The dramatic plays a very important role in framing newscasts, particularly when the news can be presented as a contest. The only possibility of a debate between the two leading candidates during the April–May 1990 election campaign was discussed in the press for five days; in the end, the debate never took place.

From the point of view of newscast producers, the emphasis on the contest theme can be explained by the following reasons:

1. The details seem more relevant and more easily dealt with, given the constraints of time and space, and the level of audience understanding. The opposing stances assumed by the principal actors of an event are considered important for explaining it.
2. There is an assumption that audiences are interested in conflicts.
3. Contest themes can be presented in the form of dramatic units. It is implicit that each opponent has an opportunity of winning; to some extent, there is also an element of suspense. It is usual for the network anchors to start their presentation of the newscasts by using a contest formula: "The polemic between the chief of police and the district attorney of the National District continues ..." (TV13); "The national hospital crisis has worsened today. The nurses and the government did not reach an agreement ..." (Colorvisión); "The secretary general of the PLD replied to the attacks of several members of the Reformist Party ..." (Teleantillas); "The controversy between the economic adviser of the government, Juan José Arteaga, and Professor Juan Bosch [leader of the PLD] continues at its hottest pitch ..." (Rahintel). Each time conditions change or any of the contenders declares something, there is a new story.
4. Contest themes offer good visual possibilities. Profound issues with several ramifications and nebulous explanations are very difficult to represent visually.
5. Debates are easily understood by the audience and by the journalists themselves. Contests can be easily decoded because ideas and persons are placed in clear opposition. For example, if concepts such as wrong and right can be determined in a given piece of information, that is an easy tool for the editor or the reporter to use, since these concepts are culturally defined in Dominican society. Also, very often there is no need to know anything about the background of a contest story in order to understand it.
6. Contests have an appearance of objectivity. Journalists favor contest themes for presenting stories in order to reduce the possibility of being labeled as partial. Coverage of more complex issues could provoke the accusation of bias. The focus of the story, for example, could be a subjective judgment, which could easily be perceived as an attempt to distort the news. Of course this does not imply that in contest stories there is no bias. The choices of what to cover and from what angle to do so are sources of bias, but it is clear that contest stories give a greater appearance of objectivity than the issues-oriented news stories do. And appearance is almost everything in television.

Emphasis on Personalities. News stories favor well-known or appealing personalities. Newscasts are largely filled with information related to the leaders of the country, in particular to those who govern (elected officials and top-level bureaucrats). The government is the primary source of stories, and the other major part of the news consists of people's responses to government actions or statements. For instance, 37 percent of the news time during the period I analyzed (see Appendix A) was devoted to stories about the activities of government officials, and very few of these were critical of the government; 21 percent of the news time was concerned with the activities of the opposition parties' leaders; and 11 percent with those of the economic elite.

Several newscast directors explained that the emphasis is on personalities because they try to produce news that will draw big audiences despite the sharp limitation of networks' resources. The production of news on Dominican television is always handicapped by time and cost limits. "Every day's news production is a struggle against the commercial elements," said a news director. The news director must juggle a heavy load of advertising, tight deadlines, and a perennial shortage of adequate and skilled staff and camera crew. Indeed, the private networks have only two or three camera crews for reporting. And Radio-Television Dominicana, the state network, has only a single camera crew to cover the entire country, and does not have complete mobile equipment. The news team of this network can count only on a videotape recorder that they use on special occasions, such as the trips of the president.

Under these conditions, the news directors tend to assign camera crews to events that have been planned in advance, and try to cover what they consider the key beats. Hence, on an everyday basis the National Palace, the highest echelons of officialdom, the economic elite, and the most important leaders of the opposition parties are covered. Only when special events, such as strikes, occur are other elements of society considered newsworthy. The focus on covering officialdom is still more intense in the state-owned network. As a programmer of this network said:

In RTVD there is only one camera and limited human resources for doing reportage and making up the newscast. Therefore, they concentrate on priorities. That is, they cover the activities of the party in power, the president of the republic, and the secretaries of state and other high-level officials, as well as the friends and political supporters of the general director of the network.

But the lack of resources is not the only reason for focusing on personalities. News teams generally assume that concentrating on personalities makes more interesting news. Furthermore, they decide whether to invest time in the pursuit of one source rather than another based on their estimation of the probable returns such an investment will produce. They favor sources that provide information easily convertible into a news story. Government activities or business associations' declarations always make news. Reliance on these bureaucratic sources is also facilitated by the tendency of reporters to accept information from them as factual. When the factual nature of information is not questioned, reporters need not invest much time to obtain it.

All these technical aspects emphasized in news production reveal a general conception of news as a particular form of entertainment. However, political-structural aspects also affect the content of news.

Political-Structural Determinants of Newscasts

Directives from network owners regarding news content are very vague and vary from one network to another. In general, there is no specific directive about what should be broadcast, but none of the networks will knowingly criticize its stockholders, according to an administrator:

> The president of the network, who is the main stockholder, makes some suggestions in order to avoid conflicts with the other stockholders. He could ask us to avoid referring to their companies critically, because they could call him and say: "What is going on? We are attacked on our own network. Are you conspiring against us?"

Usually, what has to go on the air is first suggested by the journalist/reporter who submits a given story for approval to the managing editor, who, if he judges it pertinent, sends it to the news director. On an everyday basis the managing editor reviews the draft work of the reporters and the news director generally checks the finished work. News directors do not exert their authority on a day-to-day basis, because they have other duties and because they follow the guidelines of the normal division of labor within the newscast team. Nor do they need to, since editors and reporters are likely to do what their superiors want. Reporters and editors are exposed to an informal ideological conditioning through insinuations and casual inferences. They might occasionally be advised not to lose their "objectivity" when they are producing a story that can disturb persons of wealth and power. For instance, "Some aspects of your story are too emotional. Perhaps you should try to be a little more calm."

When there are social problems such as uprisings or strikes, the news director exerts more careful control over what will be aired. This is done "to avoid the network's being considered as an agency stimulating the uprising," said a news director. Most news directors are very aware of their role, and they all recognize that there are some pieces of information they have to withhold. Following are statements from news directors who were interviewed:

> When there is a controversial story, certain information or parts of a story may be ignored. The selection of the news conforms to specific interests.

Taking over the means of communication is another way in which capitalists protect their interests. I think that in a certain way the networks respond to specific interests and in certain circumstances they should protect those interests; consequently, they should omit speaking of certain things. In fact, it is like an economic law.

We have to avoid broadcasting some information that could affect groups which have investments in the network or have some means of exerting pressure on the network. And some news that we broadcast needs to be presented with extreme care in order not to impair economic interests.

This implies that television newscast staff should conform to specific, although unwritten rules. Their presentation of news must conform to the limits of expression perceived by those who control the networks. Owners' interventions are seldom direct and explicit; most are subtle. Owners' control is also exercised by hiring persons, especially at the executive level, who know what is expected.

There is no need for omnipresent oversight; occasionally intervention is enough. The anticipation that owners might disapprove a given story is usually sufficient to deter a news director or managing editor from assigning it. At all the networks the managing editor and the news director have to play the role of censor to a certain extent, trying to avoid offending their owners and other powerful persons. As a news director put it:

For example, if vegetable oil prices increase more than they should, our department will not do a critical analysis trying to show that the increase should have been smaller, because one of the main stockholders of the network is one of the biggest oil producers in the country. This is a limitation imposed by the ownership.... No owner will hire someone who conspires against his interests. It is a basic principle of survival. We try not to touch the interests of the owners.

The freedom of choice of news producers and the news team always exists within specific boundaries. Decision makers exercise their powers only within the latitude permitted by the network. The coverage of each network generally varies as a function of how top executives and owners interpret a given situation. Hence, there are some differences in news staff autonomy. From the interviews it appears that Teleantillas concedes more independence to its journalists than do other networks; the state-owned RTVD is the most controlled.

In any case, the requirements of the network's owners and sponsors far outweigh the principles or preferences that may guide any single employee (whether news director or reporter). The news directors I interviewed clearly stated that if they questioned the system, they would not keep their jobs. "We are conscious that freedom of expression has its limits," one said. For instance, besides the technical factors explained in the previous pages, the emphasis on personalities also occurs because of the specific orientation of the network and its obligation to respond to economic and political pressure groups. In other words, choices made by the newscast teams about what to broadcast and how, are free neither of value-oriented decisions nor of external pressure. What to cover is decided within a particular organization structure.

Since most of the great capitalists in the Dominican Republic have some investment in the media, the possibilities for criticism of their activities on television are considerably limited. In addition, there is the weight of intergroup relations. There seems to be a general, although not formally established, agreement of nonaggression between major capitalists.

Capitalist firms also pressure the networks, specifically the producers of shows, through commercials. As a director of programming said:

The commercial department asks journalists and commentators not to attack their clients and to prevent persons who question a given client from speaking on this network. If a particular individual who has openly criticized a given business [network's client] is invited to a program, the commercial department will be very unhappy. This is a very important aspect that is considered in the programming.

Those producers who defend ideas that favor the interests of the economic elite—for instance, lower taxes on businesses—attract the most commercials; the capitalists view them with sympathy. And those who question actions of entrepreneurs have fewer commercials. Although there is no sharp separation between "friends" and "enemies," those who receive commercials and those who do not,[10] it is much easier for those who defend the business position to obtain commercials than for those who criticize it. As a matter of fact, a producer who questions business actions or ideas has a hard time gaining commercials. If he draws large audiences with his program, he will perhaps find some firms willing to advertise; but it is a great advantage if he does not question the economic powers.

As a result, no large firm is really questioned. Seldom is there a critical analysis on Dominican television. Criticism is never directed explicitly to a specific firm or group of firms; there is only a very general and vague reference to sectors—for example, "Some powerful sectors should modify their attitude concerning the present economic crisis" or "Some sectors are indolent in the face of the people's misery." Rarely is more damaging information reported.

However, even such limited critiques sometimes provoke discomfort among members of the corporate class, who protest vigorously. Generally they contact the president of the network—or the general director, in the case of the public network—to share their discomfort, knowing he will exert pressure on the network staff.

Furthermore, when individual members of the economic and power elite are involved in corruption and similar activities that are depicted on television, the coverage is in terms of bad/good person; seldom is there an analysis relating the action of the people involved to the organization of the state in particular and of the society in general. The implicit message is that the current social order has nothing to do with the problem.

The government, besides directly shaping newscasts on the state-owned network, also has the means to influence the private networks. The government is a powerful client of many enterprises whose owners have investments in the television industry, and it further has the ability to favor some business (through regulations, tax exemptions, etc.). This brings about an interdependence between private television networks and the state apparatus. The television networks have economic interests to preserve, and the government needs to project a positive image to the population.

FAIRNESS AND OBJECTIVITY

Code of Neutrality

The objectivity of information is axiomatic; information is considered truth that does not need to be demonstrated, that builds neutral knowledge. On television, information appears to be a photocopy of real events and a representation of public opinion, impersonal and collective. In actuality, however, the information on television is directed, codified, organized in a particular way, and, most of the time, biased. What counts in broadcasting information is determined through social processes that are necessarily ideological. Any newscast filters reality, constituting a network of exposition and exclusion. Certain news items must be chosen over others, and certain relations between elements are accentuated. Such choices are guided by ideological commitments and relations of power.

As Gerbner suggests, "All editorial choice patterns in what to make public (and in what proportion, with what emphasis, etc.) have an ideological basis and a political dimension rooted in the structural characteristics of the medium" (1964, p. 508). Since some events are privileged over others, a newscast demarcates a separation between what is excluded and what is admitted. In this way there is a restriction of the world. Inevitably, there is censorship of reality. In fact, there is a bias[11] in most Dominican television newscasts even if it is not always evident.

The logic of the broadcasting industry requires television to present topics of wide audience interest. The competition for public favor moves newscasts to be somewhat responsive to social attitudes, and to serve as a carrier for dramatic messages. Reporting on social problems such as crime, violence, social inequality, poverty, and other everyday difficulties (e.g., trash in the streets, power failures, etc.), as well as scandals (e.g., economic and political corruption, including some material critical of the government) is often the most powerful means to increase the audience. Also, while addressing these issues, newscasts must mention some of the contradictions and antagonisms of contemporary society. However, the analysis of these problems never goes far enough. In the coverage of such topics they also take care not to offend powerful economic sectors or the owners of the network. This is done by choosing sources, stories, facts, and explanations that, though they may carry some social criticism, do not threaten established cultural values and economic interests. What Dunn says about the United States applies perfectly to the Dominican Republic:

> To play it safe, the media typically adopt an ambiguous stance (the code of "neutrality") in the presentation of controversial subject matter. But at the level of framing and commentary in informational programs and framing and plot resolution in entertainment shows, the media tend to construct fundamentally conformist messages reaffirming the beliefs of vested social interests. (1986, p. 129)

In the coverage of the socioeconomic situation, for example, television newscasts limit themselves to portraying some of the disagreements among the economic elite and the palliatives that they propose within the framework of current social structures. There is a continual repetition of the same questions and analyses. Seldom is there criticism of the market rules or of the structural mechanisms of economic functioning in society.

In television news, a national consensus, common to all classes and people of goodwill and common sense, is presumed. This is particularly expressed in editorials and similar communications. Editorials rarely blame the system but constantly refer to individuals who do things wrong. The editorial below was broadcast by Colorvisión on June 21, 1989, the day following a general strike that almost completely halted activity all over the country for two days. This strike was probably the most important popular action since the bloody uprising of 1984.[12] This editorial, "Perspectives of the Present Time," is an example of traditional editorials aired on the privately owned networks.

> Although the promoters of the strike did not achieve their objectives, we can say that the strike was a success, both for those who called for the strike and for the government. The possibility for a dialogue has not been reduced, and there has not been much bloodshed.[13]
>
> However, there remains the danger that in the days to follow, both sectors will become enthusiastic in some ways with this success and could feel that a new confrontation would be to their advantage.
>
> The leaders of the strike are talking about a bigger strike and more violent methods. If the forces of the order also threaten more violent methods, then it is clear that both sectors will end up with lost lives and injured people in a future confrontation. Experience shows that popular leaders create ideals and myths with a certain ease. We have sometimes seen modest men suddenly assuming positions of greatness and even of arrogance.

The researchers of mass behavior have demonstrated... that just as the ardor of the popular struggle can produce courage and heroism, in an abrupt change of circumstances it can produce panic and fear with the same intensity. Therefore, one should be cautious regarding circumstantial success based on the real or supposed support of people as long-suffering, as confused, as hardened, as hesitant, as praised, and as betrayed as the Dominican people.

In two days it is not easy to establish how much was real support for the strike, and how much was fear, indifference, or laziness. Therefore, the popular leaders should be cautious in interpreting the support of the people for the strike, especially when they again call the people to confront... official power.

A wise use of this support without risk of losing it is perhaps the... ideal action. A new confrontation could signify a defeat for the popular forces, for the government, and for all of us. In the future, the endeavor should be to obtain the best conditions for the people without harming institutionalization and economic growth, without wasting a drop of blood, and without using one single bullet....

There is a naive intent here to appear balanced when in fact the message is clearly a sermon to the popular leaders. There is an appeal to what is considered "common sense," such as the statement that in a general strike, the real support of the people is not clear, in order to conclude that further popular actions should be avoided. The editorial makes the leaders of the strike appear irrational and self-indulgent to the point of being self-destructive. It also affirms a success of the popular forces when in fact the government had not made any important concessions to their demands. While highlighting the possible damage the general strike might do to the government and the economy, nothing is said about the damage to people's interests if the strike leaders accept the government's terms.

From this editorial we can extract some general ideas that are constantly reproduced in the newscasts of all the networks. Certain kinds of behavior are defined as both deviant and dangerous for society. The real danger and significance of the popular forces and their activities are exaggerated. This provides society with scapegoats and objects of indignation—at the same time diverting attention from real problems—which encourages people to remain fairly satisfied with the present social organization and to support the agencies of law and order. The pattern of coverage establishes the limits of a protest. Also provided is a symbolic bridge between the clearly criminal and those engaged in such forms of political behavior as strikes. The scope for dissent is thereby restricted, and repressive actions by the state forces are justified. Overall, this editorial and others like it play an ideological role, prescribing an acceptance of things as they are and suggesting to the people that their only alternative is to try to achieve something within the restricted possibilities offered by the government. In other words, pressuring those in power is acceptable only up to a certain point.

Further, in the analysis of television content it is not only what is said that counts; it is also what is not said. In twenty days of news coverage over several periods,[14] the editorials did not contain a single criticism of the basic structure of the predominant social system. Some sharp criticism was offered by representatives of the left invited to talk shows or by people interviewed in the newscasts, but never in the editorials or in the news reported by anchormen and anchorwomen. The coverage is imbalanced in terms not only of the orientation of content but also of the number of stories about the activities of the various groups in Dominican society.

Television news concentrates on the representatives of political power and the economic elite. The difference in the coverage of left-wing and right-wing politicians is very large; only 10 percent of the news time is spent on depicting activities of the Left, most of it concerned with the center-left Dominican Liberation Party (PLD), In fact, considering the PLD and other leftist parties as well as union and popular leaders, the total percentage of broadcast time granted to people who represent the working class or a political alternative to the predominant socioeconomic system is only 15.7 percent. This is true not only of the newscasts but also of the talk shows. Even on Teleantillas, the network that allows the most time to different groups of the population including the leftist sectors, there is an overwhelming presence of the economic elite and of members of the government. Of the 250 interviews that the program of interviews and information "Uno + Uno" telecasts in one year, 10 to 12 are of union leaders, 8 to 10 of leftist leaders, and 8 to 10 of professionals and technicians who espouse a leftist ideology; thus, only about 25 to 30 persons who question the basic structure of the system are interviewed. The percentage is overwhelmingly in favor of the perpetuation of the predominant social organization. On the other networks the imbalance is even larger. (See Table 5.1 for detailed data.)

In spite of this imbalance, programs such as "Uno + Uno" and talk shows still provide the best forum for sectors critical of the society to express their ideas. There are a good number of talk shows on Dominican television, most of which began in the 1970s. They were created by independent producers, some of whom had affiliations with the main political parties. Several of these programs, which generally were of poor quality, drew fairly large audiences. Since then, every network has allowed time to these programs without scrutinizing their political views too carefully—as long as they provide benefits to the network and do not express radical revolutionary ideas that call for immediate uprising. Variety shows also occasionally include segments in which intellectuals and politicians from the Left participate. Even the state-owned network allocates time for shows in which the government is sometimes criticized, especially since the late 1970s, during and after the two periods of government of the centrist Dominican Revolutionary Party.

Although the networks and their sponsors do not have much involvement

Table 5.1
Percentage of Time Social Actors Are Present in National Broadcast News

Social Actors	Colorvisión	Rahintel	Teleantillas	TV13	Radio-Televisión Dominicana	All Networks
Government officials						
President	9.7	9.1	7.5	19.1	30.5	15.3
Other officials	18.2	16.2	13.0	22.8	22.6	18.7
Total	27.9	26.0	20.5	41.9	53.1	34.0
Business and Industry Representatives	12.4	7.6	10.2	7.8	5.9	8.9
Union and Popular Leaders	10.2	7.8	9.0	6.0	4.1	7.3
Opposition Parties						
PLD	9.9	6.4	11.0	10.3	3.9	8.3
PRD	6.0	8.9	5.2	6.5	4.0	6.2

PRI	5.3	6.1	4.7	6.4	4.3	5.3
Other	2.8	2.6	4.1	1.3	2.0	2.4
Total	23.9	24.1	25.1	24.5	14.6	22.3
General Population	6.7	9.2	7.3	4.6	3.1	6.2
Independent Official Institutions						
Justice	4.1	4.3	7.5	2.1	4.7	4.5
CET	2.2	8.2	4.1	6.0	6.3	5.4
Total	6.3	12.5	10.6	8.1	11.0	9.9
International Organizations and Diplomats	2.6	5.6	6.0	4.3	2.4	4.2
Academics/Intellectuals/ Specialists	3.8	2.5	2.9	1.2	0.7	2.2
Church	2.2	2.4	2.5	1.9	3.0	2.4
Other Social Organizations	2.3	1.6	2.6	0.6	1.3	1.7
No Specific Actor	1.8	0.8	1.9	0.3	0.9	1.2

Table 5.1 (continued)

"Government Officials" refers to the president, secretaries of state, high-level bureaucrats, representatives and senators, and leaders and members of the party in power, the PRSC. This category also includes the parties allied to the official PRSC.

"Business and Industry Representatives" are leaders of the industry and business associations, entrepreneurs, and enterprise owners in general.

"Union and Popular Leaders" include union leaders and the representatives of peasant organizations and of numerous neighborhood organizations.

"Other," under the category "Opposition Parties," refers to small parties scattered along the political spectrum.

"General Population" concerns news stories that have as principal actors citizens in general, without reference to any particular organized social group or institution (e.g., people having economic difficulties, people going to the beach, etc.).

"Independent Official Institutions" refers to the institutions that are supposed to be independent of the government.

"International Organizations and Diplomats" concerns the newscasts that refer mainly to the activities within the country of international organizations and their representatives, such as OAS, UN, IMF, as well as to foreign organizations and all kinds of diplomats.

"Academics/Intellectuals/Specialists" concern newscasts that present statements and activities of these categories. This includes, for example, economists' comments about a given government measure, academics' activities, etc.

"Church" refers to the activities of any religious group.

"Other Social Organizations" refers to such organizations as cooperatives, charity associations, social clubs, and so on.

"No Specific Actor" concerns stories where no specific social actors can be explicitly identified in the coverage. These are basically pieces that establish a fact in a very general way (e.g., reportage about the arrival of summer, information about the economic situation of the country, etc.). These stories are few because most reporting is centered on people.

with social equality and are strongly opposed to any ideas that come from the Left, they know it is good business to have some leftists on the shows.[15] If specific events attract a large audience, network owners and sponsors tolerate some controversial and leftist ideas, unless they consider them directly menacing to their business or to the system they defend. It is assumed that dissident opinions will be canceled out by the predominant opinion and will not constitute a serious danger to the country's power structure. Free speech exists as long as it is profitable and does not endanger the interests of those who hold economic power and those who control the government. The limits of free speech vary from time to time as a function of the general situation in the country. If there is a political crisis, the freedom to express dissent generally shrinks.

TELEVISION JOURNALISTS' ROLE

Foucault asserts that the producer of knowledge experiences the pleasure "that comes of exercising a power that questions, monitors, watches, spies, searches out, palpates, brings to light" (1980, p. 140). In the process of producing information for broadcast, journalists[16] very often experience the same feeling. They also know that they should be perceived by the audience as competent to understand the events they report, and are also expected to be objective. These requirements are not easy to fulfill.

Theoretically, and according to a general assumption within the field, to be knowledgeable, a journalist or news commentator should be able to analyze a given problem in all its ramifications. The basic necessity is to understand the multiple elements that constitute reality, in order to be able to transmit accurate information to the audience.

However, in reality that is not the case. Events occurring in Dominican society are the result of many causes whose interpretation involves infinitely diverse domains of knowledge. No journalist can hope to be a specialist in all fields, and so the capacity of journalists to describe and analyze national as well as international events is necessarily limited. If they are not aware of this limitation and present their perceptions of reality as accurate and "objective" information, as frequently happens, the nature of a given event is distorted. Even if they have no intention of deceiving their public, they are in fact doing just that. This is observable in the morning information programs (e.g., "Uno + Uno," "Buenos Días," etc.), which usually feature news commentaries.

Yet the general organization of television broadcast news in the Dominican Republic, with its emphasis on the spectacle, favors simplification, particularly in the daily newscasts. Journalists are not required to be very knowledgeable. If newscasts do not avoid topics that seem too complicated, they simplify them enormously. Journalists tend to seek the most obvious facts of events, and avoid dealing with the more subtle causes.

As a matter of fact, television news is based on the concept that most consumers of news are merely observers of stories that journalists unfold for them. The type of information (and in particular the way it is presented on television) implicitly suggests that the citizens are too lacking in seriousness to have an interest in difficult problems, and too limited intellectually to understand them. And these assumptions seem justified if statistical data alone (such as ratings) are considered; most heavy viewers of television (the less educated) are not interested in a profound analysis of the news. Therefore, a vicious circle operates in the newscasts, as in entertainment programming: "The popular mind will decide which sources and ideas make the news, but the popular mind knows nothing of a wide range of alternative sources and ideas, because they have not made the news" (Meyer and Exoo 1988, p. 36).

There is a strong tendency to reduce nuances to simple statements about right and wrong, as well as to assertions that do not hurt the political and economic elite. Further, as we have seen, news is usually presented in such a way that it fulfills the "show business" role of television. This follows from the principle that the audience always looks for mindless distraction. As an editor told me, "Our basic concern . . . is to make simple and direct statements about events, in a more or less . . . entertaining way."

Indeed, fascinated by images and infatuated with violence, television reporters generally look for the sensational and the spectacular, privileging above all dramatic events charged with emotions, pathos, and death. Therefore, they neglect to cover stories lacking noise and action, though these might affect the citizens in a radical way. Following this logic of looking for effect, reporters give a disproportionate importance to small mistakes of politicians or other public figures in their speeches or press conferences, a practice that does not help viewers understand the basic issues. An example is the continuous attention that journalists paid to the words of the presidential candidates during the 1990 campaign. Some, of course, displayed malice stemming from their personal political positions, but most of them followed the structure of information organization, which is almost at the level of gossip.

Not only news stories are communicated in a simplistic and reductive mode; there is also a strong tendency to follow a mechanical and positivist approach in news commentary. Taking as an example the coverage of economic issues, it is noticeable that television newscasts' depiction of economic measures are not extensively explained. The economic considerations of most journalists/commentators tend to support the idea that the factors which can be measured (GNP, money supply, balance of payments, etc.) allow us to direct the economy scientifically. For instance, most analyses of a monetary policy rarely include an examination of the social and political context.

These, together with other aspects of the organization of television broadcast news (e.g., the commercial requirements, the limited airtime, the need for speed, and the desire to present a sensational "scoop"), fragment news stories in such a way that the audience gets only bits and pieces of information. Events and issues are presented in such a manner that the links between them are oversimplified. As a result, understanding the total picture is very difficult, especially when the information relates to unfamiliar places, events, and circumstances, as it does in international news stories. Television newscasts produce only an apparent knowledge of events. The in-depth analysis of events and issues is left to other programs, such as "Uno+Uno" on Teleantillas and "Buenos Días" on Rahintel. However, these shows are not watched by as large and varied an audience as the newscasts.

Furthermore, any journalist makes conscious or unconscious use of a personal hierarchy of values and ethics. One fundamental ethic in journalism is not to hide the truth, not to spread falsehood; but this is not enough. Two journalists who depict the same event differently are not necessarily consciously deceiving the public. They see the same elements, but the importance allowed to each element depends on whether their personal values favor equality or productivity, freedom or efficiency, order or justice, economic prosperity or dignity, and so on. All these values coexist within the general cultural structure, although one can observe that the need for production and order is more often emphasized than the need for freedom and dignity. This is due in part to the acute economic crisis in which the Dominican Republic is enmeshed (insecurity, lack of electricity, transport difficulties, etc.), and in which journalists have been socialized; but it is also due to the particular view that is encouraged by the networks' owners and the economic elite in general.

Thus, objectivity in information, for all practical purposes, is relative. Journalists inevitably show different degrees of sympathy for a given cause or political party. Their inclinations could misrepresent to them some elements of an event or issue, or make them blind to the faults of a given social actor (entrepreneurial organization, political party, union, etc.).

For instance, some television journalists sincerely share the political view of the power elite and thus believe that the news they produce is objective; others are fascinated with people who have fame and power. As a matter of fact, numerous newspeople in the Dominican Republic are drawn to the power elite, finding it more comfortable and financially more secure to support it than to fight it. This is particularly true of the more veteran journalists. Some of them even believe that they may exercise influence over the economic and political power elite.

On the other hand, newspeople are not free agents. They work in a context of hierarchical authority, for someone who pays their salaries and who can fire them. They are forced to accept the power of those who control the television network and hence must carefully consider what they can reveal, what they can say, and what they should not say. Consequently, many of the restrictions on reporting do not derive from direct censorship exerted by owners or sponsors but from self-censorship by reporters and editors who arrange their stories so as to avoid objections from their bosses.

This implies that although television newscasts in the Dominican Republic have contributed considerably to public awareness, they do not provide the information to participate in a democracy. Only information users in the higher strata and professionals and intellectuals in the middle strata, who generally have more education and analytical skills than people in the lower strata, can fill in the blanks left by the television newscasts, by reading newspapers and through professional journals, interpersonal contacts, and so on. In other words, even in this television-mediated society only elite, highly motivated segments have access to more accurate and deeper information.

SPECIAL INTERESTS MAKE A DIFFERENCE

There is a general tendency in the Dominican television industry to broadcast messages that contribute to the perpetuation of the present social structure. But this does not mean that there are no differences among the networks. Indeed, the specific content of each network reflects the interests of those who control it economically.

As a concrete example, the following pages contain a comparative content analysis of a news story about a general strike on two private networks, TV13 and Colorvisión. Specifically, I will examine their portrayal of the general strike of June 19 and 20, 1989, on the evening newscast of Thursday, June 22, two days after the strike ended. All the newscasts on all the networks were filled with stories about the strike during the days that followed this popular movement. This particular story concerned the meeting of a dozen representatives from about 300 associations that called for a national strike. The meeting had as its objective a discussion of the reaction of the government to their demands. My analysis does not focus on a sharp opposition between the two networks; one defending the promoters of the strike and the other defending the government. Neither network was on the side of the promoters of the strike. As a matter of fact, both networks are relatively conservative in their general newscast content. But even within this frame of reference it is possible to see some differences in the positions held by each network.[17]

The camera is not used very creatively in the television newscasts, and the differences in presenting the visuals are not significant. Therefore, I do not emphasize this aspect.

The news story examined here was the second in both newscasts. On TV13 it followed a report on the same topic emphasizing a supposed concord between the entrepreneurial sector and the government, and on Colorvisión, it followed a story about the president's defending the official economic policy.

TV13 offers a positive presentation of the president's response to the popular forces and emphasizes the negative aspects of the popular leaders. The length of time the popular leaders met and the supposed fact that they did not reach an agreement are accentuated. The reporter and the anchor contradict each other (one says that the meeting lasted four hours and the other, five hours). Their claims regarding the duration of the meeting differ from Colorvisión, which reports that it lasted three hours. Although Colorvisión mentions "long hours of debate without reaching a definitive agreement," it tends to be more neutral than TV13.

This story was presented a little more impartially on the other private networks, Teleantillas and Rahintel, than on TV13. These networks did not present the meeting as a response of the popular forces to the proposals of the government, as TV13 did, since the proposals were not concrete measures but propositions placed before the Congress. A response to concrete measures differs from a response to possible measures. The first implies that the popular leaders were unable to agree on the response to concrete propositions that needed an immediate reply; the other indicates that an immediate reply was not required because these were general propositions that had to be debated in Congress.

From the point of view of the organizers of the strike, this meeting was to discuss the reaction of the government to their demands; in order to formulate a common position, they considered it necessary to hold a second meeting of the national representatives of each organization that had participated in the call for the strike. In other words, they planned that each representative would consult the other leaders of the organization to which he or she belonged so that all the organizations which called for the strike could participate in forming the position in response to the government measures. This was not made clear in the newscasts.

Furthermore, in the fourth position in the same newscast, TV13 broadcast a story in which President Balaguer stated that the strike was called by isolated sectors. This story lasted two minutes and twenty-five seconds, slightly more than the time allowed to the story concerning the organizers of the strike (two minutes and ten seconds). The president, always shown in a neutral or positive manner, appeared in two stories about other matters. These other stories occupied a total of four minutes and forty-five seconds. Thus, in this newscast the president was present for more than 30 percent of the time (not counting the time spent on commercials). Half

TV13

Text	Time[18]	Subject/Object Movement Setting	Type of Shot Camera
Anchorman: The organizations that called for the national stoppage of work did not reach an agreement tonight concerning the proposition made by President Balaguer to satisfy their demands. The representatives of the organizations met for four hours on the premises of the Dominican Association of Professors.	20 sec.	Anchorman reading	Chest Shot Camera steady
Reporter: The meeting, which was supposed to start at four o'clock, started closer to five o'clock. The leaders of the organizations that sponsored the national stoppage of work for forty-eight hours analyzed two issues during five hours : the development of the general strike and the decree. . .	20 sec.	Popular leaders around a table	Camera moves in Eye level
. . . released by the president of the Republic calling a meeting of the legislature and creating a committee to study the unions' demands.	10 sec.	External view of the National Palace	Camera tilting

The spokesperson of the group, Rafael Santos, declared, however, that they will keep up the struggle.	5 sec.	Popular leaders around a table	C. moves in Eye-level
<u>Union leader</u>: The collective of unions, peasants, professional, and popular organizations reached a first evaluation of the protest movement over the country, and in particular the forty-hour strike of June 19th and 20th, and we reached a unanimous conclusion. The document containing these conclusions will be delivered to the press in the next hours, once the synthesis in preparation is approved. However, we say now that the movement has been positive, that we need to continue the struggle because the grievances that motivated the movement have not been satisfied.	50 sec.	Union leader speaking	Camera moves in Chest shot
<u>Reporter</u>: The popular organizations will meet again this coming Friday at five o'clock in the offices of the CNTD. We unofficially heard that today they did not reach any agreement because of differences among the various organizations.	25 sec.	Popular leaders around a table	Camera moves in Angle down and tilting

Colorvisión

Text	Time	Subject/Object Movement Setting	Type of Shot Camera
<u>Anchorman</u>: The representatives of the unions and popular organizations that called for the national strike deferred until tomorrow a unified response to the proposals of the executive power responding to their demands.	10 sec.	Anchorman reading	Chest shot Camera steady
<u>Reporter:</u> The popular forces' leaders had a meeting for more than three hours and have acknowledged the proposals of the executive power. After long hours of debate without reaching a definitive agreement, the assembly of the popular organizations, after evaluating the recent general strike as positive . . .	20 sec.	Popular leaders around a table	Camera moves in Eye level and tilting
. . . decided to postpone until this coming Friday a unified response to the executive power. Rafael Santos assumed the role of spokesperson.	10 sec.	Union leader speaking; we hear the voice of the reporter.	Chest shot Camera steady

Union leader: Our collective of organizations has made a first assessment of the decrees of the executive power and sent them . . .	10 sec.	Union leader speaking	Close-up Camera moves in Eye level
. . . to our respective executive national committees that must meet tomorrow, and arrive at an organizational opinion. At five P.M. tomorrow we will have a definitive response.	25 sec.	Union leader speaking	Chest shot Camera steady

of the stories on TV13 newscasts that day concerned measures taken by the government as a consequence of the strike, presenting the government as having seized the initiative and showing these measures in a favorable way. On the other hand, the organizers of the strike were presented as negatively as possible, although always within a frame of apparent objectivity—the owners of TV13 know that it is poor business strategy for a private network to appear excessively imbalanced; therefore, they try to combine their political concern with their economic interests.

But the evidence suggests that contrary to what a TV13 newscast staff member declared during an interview—"Precisely because our main owner is a politician belonging to the party in power, we make a greater effort than the other networks to be neutral"—TV13 newscasts are biased in favor of the government and endorse the political position of its principal stockholder, Jacinto Peynado. During the period I analyzed the newscasts, TV13 consistently aired ideas and news favorable to the government position.

The other private networks also presented Balaguer criticizing the people who called for the strike. Colorvisión presented this in one minute and thirty seconds, as the fourth story of the telecast; Rahintel, in one minute and forty-five seconds in the third position; and Teleantillas, in one minute and twenty-five seconds as the first story of the newscast.

On the state-owned network, RTVD, the story about the meeting of the popular leaders was presented in one minute and forty-five seconds, and the one about Balaguer criticizing the organizers of the strike in three minutes and ten seconds, giving ample positive coverage to the governmental position throughout the newscast. In fact, during the two days of the strike and the days that followed, eight out of ten stories on RTVD newscasts presented statements of the president and other officials criticizing the strike and minimizing its success.

This enormous amount of news covering government activities is not limited to specific events of crisis, such as the general strike. The newscasts on RTVD are almost exclusively propaganda for the party in power. For example, in a newscast during a period when no important political events were occurring (the debate about the strike being over), on June 29, there were fourteen news stories. Three of them related to international affairs, and eight out of the remaining eleven were positive depictions of government activities: Six described Balaguer's activities and statements, and the other two were about other government officials. All the headlines at the beginning of the show referred to government decisions and actions. Not one story carried even the slightest criticism of the government.

The other national stories were not even mentioned in the headlines and came in fourth, eighth, and ninth positions in the telecast. The first of these concerned a statement by the International Corporation of Executives Services (a U.S. firm whose president was visiting the Dominican Republic) emphasizing the importance of private enterprise for the development of any country. The second alluded to a statement by the president of the Latin American Savings Association about the economic crisis in the area, and the third referred to the declaration of the president of the Association of Industrial Enterprises of Herrera (one of the most important industry associations of the country) about the necessity for entrepreneurs to exert leadership in order to improve the living conditions of the Dominican people.[19] The editorial and a commentary, "The Theme of the Day," were strong defenses of the presidential policy and of the secretary of state for public construction.

The total time allotted to government news by this network was eighteen minutes and ten seconds (twenty minutes and thirty seconds, including headlines); the time allotted to other national news was one minute and twenty-five seconds, and to international news, four minutes. The rest of the thirty minutes of the evening newscast was devoted to commercials and the credits. A similar observation can be made about the newscasts of September 29 and 30, 1989. During the period close to the elections (April–May 1990), the newscast time allotted to the government and the party in power increased to an average of twenty-three minutes per newscast (on the other networks it rarely exceeded fourteen minutes).

The president makes news whenever he acts, and his presence is notable on the newscasts of all the networks, though the coverage of his activities on the public network far outweighs that on the private ones. As a journalist who worked for the public network put it, "The public network is a microphone for high-level government officials." The news director of RTVD recognizes this tendency in part:

Of course, on the newscasts we have a great interest in all the information from the government sectors and official agencies. But independently of that, the information service of this network is open to all the social, cultural, and political concerns of the country, inasmuch as these accommodate the democratic and civilian spirit that guides the politics of the state.

The level of dissent to which the public network is open has varied from one government to another, but since its creation by Trujillo and throughout the electoral democracy existing since 1961, there has been an overwhelming tendency to promote government activities on its newscasts. All governments have considered this network to be a propaganda tool. During the long period of transition to electoral democracy between 1961 and 1978, government control over the state-owned network was absolute. After 1978, with the coming to power of the centrist Partido Revolucionario Dominicano (PRD; Dominican Revolutionary Party), there have been modifications allowing some expression of dissent on the news.

But in its second period in power (1982–86), according to interviewees who worked for this network at that time, even the PRD tended to control the content of the state-owned network. At certain times, the general director of the network requested that all programs be prerecorded, to prevent negative images of the government from being broadcast. Even those who risked their lives for democracy and free speech against Trujillo's government and the semi-dictatorship of Balaguer (in his first two periods of government), as several leaders of the PRD did, ended up trying to control the ideas broadcast once they were in power. Today, under the new government of Joaquín Balaguer, people who work for the public network are members of the party in power (with the exception of a few independent producers).

WHO LEADS THE MERENGUE?[20] THE LOGIC OF INFORMATION SUBSIDIES

Most Dominicans assume that information is an important input in the production of influence. And television newscasts are viewed as primary means for dispensing information. Business enterprises, government agencies, political parties, most trade unions, and even individuals[21] try to be on the television newscasts as much as they can, and newscasts have a continual need for stories.[22] As Gans says, "The relationship between sources and journalists resembles a dance, for sources seek access to journalists, and journalists seek access to sources" (1979, p. 116).

Newscasts, because of the credibility associated with them, allow sources more access to the audience's attention than the usual propaganda spot. Therefore, from the point of view of the sources, it is worthwhile to have a message delivered in a news item rather than in a commercial. In fact, numerous events covered by television are staged events designed for coverage, "pseudo-events" in Boorstin's (1978) term. Firms' public relations departments create news in order to promote their products or activities. For example, newscasts sometimes present as news the opening of a bank's branch or cover the ventures of a particular firm. These kinds of activities deliver more powerful messages when conveyed as news stories, objective facts, rather than as part of a promotion campaign. This kind of information increases in value to the extent that the promotional self-interest of the information is hidden. This also happens with political items. During the political campaign many activities were undertaken in order to attract the media, television in particular.

Political parties and businesses try to be on the television screen as much as possible, using the network resources. Commercial firms pressure the networks to cover their activities. Some argue that because they advertise on the network, the network should be willing to promote their activities. However, there is strong competition for time, equipment, and crews. Therefore, enterprises, as well as government agencies, political parties, and so on, feel compelled to submit much of the information they want to have broadcast; in Gandy's (1982) terms, they subsidize the information.[23] Television newscasts make extensive use of subsidized information, since it reduces the cost of producing news and simplifies the reporter's job.

The government, large enterprises, associations of entrepreneurs, political parties, and most trade unions stay in continuous contact with the television news departments, sending them information about their activities, and even press releases and videos prepared by their public relations staff (the latter is more intense during political campaigns).[24] It is no coincidence that more than 70 percent of the television newscasts on all the networks considered in my study are inspired by press releases, press conferences, political party rallies, meetings, and other prerecorded events.

In order to be able to deliver information to television, sources need to have some financial and organizational resources, which often go hand in hand with economic and political power. This is a great disadvantage for nonprivileged groups of the population, political parties, or other organizations.

As a matter of fact, sources select channels, decision makers, and techniques according to their assumed relative effectiveness in the production of influence over the opinions and behavior of others, and also as a function of the personal or economic connections that they have with the people who control a given network or newscast.

The government in particular extensively subsidizes information. A great deal of the national news is made up of what the officials want the press to report. Government officials utilize the public network, but they also try to send their messages through the other networks that have larger audiences, making use of press releases, of pseudo events such as the press conferences of government officials, and of briefings. Very often at these conferences and briefings reporters are supplied with summaries of speeches by key administration officials. Nobody has established how much money the Dominican government spends on promoting itself through the media, but it is probably a large sum that could be used for social services or productive investments.

The supply of information to newscasts is particularly evident during political campaigns. Dominican networks do not have enough crews to cover all the activities of the various political parties, and cannot send crews to distant locations. Therefore, visuals of political rallies and meetings are frequently handed to the networks by the parties themselves. The public relations or press relations departments of the political parties prepare videotapes ready to be edited, some complete with scripts. In this way the parties increase the probability that their information will be broadcast. The media need stories, and the political parties need publicity to attract voters. Each is useful to the other, and each exerts some kind of influence on the other; but it seems that especially during the political campaign, the political news is largely provided by the political parties themselves.

The effort of the PLD to appear on television is an example of extended political information subsidy by an opposition party. The PLD started giving journalists videos about its activities and its leadership during the 1986 political campaign, when it had few resources and was a distant third with no possibility of winning the presidency. It did so even more intensely in the 1990 electoral campaign, with more resources. In this election it won many seats in the Senate and the Congress, and missed winning the presidency by only 2 percent of the votes.[25]

Public opinion surveys are another device used by political parties to promote their candidates on newscasts. Television newscasts are very receptive to polls. Companies close to certain political parties, or firms that the parties hire, report results in which the party that financed the poll is in the leading position. For example, on May 10, 1990 (six days before the election), TV13 presented the results of a poll sponsored by a group supporting the reelection of Joaquín Balaguer, leader of the conservative Social-Christian Reformist Party. The results of this poll were described extensively at the provincial and national level. Balaguer and his party were, of course, the winners. No explanation of methodology and the sample was provided.

The ultimate consequence of information subsidies is control over what will be broadcast. In normal coverage the events are outside the network's control, but the time allowed to presentation of a given event and the type of shots, camera angles, and editing are not. Besides, to make up the newscasts, news teams choose from a battery of sources and events on the basis of perceived utility in producing news that will meet organizational needs. But when the information has been delivered by the source, most of these elements escape network control. For example, if a video is submitted, the shots and camera angles are under source control.

In fact, through the provision of information subsidies, those with economic and political power are able to fill a large part of the television newscasts with their ideas. During the period in which I analyzed newscast content, 72 percent of the stories came from official bureaucratic channels, political parties, and other organizations (press releases, press conferences, official proceedings, and so on). Less than 20 percent of the stories could be considered a result of enterprise or investigative journalism. And to the extent that interviews could be seen as the result of access to official or business speakers, very little of the news is derived from investigation. The morning information programs (three out of the four private networks I studied have one: Teleantillas, Colorvisión, and Rahintel), which generally invite politicians or key officials to be interviewed while having breakfast, serve as important sources for evening newscasts.

INTERNATIONAL NEWS

Dominican networks, already enormously dependent on U.S., Mexican, and other Latin American companies for their general programming, rely almost completely on foreign sources for their international news. The fundamental reason is economic: Producing their own international stories is very expensive, and therefore out of the question. On a very few special occasions, such as the official visits of the president to a foreign country, do some of the networks send their own reporters (with the financial support of the government).[26] No network in the Dominican Republic has the desire or the economic resources to have a permanent information service.

However, newscasts have to have some international information; Dominican audiences are generally eager to know what is happening in other parts of the world. The time allotted to international news on Dominican television varies from 6 percent to 17 percent of each newscast. On average Rahintel carries more international news than the other networks (between 10 percent and 17 percent of newscast time).

Each day U.S. agencies linked to the networks NBC, ABC, CNN, and Univisión, and the Mexico-based companies SIN and ECO, furnish a selection of images of international current events to the networks of the Dominican Republic. The most important wire agencies are United Press International (UPI), Associated Press (AP), Agence France Press (AFP), the Spanish Agency of Information (Efe), the British Reuters, and the German DPA.

The number of sources from which the Dominican networks draw their international news varies. Private networks have two or three sources for visuals and two or three wire services. Teleantillas edits information from CNN in Spanish and from ABC. The international wire agencies of Teleantillas are Efe, AFP, and DPA. TV13 has CNN and AP as partners for international news. It also has an agreement with a Puerto Rican network from whose archives it sometimes acquires visuals. Rahintel receives all its international information by satellite from the Spanish-language, U.S.-based network Univisión, while RTVD receives visuals and audiotapes from ECO and wire service from UPI. News that comes in English is translated by the networks.

The fact that they have to rely on international agencies, especially U.S. television, for their broadcasts is considered a problem by international editors of the networks:

In U.S. networks Latin America appears very little, they have very little interest in news about Latin America; furthermore, they present their vision of the world.

To make the news in the U.S. networks and most international agencies, the countries of Latin America must be experiencing some disastrous or violent situation. Therefore, frequently important events for Latin Americans are ignored on U.S. networks, and they also interpret . . . reality from their perspective.

By editing the visuals we try to make a balanced presentation. It is not ideal, but it is the only thing we can do with our resources.

Indeed, the flow of news from U.S. television and international agencies is generally imbalanced, with heavy coverage of the United States and other developed countries and little coverage of most Latin American countries (Univisión is an exception). Furthermore, the events carried by international wire services and U.S. networks do not necessarily correspond to news that a Dominican journalist may judge important. For example, in 1987 the *New York Times* editor E. Clifton Daniel prepared a chronological list of the ten top events of the twentieth century, without judgments about their relative importance. This list was reported by an essayist in *Time* (Friedrich 1987).

1. Man's first flight in a heavier-than-air machine (December 17, 1903)
2. The great powers go to war in Europe (August 1, 1914)
3. The Bolshevik Revolution in Russia (November 7, 1917)
4. Lindbergh flies the Atlantic alone (May 21, 1927)
5. Hitler becomes chancellor of Germany (January 30, 1933)
6. Roosevelt is inaugurated as president (March 4, 1933)
7. Scientists split the atom, releasing incredible power (January 28, 1939)
8. The nightmare again—war in Europe (September 1, 1939)
9. Surprise Japanese bombing of Pearl Harbor (December 7, 1941)
10. Men land on moon (July 20, 1969)

Would any Dominican television or newspaper editor agree with Daniel? Probably not. Neither would the editors of *Le Monde*, or *Pravda*, or *Corriere della Sera*, or *El País*. Daniel's classification reflects his own point of view. For example, he made Roosevelt's inauguration one of the most important events of the century because he sees things as a U.S. citizen. A Dominican would include among these events the assassination of Rafael Leonidas Trujillo, while a French journalist would perhaps consider the inauguration of Charles de Gaulle more important, and a Chinese editor would include the Chinese revolution.

In other words, international information has been selected according to the interests of those who are editing the news at the source. Thus, the dependence on international wire agencies and foreign television networks inevitably involves some elements of transculturation and some bias. This confirms Boyd-Barret and Palmer's (1981) assessment of the importance of international information agencies to the interpretation of world events, even though these agencies are not usually recognized by the final recipient of the information. This is especially true because Dominican audiences have fewer means to judge international news than national news. Indeed, in some cases viewers can contrast the information provided concerning national news with direct experience or with their personal knowledge of the situation. Therefore, what television conveys as international news is even more important for establishing a public agenda or influencing the audience than the presentation of local news. In fact, I ascertained during field research that the international issues that people identified were the ones presented on the television newscasts of that time.

Furthermore, the small number of international wires subscribed to by each Dominican network—economic constraints do not allow a network to have dozens of visual and wire services—limits the choice of the newscast staff. International editors have to choose among those wires and visuals which are sent to them. As a result, international news on Dominican television is a sampling of a sampling made by international agencies of what is happening in the world. "We take from the international news those stories which have a Latin American interest," said an international editor.

Given the offerings of these international agencies and because of the overwhelming number of visuals and wires that reach the Dominican Republic from U.S. agencies, one would expect that international news in the Dominican Republic extensively depicts the U.S. networks' vision of the world and their interpretation of events—that is, more often than not, the economic and diplomatic interests of the United States.[27] But this is not what actually happens. On the contrary, Dominican international editors are able to sort the content of the information and the quantity of news so that Latin America is adequately covered: 55 percent of international news over the period studied concerned Latin America; 23 percent, the United States; 17 percent, Europe; and 5 percent, other parts of the world. (See Table 5.2.) International editors also present the information in such a way that they considerably limit any bias that the international news could have carried. With the exception of Rahintel, which receives its international information directly from the U.S.-based Spanish-language network Univisión—which is strongly favorable to the views and regional interests of the United States—the other networks have a fairly balanced presentation of international news. And once in a while we can also find specific information biased in favor of a given government in Latin America (the Sandinistas, for example). As a matter of fact, very few of the journalists interviewed were favorable to the Contras in Nicaragua, and this was sometimes manifest in the newscasts.

Audience interviews also indicate a tendency to adopt the views of the oppressed against what they perceived as "the aggression of foreign powers": 52 percent of the people interviewed saw the problem of Central America as caused by foreign intrusion. Specifically, 61 percent of people in the lower and middle strata criticized what they considered U.S. trespass. However, this tendency is not just a result of television information. The experience of two U.S. invasions in less than fifty years also probably has strongly contributed to stress on anti-interventionism in other countries.

DRAWING NEWS WITHIN GIVEN STRUCTURES

Television newscasts bring a general awareness of what goes on in other societies, and in the country. But the Dominican Republic is far from a society in which the explosion of information and communication has created a more educated and informed people. The organization of television information does not allow a total understanding of events, and does not lead people to question existing structures. On the contrary, most of the time newscasts are superficially descriptive. There is disinformation through simplification. Also, because of the importance given to spectacle, there is an increasing difference between the world as it is and its representation on television. The marriage of a celebrity or the verbal lapses of politicians occupy more newscast time than the daily deaths of children from the lack of food and medication.

As a matter of fact, the market imperatives that underlie television newscasts often dilute the information ethic. News teams have to keep newscasts marketable. Information is costly, and the networks' owners are not ambitious to further talent, intelligence, or culture in general. Sure of their rights as owners, they profess their objective: to engender benefits.

It has been demonstrated in this chapter that in deciding what to cover, reporters, editors, and news directors are above all influenced by commercial imperatives. Other factors, such as organizational routines, internal power struggles, and decision makers' specific ideas, also play a role in the

Table 5.2
Percentage of International News on Dominican Television, by Continent

	Latin America	North America (USA and Canada)	Europe East	Europe West	Other Continents
TV 13	54	26	5	7	8
Teleantillas	51	24	10	9	6
Colorvisión	46	24	10	13	7
Rahintel	64	22	5	7	2
RTVD	52	27	8	11	2

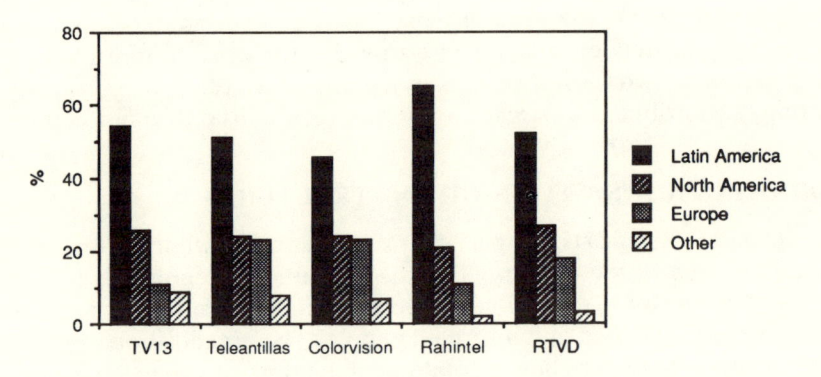

Source: Author's data.

production of news, but to a lesser extent. It has been shown that news presentations are made within a given framework, whose limitations are imposed on the newscast team, in the coverage of events and issues that could be seen as controversial, by the owners of television networks or by sponsors. Institutional and group interests play a critical role in determining what to broadcast. As Tuchman (1978, p. 210) writes, "News both draws upon and reproduces institutional structures." Although there are exceptions, the staffs of the television networks generally are subservient to those who control the media: owners, stockholders, or the government. We have seen how the political affiliation and the economic interests of those with economic control over the networks play an important role in influencing their overall message. As a result, expressions of dissident values are rare on television newscasts.

Even if the political consequences of television newscasts' messages are not always conscious or intentional, they are nonetheless present. Overall there is a strong avoidance of anti-business ideologies and a sharp tendency to reproduce dominant ideas. The democratic assumption of the right to information is significantly subverted by the free market economy.

Thus, my research indicates that in the Dominican Republic, the economic structure and corresponding power relations in which television networks are enmeshed determine in different ways (through ownership, sponsorship, and pressure groups) the general content of television newscasts and, therefore, limit the extent of pluralism. This tendency, as we will see in Chapter 6, is accentuated during elections.

NOTES

1. In the McBride Report information is considered as a natural resource, like energy and other material resources, as well as a collective right of the communities and the peoples of the world. The Report also questions the role of advertising and the commercialization of information. All the media owners in the Dominican Republic opposed this report, as did the media owners in most countries of Latin America, North America, and western Europe, as was made clear at the thirty-fourth Congreso Internacional de Editores de Periódicos, at Madrid in 1987.

2. A functioning television station in the United States—from which country Dominican firms imported most of the equipment to establish the networks—had an average price of $24 million in 1984, with some stations as high as $510 million. To open a new television station cost between $5 and $6 million (without considering cost of operation). A typical television outlet (the emitting device itself) cost about $680,000. Television news requires between fifteen and twenty people as well as sophisticated machinery. Earth stations that send signals to satellites (the uplink) range in price from about $600,000 to $750,000 (Head and Sterling 1987).

3. According to government data, 45 percent Dominicans are illiterate.

4. Dominican networks have three newscasts a day: one early in the morning, which on networks such as Teleantillas is part of a talk show; one at the beginning of the afternoon; and a third in the evening. This last attracts the biggest audiences. On most networks, the evening newscasts last for thirty minutes. The exception is Rahintel, which has a forty-five-minute evening newscast, ten to fifteen minutes of which is dedicated to regional information from the second most important economic area of the country, El Cibao. The newscasts carry a great number of commercials. The number of commercials broadcast and the time allowed for them vary from one newscast to another on the same network. One day a given network will broadcast ten commercials, and the following day, eighteen; one day the commercials will occupy 20 percent of the newscast, and the following day, 35 percent. On an average the percentage of total time allowed for commercials during evening newscasts by each network is as follows: Rahintel, 29.1 percent; Colorvisión, 28.9 percent; Teleantillas, 27 percent; TV13, 24.1 percent; and RTVD, 6.4 percent.

5. The term "political" is used here in its broadest sense.

6. These assessments derive from the statements of journalists, editors, and news directors interviewed, as well as from my content analysis of the news.

7. Dominican television newsroom structures are very similar from one network to another. There is a news director, who is responsible for everything that goes on the air. At some networks he produces other programs of information, such as the two-hour morning programs (e.g., "Uno + Uno"). He is also in charge of the newscast personnel. Next in authority is the subdirector or managing editor, who is in charge of operations. He is expected to direct news gathering, preparation, and production. Both the news director and the managing editor act as executive producers of the newscasts. Next in rank are editors (international, sports, etc.), reporters, anchors, picture editors, and cameramen. In the Dominican Republic the anchors are only readers of news. News directors, managing editors, editors, and reporters are journalists, most of whom worked for newspapers. The anchors have diverse professional and education backgrounds. Among them are journalists, actors, psychologists, and lawyers.

8. The fact that visuals are not used to their full potential does not imply that there is no awareness about their possibilities; rather, the limitation of resources (human and technical) does not permit much sophistication. There is no school that trains people for television production. The visual work is very well done in political propaganda spots—which are handled by experts, most of whom are foreigners, and most of the technical montage is done in the United States or some other foreign country.

9. The gap between the camera coverage and the narration may create confusion among audiences. As Salvaggio (1980) suggests, the visual image is important in itself, and it is particularly crucial in its interactions with the audio.

10. The group interests are so interrelated that sometimes sponsors prefer to pay a "quota" in order not to appear as enemies of certain views. This also happens with the political parties. Even leftist parties receive some kind of financial support from the sponsors who want to be on good terms with them.

11. Golding (1980) suggests possible biases in the television newscasts. Deliberate short-term effects may be considered as bias; short-term, nondeliberate effects fall under the heading of unwitting bias; deliberate and long-term effects indicate policy; and long-term, nondeliberate effects are ideology. All of these are present in the state-owned network. As for private networks, my research shows evidence of bias, unwitting bias, and ideology; I found no proof of policy.

12. On April 24, 1984, discontent with the sharp increases in the price of gas and food led to several uprisings in the country. Dozens of people were killed and hundreds injured by the police and the army.

13. This is, of course, relative. Three people were killed by the police and the army during the strike, and several injured. This can be compared with the general strike of August 1990, in which twelve people were shot, several dozen injured, and, according to Caroit (1990), correspondent of *Le Monde*, thousands imprisoned.

14. I recorded newscasts for six days in June 1989, two days in September 1989, and twelve days in April–May 1990.

15. One of the programs presented on RTVD, "Revista 110," was judged by opposition politicians to be one of the most democratic on Dominican television. "Anyone can go and talk on this program. At least for now, that we are not yet

in a political campaign," said the president of the leftist Socialist party in June 1989, a year before the elections. This idea was shared by all the politicians interviewed.

16. I use the term "journalist" to include all the members of the newscast staff who perform a professional activity related to journalism: reporters, editors, managing editors, and news directors.

17. The biggest stockholder and the president of TV13 is Jacinto Peynado, owner of a large import firm and other enterprises, and one of the most prominent leaders of the conservative Social Christian Reformist party. The major stockholder of Colorvisión is the Bermúdez family, the biggest producers of rum and actively involved in the most important agro-industries of the country.

18. The plots (scenes or stage sets) are arranged according to the type of shot. Considering that for the purpose of this research a difference of one or two seconds is not significant, I rounded off the time to the closest five seconds.

19. Since the early 1980s it has become very common to hear such statements, which sometimes reflect a real concern of some individual entrepreneur. However, concrete actions rarely follow these declarations.

20. The merengue is a very popular dance in the Dominican Republic.

21. There are numerous examples of efforts by individuals in the government or in private firms to gain advantages for themselves through self-promotion in the mass media.

22. Lately, even politicians from what has traditionally been called the revolutionary Left have learned how to make the journalists' code work for them. They are often interviewed on television in suits and ties, sitting behind desks or in front of bookshelves, embodying solid expertise and mainstream reliability.

23. I consider Gandy's definition particularly appropriate. In his words: "An information subsidy is an attempt to produce influence over the actions of others by controlling their access to and use of information relevant to those actions. This information is characterized as a subsidy because the source of that information causes it to be made available at something less than the cost a user would face in the absence of subsidy" (1982, p. 61).

24. In choosing techniques to attract the attention of reporters, sources are concerned with cost effectiveness. They tend to select those techniques which ensure the widest coverage for the least effort. Press releases, press conferences, and briefings are considered economically efficient because they provide sources with access to several reporters at the same time. Sometimes, though, network press departments try to obtain exclusive interviews.

25. Although this party received more votes than the governing PRSC in the 1990 elections, it did not win because the latter was allied to right-wing small parties. There have also been strong claims that fraud helped the PRSC and its allies to win.

26. The visit of Juan Bosch to New York (around 800,000 Dominicans live there) at the beginning of the electoral campaign was covered by Rahintel.

27. Although the U.S. networks are apparently independent of the government, and criticism sometimes appears in their news, on the whole they strongly favor the foreign policy of the United States. This can be observed in the treatment of information in daily newscasts, but also and more dramatically in situations of international trouble, such as the invasion of Panama or the Persian Gulf crisis.

Besides, the U.S. government in general gives great importance to mass communication as an instrument of international policy. Examples are Radio Free Europe, Radio Martí, and "Project Worldnet." This last program was described by the White House "as a means with no precedent and with no limits to reach the spirits and the hearts of the peoples of the world and to attract them to the ideals and objectives of the US government" (Eudes 1988, p. 11).

Chapter 6

Election Ritual and Television

The electoral process in a representative democracy like the Dominican Republic usually involves long political campaigns.[1] Candidates for official positions need to present themselves and their programs to the electors. Voters' choices are largely the result of the contending candidates' and political parties' attempts to communicate appeals that are sufficiently persuasive to attract mass support.

Until the mid–1970s, the promotion of Dominican political candidates was accomplished by personal contact of candidates and party members with the population through meetings, rallies, and home visits, as well as through radio, newspapers, and posters. Television was barely used. In the 1990s, candidates are publicized primarily by television, advertising agencies, and opinion research firms.

Political parties, unions, and neighborhood organizations are substantial factors in political promotion and make it possible to recruit large numbers of voters. Also, the insight of the political candidates and party leaders into the political culture of the country are important in determining the outcome of an election. Other determining factors include how well the incumbents did their job, and the economic conditions during their term of office (bad conditions could bring people to vote against those in power). But, however these factors affect the election, it is clear that the larger society becomes, the less people have personal contact with those who are seeking their votes. Television replaces this contact by allowing the voters to see the candidates up close and to hear what they have to say. Besides, being informed, understanding, knowing how to choose, making decisions, and voting require time and energy that voters are not always inclined to take. Television quickly brings audiovisual information about the candidates to the voters' homes, thus saving them time and energy.

The media play different roles in a political campaign. The newspaper is the most effective medium for conveying elaborate, complex messages. Print is most often directed to the upper classes and to the intellectuals, the ones who usually read the political items in the newspapers. The radio brings the voices of the candidates to sectors of the population such as peasants and maids. But the possibilities of mass communication that television offers across class lines have made it the most attractive medium for political strategists.

TELEVISION AS MASTER OF POLITICAL CEREMONIES

Most Dominican voters today become familiar with political candidates through television. The majority of voters never attend a meeting; their contact with the candidates is essentially through the television screen. Television allows candidates to be known in almost all homes, and gives the impression of direct and spontaneous communication between the candidate and the voter. Intermediaries, such as other members of the party, are now less necessary.

Television transmits political information even to those who are not seeking it. Indeed, viewers may consume political information involuntarily through political spots aired during entertainment programs and through political interviews conducted during variety shows.

Television became a major instrument for political promotion in the Dominican Republic during the 1980s. The centrist Partido Revolucionario Dominicano (PRD; Dominican Revolutionary Party) started to campaign using television, polls, and computers extensively in 1978. The conservative Partido Reformista Social Cristiano (PRSC, Social Christian Reformist Party) followed suit almost immediately. In subsequent campaigns television has been the primary medium of promotion used by these parties (before, it was used to complement meetings and other traditional forms of campaigning). The other parties, especially those on the Left, have been slower to recognize the need for television in the political campaign. The center-left Partido de la Liberación Dominicana (PLD; Dominican Liberation Party) started to use television only in 1986, and by 1990 had developed a fairly extensive use of political spots and television in general.[2] In fact, during the 1990 campaign most political parties used television with such frequency that the presence of politicians on the screen was almost constant.

Lately the party in power has used television exhaustively, and not only in political campaigns. Since the 1980s shows promoting economic or sociopolitical actions of the government have occupied an increasingly large amount of airtime. Likewise, most groups of the power elite have been using television to promote or defend their ideas and interests.

More and more in the Dominican Republic a candidate's chance of being elected increases as television information and advertising about him increases. Even meetings and political rallies are usually organized for maximum television coverage. In politics today, for a large part of the Dominican population, what is not shown on television is as if it never happened. As in other societies, television has become the master of political ceremonies. This is openly and clearly recognized by several top politicians of the Dominican Republic whom I interviewed:

Television is an important instrument for political promotion today. It can destroy the political image as well as the physical image of a candidate. (Juan Bosch, president of the PLD and candidate for president of the Republic)

According to a survey financed by our party, ... the most important medium in politics today is television. Given the influence of television, our campaign will concentrate on using this medium. (José Francisco Peña Gómez, president of the PRD and candidate for president of the Republic)

I think that some of the Dominican politicians have been very slow to assimilate the importance of television in politics, especially those on the Left. They did not understand the signs of the time, they did not understand the dynamics that exist between the people's consciousness and the medium through which the message is sent. They did not understand the role that television plays today in conforming tastes and political preferences. Today, personal contact through meetings and rallies is not enough; the popular forces need to use the mass media in order to reach the popular consciousness, and television is the most important of the mass media for this purpose. (Rafael Taveras, president of the Socialist party)[3]

The importance of television to politics is also clear to those in charge of the political campaigns of most parties. Their view is illustrated by the words of a campaign directive of the PRSC:

The value of an event does not depend on itself, but rather on the capacity that one has to diffuse it through the media, in particular television. In this sense, if a party has not the resources to reproduce its activities on television, this party will not have much impact on society.

Most political analysts and researchers agree that television's power to attract attention and to inform the audience about political matters is unsurpassed. My observations of the 1990 campaign confirm that television in the Dominican Republic does play a significant role in influencing the way voters think about the candidates and their political agendas, although such influence is not uniform. Each voter is affected differently by television, based on political predispositions (e.g., whether undecided or strongly supportive of a given candidate) and interests (e.g., if some personal advantage is expected from a particular candidate, such as a job).

Clearly the work of party members, and their meetings and rallies, are not enough to win elections. For example, the PLD has had more members than the other parties since 1982, and perhaps even before. The PLD was also by far the best-organized party in the country. These factors did not result in a correspondingly great number of votes. In the 1986 election the PLD had the biggest rallies and meetings, and even though it experienced a huge growth in the number of votes compared with the 1982 election, it came in distant third with around 12 percent of the votes. In the 1986 campaign the PLD started to use television, but it was not yet the basic campaign tool. In the 1990 election it received more than 32 percent of the votes and became the largest party in the country (the PRSC won the election with the support of four other parties). In this campaign, besides the traditional work of its members, the PLD enormously intensified its television propaganda. This suggests that television propaganda does help to make the difference, and may be essential. A party that cannot make extensive use of television has a hard time getting its candidates elected.

However, this is not to say that the number of votes will be proportional to the time spent promoting the candidates on television. For example, in the 1988 election in Ecuador, the right-wing candidate, Abdalá Bucaran, broadcast three times as many political spots on television as the winning president, Rodrigo Borja, broadcast. Similarly, during the 1989 referendum in Chile, the dictatorship imposed clear limitations on the access the opposition had to television, but Pinochet lost anyway.

In other words, the appropriate and intensive use of television increases the chances for a candidate to win an election, but it does not guarantee victory.

Agenda Setting

In the 1990 political campaign, television strongly influenced the agenda for public discussion. Events that were given little emphasis on television did not attract much public attention. In this political campaign television played a very important role in defining the limits of political debate and specifying the issues upon which voters would decide how to vote. By placing certain campaign events repeatedly and prominently in the news, television coverage signaled their importance to the public. As Iyengar et al. (1984, p. 58) stated: "by ignoring some problems and attending to others, television news programs profoundly affect which problems viewers take seriously."

Television's influence on agenda setting is illustrated by the controversy that arose about alleged tax evasion of the PLD vice presidential candidate during the 1990 election. The government accused this candidate, who owns a shoe company, of avoiding the export tax on shoes sold to Cuba. The candidate argued that since the Cuban government had not paid him for the shoes, he could not pay the tax. The information was released by the government with the clear intention to harm the PLD, two weeks before the election.[4]

Television newscasts and other media followed this story during almost all the rest of the campaign. It became one of the major issues of the last two weeks of the campaign on all the networks, particularly the state-owned RTVD, TV13, and Rahintel. This was a juicy story, with all the controversy (accusations and counteraccusations) that news executives assume attracts an audience, but for some groups with network control, it was also an opportunity to discredit a party that they saw as a possible danger to their interests. Similar coverage of other stories, such as the Bosch declarations about equal rights for all religions and the selling of state enterprises to the private sector, provide further evidence of the role of television in setting public agendas in the Dominican Republic.

These news stories were followed by the public, who referred in their conversations to the arguments and points of view presented in the telecasts. Therefore, one can deduce that television messages affect the decision-making process in voting, particularly among the undecided. In other words, what is emphasized by television has significant consequences for the electoral process.

Telepolitics: The Spectacular Game

The problem with the agenda-setting role of television is not only that it emphasizes some aspects over others, but also that it does not really inform the population about the most important issues in an election. More than 60 percent of network reports on the Dominican elections in 1990 were done in terms of a contest or game; others just provided information about meetings and other activities; and less than 15 percent of newscasts actually gave information about the issues.

The political intentions of each candidate were not covered extensively in the news. From time to time the more substantial issues were debated in interviews on morning shows such as "Uno + Uno" and "Buenos Días." But these programs do not have as large an audience as the newscasts. In fact, to a large extent, through these morning shows the reports on issues reach people more directly involved in politics, such as party members and intellectuals.

Television focuses on the particularities and personalities of the presidential candidates, to the detriment of their political projects. Even documentaries about the most important presidential candidates that were broadcast during the 1990 election, emphasized their personal histories but said little about the policy they would follow if they won the elections. In fact, television portrayals of the politicians encourage the acceptance of demagogic and autocratic politicians. The caudillismo that has characterized Dominican political organization has been complemented by personalism throughout television. Also, television newscasts' continuous quest for spectacle caused them to pay excessive attention to the gaffes of presidential candidates: Bosch forgetting something during a speech, or Balaguer not having the answer to a question. Furthermore, they cover the election in terms of who will win, who is ahead, and other details more suited to games.

A political commercial of the centrist PRD aired during the last two weeks of the political campaign is an excellent example of how the Dominican television newscasts tend to cover the elections. This ad used cartoons to depict the elections as a horse race. According to most polls made public during the political campaign, the PRD was third behind the PLD and the PRSC. In order to project the idea that the PRD was quite close to winning the election, this commercial depicted a horse race with three horses in the colors of the three parties: violet (PLD), red (PRSC), and white (PRD). The race started with the violet horse leading, followed by the red horse and the white horse. But as the race went on, the white horse approached the leader and eventually won. The commercial used crowd noises and commentary typical of an actual horse race: "The violet is ahead, followed by the red, the white is behind... but wait, the white is coming up fast on the outside, he is now very close to the violet, he is now head to head...."

By concentrating on the more spectacular part of a story, television journalists mislead the public because they are not reporting the hues and lights of a given story. Television provides superficial information that favors imagery and immediacy of reporting over discussion. Because of the way television newscasts covered the election campaign of 1990, voters learned little about the concrete policy positions of the candidates. Only a few controversial statements by Juan Bosch created some debate about specific issues.

"TELEMARKETING" THE CANDIDATES

Television has influenced the form and the style of the political campaign. Through the bias of television the electoral campaign has become more and more a contest not only between candidates but also between experts in marketing and communication.

The more frequently used promotional tools in the 1990 political campaign were political spots, press conferences, press releases, supply of audiovisual and written accounts of parties' activities to the media, and meetings and rallies (activities that usually attract news coverage).

Television newscasts also directly or indirectly promoted the candidates by organizing panel shows with the candidates, sponsoring debates with political specialists on the characteristics of the candidates and parties, interviewing people in the streets about their opinions on the candidates, and inviting candidates to variety shows. Some networks also showed short documentaries on the lives of the most important candidates: Bosch, Balaguer, Peña Gómez, and Majluta.

Political parties always want as much access to television as they can get, but they are not always sure that newscasts will carry all the messages they want. Indeed, because of the costs, networks do not always cover all the activities of the parties and candidates (for example, the trips of candidates to distant parts of the country), and decision makers do not always correctly interpret what the parties would like to project in a given story.

In addition, the goals of the parties and the networks are sometimes contradictory. Political parties aim to inundate television with information suitable to the election of their candidates, while newscasts seek news containing controversy and scandal. Besides, for diverse reasons that are not always intentional, broadcasts may fail to report a positive image of a candidate. For instance, all the plans of consultants and party staff will not necessarily give the presidential candidates attractive appearances on television in briefings, interviews, or press conferences. Their performance in front of the television cameras is often far from appealing. For example, the candidate of the PRSC was almost completely blind and appeared very awkward, looking for the microphone or pausing at length before answering journalists' questions with difficulty. During most of his television appearances, the leader of the PLD, Juan Bosch, talked excitedly, aggressively, and angrily. Most of the other candidates were equally unimpressive. Majluta, the candidate of the Independent Revolutionary Party (PRI), was pompous, and Abinader, the candidate of the tiny Constitutional Action Party (PAC), was dull. Perhaps Vincho Castillo (Progressive National Force, FNP) and Peña Gómez (PRD) were the least bad, although the latter was far from using the television image in all its potential.[5]

Given this situation, the parties want as much control as possible over what will be broadcast; therefore, the parties with resources send their own reports to the networks and buy time to transmit their political spots.

Political Spots

In the 1990 campaign, the political propaganda spots were the most systematic mechanism for creating positive and attractive images of the principal presidential candidates. The function of political spots tends to be the same as that of ordinary commercials. The voters are considered consumers of politics. Conceived as merchandise, the political product is offered in the Dominican electoral market, where all means are used to influence the voters' choice, treating voters more as targets of a promotional campaign than as responsible citizens. "Sell your candidates in the same way that businesses sell their products," advised Leonard Hall, director of the U.S. Republican Party electoral campaign, in 1956. Since then, little by little, the lesson has been learned by most electoral democracies around the world. In the Dominican Republic, the tools of the television advertising industry have been applied to politics with particular intensity since the end of the 1970s.

The party leaders, and party members or sympathizers who are journalists or in some way connected to the communications industry, traditionally have played an important role in defining the basic objectives of the campaign and its direction in most Dominican parties. But in the campaigns of 1986 and 1990, most parties also received insights from international specialists, particularly in the design of political spots. They were also helped by experts from allied international parties: The PRSC was helped by the International Social-Christian Party; the PRD, by the Socialist International; and so on. In the 1990 campaign the foreign consultants started to play a more prominent role.

Political spots were produced following the logic of commercial advertising, with meticulous staging to present a candidate's positive image. Spots are artistic enterprises of a team composed of television producers, advertisers, public relations personnel, and all manner of consultants. They constitute a kind of theater production done in such a way that it will be received with interest and satisfaction by the voters and thus gain their votes. The scenario is based on the propaganda team's supposed knowledge of voter psychology. The point is to sell an image that will respond to the voter's fantasies and desires. As Graber asserts:

Aware that the audience's interest needs to be aroused, the media cast political tales as stylized, familiar dramas. The audience incorporates these media-created scenarios and stereotyped characters into their personal or group fantasies about the nature of the political world. These fantasies then become the realities to which people respond with political action. (1984, p. 149)

The idea behind television campaigning, especially the production of spots, is not to change profound beliefs but to appeal to the voters' feelings, stimulating them to vote for a given candidate. The image and sound of the television propaganda tend to be subliminal. "The intention of the political spots is to connect the candidate to the internal emotive signals of the voters, to adjust the message to their state of resounding," said a political campaign adviser.

In form as well as in content, the political spots in the 1990 campaign were designed to establish a face-to-face relation with the audience. There were no rational, long, and technical explanations of issues in these spots, for they were oriented to reach emotions more than reason. The message was simple, using everyday language and short sentences. The spots concentrated on two or three basic themes. The propaganda teams of the four most important parties in the 1990 campaign apparently had incorporated Saussez's (1986) claim that in a short time the communicator should aim to seduce, since it is impossible to convince.[6]

Staging for Television

As in the production of the propaganda spots, most promotional activities were calculated by the party campaign team. Each day of the campaign was planned, and the scenarios for an event were often prepared days in advance and in such a way that the presentation of negative images would be highly improbable. The campaign team organized things to facilitate television coverage. Each day of a campaign contained a certain number of events that generated news. Sometimes the candidates were in three or more cities or places in a single day. On those occasions the telecasts edited the images of the presidential candidates in such a manner that the audience could have the impression that they were only getting in and out of a car or getting on and off a helicopter (in the case of the incumbent, who often used an official helicopter). Although only the most important events of each candidate's campaign were followed by television reporters, most large parties managed to send the newscasts their own videos of the events they wanted to have reported.

Rallies and meetings are important in measuring the support of the population and projecting a given candidate as the winner. Pictures are used extensively to show which presidential candidate drew more people to the meetings. Showing such pictures on television is seen as crucial to attracting voters. As a matter of fact, meetings are largely staged to be shown on television. People's reaction in front of the television set while these meetings are telecast is symptomatic of the role that television plays: "Look at this crowd; Bosch will probably win the elections" or "This meeting is as big as the one that the reformists did last week; Peña Gómez has enough people to win the elections."

In the Dominican Republic a rather large part of the population, compared with other countries, is involved in the political process. People talk about politics very often, but this is particularly intensified in the election period. Politics dominates conversation for several months: at social gatherings, on public transport, at the universities, and, of course, in the media. Rallies and meetings of more than 200,000 persons in the capital city and in other important cities were not rare in 1986 and 1990. Most parties spent considerable sums bringing people to the meetings and rallies. In 1990, in addition to numerous rallies and local meetings, the four most important parties organized a minimum of three special gatherings, the largest ones a week before Election Day. These were covered by television newscasts, with the crowds shown from multiple angles. The networks estimated that the four major parties were able to bring around 300,000 people to each of these gatherings. For these large meetings—which took place in Santo Domingo and Santiago—transport companies were hired to bring people from all over the country.

However, not all the people who attend these meetings are fervent members of the organizing party. A good number attend because they receive some form of contribution from the sponsoring party. Some receive a small stipend; others get money for expenses; and for many attending the meetings is an opportunity to travel with all costs covered. The party in power also strongly encourages government employees to attend these meetings. They risk their jobs if they do not attend. This was particularly true during the governments of the PRSC.

The political interest that is created during an election is not the result solely of ideological commitment. In addition to the preference for a given candidate because their views are similar to his, numerous Dominicans expect direct material gains from a change of government. Some expect to get a job, others expect to lose their jobs (the government is an important supplier of jobs), and business owners expect to do business with the government according to their relationship with those in power. In other words, "What's in it for me?" plays a significant part in the interest that large groups of Dominicans have in politics. This is known by the political parties, and some of them do not hesitate to offer positions to their followers before they are in power.

Parties are above all concerned with having enough people attend these meetings, which are important demonstrations of force shown to the entire country on the television screen. The basic content of the principal candidates' speeches at these meetings is merely expressions of triumphalism.

Vague and Generic Expressions of Platforms

By using television, political strategists try to transmit a personal image of the candidates that is attractive, acceptable, and desirable to voters. In the 1990 campaign each candidate tried to convince voters in a rather abstract way that he had the personal qualities to confront the economic crises and to find solutions to basic problems, such as the numerous electrical power failures. The party in power, the PRSC, argued that its candidate was the only one able to modernize the country peacefully, while the major opposition parties presented their candidates as the most honest, intelligent, and able.

Concerning their political projects, the candidates in general tried to be careful to avoid alienating voters and economic supporters. They attempted, as the politicians of other countries usually do, to be the least objectionable by making very general statements, avoiding as much as possible controversial presentations of their intentions. Most of the candidates did not present a clear, written program of government, limiting themselves to general and vague ideas of how well they would govern. Only occasionally did they give true indication of their intentions, because they know that the Dominican people in general vote for persons and not for programs. It is advantageous to stay ambiguous and imprecise. Balaguer has never presented a written program to the population and has been elected for six terms. People vote more for a messiah than for a program.[7]

Only Juan Bosch, among the most important contenders, made some concrete pronouncements about his intentions. He said that he would sell the state enterprises to the private sector if he was elected, and that all religions would have the same privileges. The way television networks and other media reported these statements created a strong controversy. The report on the selling of the state enterprises provoked a negative reaction (amply enhanced by the PRSC) among a good number of state employees, who, afraid of losing their jobs, strongly disapproved of Bosch's intentions. And concerning equal rights for all religions, Bosch's statements, as they were reported, elicited the fury of the Roman Catholic hierarchy, as well as the alienation of a good number of Catholic voters. There is a special agreement between the Dominican state and the Vatican that makes Roman Catholicism the state religion. This agreement was established by Rafael Leonidas Trujillo and the Vatican in 1956.[8] Several political analysts agree that these declarations probably hurt Bosch's chances of winning the election.

In fact, judging by what the people on the street were saying, as well as by the remarks of several journalists and political analysts—who wondered if Bosch really wanted to win the election, since he committed so many gaffes in the last two weeks of the campaign—it has become acceptable to the voters that the candidates not reveal their real intentions during the campaign. In this situation, the electoral process is more a confrontation of persons than of ideas and political issues. This is reflected and amplified on television.

The candidates with a chance of winning the presidency in the 1990 campaign were well known.[9] Therefore, the promotional campaign in television and other media was oriented to showing which candidate would best solve the problems of the country by emphasizing personality traits that the political strategists believed the population appreciated. Although the vast majority of the population were very familiar with the principal candidates, there was a large group of voters who had not yet made up their minds three weeks before Election Day. This indecision occurred because the country was in such crisis that many people were desperately looking for a savior, and they were not sure that the traditional leaders could do anything. In addition, it was the first time since the fall of the dictatorship in 1961 that more than two parties had a chance of winning the election. Therefore, people had a harder time making up their minds. Traditionally the elections have been a duel between the PRD and the PRSC, but in the 1990 election the PLD was ahead in the polls.[10]

Most campaign strategists were conscious of the need to accommodate the campaign at several levels: (1) to reinforce the convictions of supporters; (2) to convince the undecided who were somewhat in favor of their candidate; (3) to lead voters predisposed to vote for another candidate to vote for their party, or at least to make them undecided; and (4) above all, to win over the undecided and those who did not intend to vote. In the 1990 elections more than in previous elections, the number of people undecided was particularly large. According to some polls and advertisers, it was around 25 percent one month prior to the elections. A political leader interviewed three weeks before the elections said:

Because of the continuous economic crises that we are experiencing in this country, it is not easy to predict the trend of the vote in advance. We know that right now the PLD is the first party in the polls, but it is very easy for a large group of the population to change from here to the elections. This group could be as large as 20 percent or more.

If a party could win over even a small proportion of the undecided, this margin could be enough to win the election. In the 1990 campaign four candidates had a chance to win the presidency. The difference in the polls between the two leading candidates, Bosch and Balaguer, was minimal; and the third-place candidate, Peña Gómez, was not far behind. The other candidate with some chance was Jacobo Majluta, leader of the right-wing PRI.[11]

Polls

The polls of electoral preferences produce material to feed the campaign and the television newscasts. The polls generally have two basic functions: to inform the political leaders and the population about the leanings of the voters, and to induce the voters to favor a given candidate.

In the United States and Europe, opinion polls play such an important role that the candidates try to adapt their discourse to the results of the polls. Parties continuously take polls to evaluate the campaign on an almost daily basis, to localize the weak points of the campaign, and to establish the strategy to follow in the next days. They also store information in computers. No politician could be elected to an important position without a heavy load of demagogy in his speeches, and that demagogy is amply based on the data obtained from the polls.

This level of demagogic technology is not yet applied with great precision in the Dominican Republic, but that does not mean there is no demagogy in Dominican politics. Some politicians, such as Joaquín Balaguer, are naturally great demagogues. It is no accident that he won six elections (even if he was sometimes suspected of cheating, he always managed to have a relatively large support among the population).

In the Dominican Republic the polls are used more as instruments of promotion. Most major parties hire polling firms to indicate their chances of winning the election, and the biggest parties tend to find at least one poll whose results give them the lead or a position with a chance of winning. Those specific poll results are diffused extensively through television and other media. It is expected that a poll indicating a given candidate as the winner will attract more people to support him. Indeed, according to my interviews, this plays a significant role in attracting more votes and raising money. Most people's opinions about a given candidate tend to conform to the perception of his chances, especially among those who are not strong followers of a particular party. If they regard a candidate as having a good chance to win, they will be more inclined to vote for him. On the other hand, they usually will be less likely to vote for a candidate who does not have much of a chance. People vote for those candidates with chances of winning who will be least harmful (from their point of view). Furthermore, the government is an important source of jobs to which numerous Dominicans aspire. Thus, those who are looking for a job will tend to align with the possible winner they expect will give them a job.

In other words, if a voter prefers a particular candidate whom the polls and the media do not present as a possible winner, this voter will tend to vote instead for a candidate who does have a chance of winning and who is close to his/her ideas or interests. Likewise, the capitalists will invest more in the candidates who are more likely to win, in order to ensure specific advantages.

For the networks, polls are important not only because they make good news; polls also give insights about the support the candidates have among the population, and newscasters therefore act accordingly in their coverage.

DIFFERENT POLITICAL VIEWS ON TELEVISION

All the political views that exist in Dominican society are displayed on television. This is recognized by leaders of the self-proclaimed "revolutionary Left" in these terms: "Although we are far from being perfect, from what I know, Dominican television is probably the most pluralistic of Latin America" and "if we compare with other countries of the Caribbean and Latin America, Dominican television is relatively open to diverse opinions."

This relative political pluralism results from the fact that within the networks there is a certain degree of leeway for journalists and producers, and also from the fact that much television airtime is sold to independent producers who have more freedom of action than do employees.[12]

But the fact that most political views are present on television does not mean that every political party receives the same amount or quality of television coverage. Juan B. Mejía, leader of the Revolutionary Workers Organization, or Organización Revolucionaria de los Trabajadores (ORT), evaluates the coverage of the Left in this way: "despite a relative openness, the parties of the Left do not have the same reception in the networks. A declaration of the Left is abbreviated enormously, while a declaration of a right-wing party is more emphasized."

And Narciso Isa Conde, general secretary of the Communist Party, gives his impression of his party's presence on television as follows:

We can say that in general the journalists themselves have a fairly open position. But of course some networks allow us a little more access than others. For example, we have been denouncing the group Financiera Universal and particularly its owner, Leonel Almonte, as an embezzler of public goods. Therefore, Rahintel, which belongs to him, does not allow us much opportunity to express our ideas in its airwaves.

A member of the National Committee of the PLD argues that the time the PLD was on the air during several months in 1989 "was a lot less than the other big parties, the PRSC and the PRD. The PLD had around 20 percent of the ... coverage that the PRD and the PRSC each received separately."

In general, the fact that the Left is not on the air as much as conservative parties are is more a question of organizational priorities and ideological biases of those who control the networks than a conscious policy to ban the ideas of the Left from television. Newscasts tend to emphasize personalities, and of course those parties which have been in power, such as the PRSC and the PRD, have more known figures than parties which have never been in power. Also, the conservative parties, even if they have never been in power, have more personal relations with owners and sponsors due to social class origin and similar interests. Some of the network staff also have personal relationships with the economic elite. Consequently, very often the opening of a branch of a business has higher priority on newscasts than the political activity of the Left.

However, near Election Day politics becomes a primary theme. As the 1990 elections were approaching, this difference in the extent of newscast coverage of the various parties changed; the moderate-left PLD occupied a large share of the newscasts. This was basically because this party conducted an intensive campaign on television—since the beginning of the campaign it had had a policy of continuous contact with the newscasts—and because of the enhancement of its political power—polls had shown a strong growth in those who said they would vote for the PLD. This apparent growth led to additional television coverage for commercial reasons. The PLD had more followers and more voters, and therefore a larger audience. Thus, networks covered the PLD activities because they did not want to be separated from people who could be in power; nevertheless, the coverage of this party was not always objective and positive.

Indeed, the amount of coverage is not everything. How the different parties and views are covered in the newscasts, and how a story is framed, also determine the message sent to the audience. The news is probably more relevant to the vote than are the propaganda spots. News stories appear to be independent of the parties and to be controlled by journalists; therefore, they are less likely to produce defense mechanisms than is direct promotional material, such as propaganda spots. Television coverage of the political campaign (speeches, rallies, meetings, etc.) is extremely important for voters' decisions. Coverage of the economy, relations with foreign governments (especially with the United States), and the international political situation will also influence some sectors of the population in their choice of leadership.

The fact that television information is usually superficial and frequently manipulated is not considered or not known by most of the audience. The audience is not always conscious that the "window to the world" which television represents is not innocent. The message broadcast, especially during the electoral process, is calculated: the way of presenting the news, the focus on particular aspects, the tone of voice, and so on. For example, during the 1990 political campaign there was a general tendency on the Dominican networks to mention the incumbent first. Even if most polls showed that Juan Bosch (presidential candidate of the PLD) was ahead of the other candidates, when television newscasts mentioned several parties in their headlines or news stories, they always mentioned the PRSC first the PLD second, the PRD third, and the PRI fourth. This tended to create the idea that this was how the relative political power of the parties was really distributed, an impression that could affect a candidate's chances of winning.

Also, some aspects of news stories were emphasized while others were ignored, thus affecting the public's perception of an event or person. There were several differences in the ways the various networks treated information during the 1990 campaign. The following table is a concrete example of how the four private networks I studied presented a story that was broadcast on the evening of May 8, 1990. It is a story with the spectacular and sensationalist content that television newscasts like.

This news story came out when the PRSC, the party in power, asked the Central Electoral Junta (JCE) to allow people to vote even if they were not on the official list of the particular electoral center where they were supposed to vote. They argued that these lists were incomplete because

TV13

Text	Time	Subject/Object Movement Setting	Type of Shot Camera
<u>Anchorwoman:</u> The Dominican Liberation Party today presented to the Central Electoral Junta more than two thousand allegedly falsified electoral register forms, with which this party will try to prove its charge that the official party is planning a fraud for the coming elections.	15 sec.	Anchorwoman reading	Chest Shot Camera steady
<u>Reporter:</u> The register forms were given to the electoral organization by the chief of campaign of the Dominican Liberation Party, Félix Jiménez, who said that . . .	11 sec.	Félix Jiménez standing, showing the electoral register forms, and talking	Entire body
. . . the forms had been offered for sale to the PLD by an employee of the electoral tribunal, but he did not explain how the supposed fraud would be achieved.	10 sec.	Documents	Close-up of documents
Jiménez said also that the electoral register forms delivered to the Electoral Junta are more than enough to determine that a major fraud is planned.	9 sec.	Félix Jiménez standing, talking	Entire body

Jiménez's voice: . . . if they do not take into account the demand that we made, the Dominican Liberation Party and the Dominican Revolutionary Party with the support of the National Progressive Force and other parties from the opposition to the present government of President Balaguer. If they do not listen to us who represent 70 percent of Dominicans with the right to vote, then the elections should be put into question and it should be analyzed if it will be convenient that the Dominican people participate in the election on May 16.	40 sec.	Félix Jiménez talking	Chest shot Camera steady
Reporter: The leader of the PLD reiterated the opposition of his organization to the proposition that persons who are not on the official lists could vote.	10 sec.	Image of Félix Jiménez standing and talking	A little more than entire body

Jiménez's voice: We say that we go to the elections on May 16, that we are prepared to confront that fraud, but the Central Electoral Junta must adopt the necessary measures to avoid materialization of the fraud. And one of the measures that the Electoral Junta could take is, with enough time, to prevent from voting those Dominicans who do not appear in the lists of voters in each electoral center. To have a national identification card or an electoral register document is not sufficient. We have demonstrated here that these documents could be falsified.	35 sec.	Image of Felix Jiménez	Camera moves in Chest shot
Reporter: Félix Jiménez stated in addition that the PLD will let the Electoral Junta investigate and warned that after the investigation the PLD will determine if it is of any value to participate in the coming election.	10 sec.	Image of Félix Jiménez standing and talking	Camera moves far Entire body

Colorvisión

Text	Time	Subject/Object Movement Setting	Type of Shot Camera
<u>Anchorwoman:</u> The political delegate of the Dominican Liberation Party to the Central Electoral Junta presented alleged proofs of a supposed fraud intended for the approaching elections that would be prejudicial to the Dominican Liberation Party.	15 sec.	Anchorwoman reading	Chest Shot Camera Steady
<u>Reporter:</u> Mister Félix Jiménez, who is also PLD's chief of campaign, warned that if the Central Electoral Junta adopts a resolution that will allow those with an electoral register [document] to vote without appearing in the lists, the fraud will be carried out. He stated that if this happens, nobody will believe the results of May 16 elections . . .	22 sec.	Hall of the Central Electoral Junta building. Félix Jiménez standing, talking, and pointing to the electoral register forms that another person, next to him, shows to the camera	Entire body
. . . Jiménez presented thousands of electoral register forms as proof of a quantity of these documents that allegedly had been offered for sale to the PLD by a presumed employee of the Central Electoral Junta.	18 sec.	Close-up of the documents	Close-up

Jiménez's voice: Probably more than one person has been selling these electoral register forms. The person who has made available to us these almost two thousand electoral register forms, as a proof, said to the companion through whom we received these documents that he could obtain for us thousands of electoral register forms, as many as two hundred thousand.	35 sec.	Jiménez talking	Chest shot
Reporter: However, the delegate of the PLD did not identify the presumed employee of the Electoral Junta.	10 sec.	Félix Jiménez standing, talking	Camera moves back Eye level

Teleantillas

Text	Time	Subject/Object Movement Setting	Type of Shot Camera
Anchorwoman: The Dominican Liberation Party deposited in the Central Electoral Junta more than two thousand electoral register forms and argued that these were part of the proof of an alleged fraud that the Social Christian Reformist Party was organizing for next week's election.	20 sec.	Anchorwoman reading	Chest shot Camera steady

Reporter: Prior to delivery of the electoral register forms, Félix Jiménez, president of the National Electoral Committee of the PLD, gave a press conference in the facilities of the Central Junta . . .	12 sec.	Hall of the Central Electoral Junta building. Félix Jiménez standing, talking	Chest shot
. . . where he showed the documents. According to Jiménez, it is because of this possibility of fraud by using false register forms that the Social Christian Reformist Party is asking the highest electoral authority to allow the persons who are not in the list of the electoral centers to vote.	18 sec.	Félix Jiménez standing, talking and indicating the electoral register forms that another person, next to him, shows to the camera	Full body shot Long shot
Jiménez's voice: The PRSC asked the Electoral Junta that any Dominican with an electoral registration [document] be allowed to vote even if he did not appear in the list of voters in the electoral center.	20 sec.	Félix Jiménez standing, talking	Chest shot Camera steady
Reporter: Félix Jiménez indicated also that the person who brought the electoral register forms to the PLD identified himself as an employee of the Central Electoral Junta	15 sec.	Documents	Close-up on documents Camera moves in

<u>Jiménez's voice:</u> The envelope said President of the Central Electoral Junta, Santo Domingo. This seal is from the Municipal Electoral Junta of Azua. It came by mail, and look what is inside: thousands of electoral register forms with the corresponding number...	28 sec.	Jiménez talking	Chest shot Camera moves in
They have been taken from the Central Electoral Junta or from Azua's Municipal Electoral Junta.	12 sec.	Documents	Close-up on documents Camera moves in
<u>Reporter</u>: Félix Jiménez submitted the electoral register forms to the secretary of the Central Electoral Junta, Amable Díaz. The security agents of the highest electoral organization did not allow the journalists access to the official's office.	10 sec.	General view of Félix Jiménez standing, talking	Camera moves back Eye level

Rahintel

Text	Time	Subject/Object Movement Setting	Type of Shot Camera
<u>Anchorwoman:</u> The Congressman Félix Jiménez, chief of campaign of the Dominican Liberation Party, announced this afternoon in the Central Electoral Junta that the Social Christian Reformist Party was organizing a major fraud for the coming elections. In this context some measures are being taken by the high electoral tribunal, given the proximity of next week's elections.	25 sec.	Anchorwoman reading	Chest shot Camera steady
<u>Reporter:</u> Congressman Félix Jiménez's announcement is made within the context of the Electoral Junta intensifying security measures as the election approaches . . .	15 sec.	Police inspecting the documents of the people who enter the Central Electoral Junta building	Full body shot Eye level Tilting
. . . Jiménez said that the reformists are providing electoral registrations from deceased people and from people who live overseas to members of that organization in order to allow them to vote fraudulently on May 16 . . .	18 sec.	Félix Jiménez standing, talking in a hall of the Central Electoral Junta	Full body shot

. . . Concurrently with Félix Jiménez's announcement, the Central Electoral Junta has taken several security measures because of the great number of visitors at this time and to avoid, according to the staff of the Junta, any kind of action that will obscure the electoral process . . .	22 sec.	Félix Jiménez showing the envelopes containing the electoral register forms, and people around him in semi-circle	Full body shot Camera moves in Tilting
. . . The speaker of the purple party explained that it is estimated that the governing PRSC could obtain 200,000 votes if the Central Electoral Junta allows voting without matching each person with the electoral list in each electoral center, as the PRSC is asking.	20 sec.	Félix Jiménez standing, talking	Medium shot Camera moves in
Jiménez's voice: If the Central Electoral Junta allows anyone with an electoral registration to vote without appearing in the lists produced by the data center of the Junta, if the Central Electoral Junta accepts the proposition of the Social Christian Reformist Party, the latter could end up committing electoral fraud.	30 sec.	Jiménez talking	Chest shot
Reporter: Félix Jiménez said that the PLD will not permit the occurrence of an electoral fraud because the Dominican people will reject such an act.	10 sec.	General view of Félix Jiménez standing, talking	Full body shot Camera steady

many new voters (people who were eighteen years old that year) and other people, for diverse reasons, were not included. Therefore, they considered it unjust to prevent these people from voting. Most parties of the opposition, in particular the PRD and the PLD, fearing fraud by the PRSC, were opposed to such a measure. Eventually, two days before the election (and six days after this story was broadcast) the JCE announced that people would be allowed to vote, that these votes would be checked after the election, and that it would then be decided if they were valid. After the election, which the PRSC won by a tiny margin, there were charges of voting irregularities in several parts of the country, with documents sustaining these charges (e.g., votes and electoral lists that did not correspond to the numbers the JCE had assigned to each list to prevent fraud). As a consequence, only after two months was an official announcement of the election winner made.

TV13 newscasts, in reporting PLD's accusation of fraud, put particular emphasis on the possibility that the PLD would not participate in the election, editing the information in such a way that the central point of the story appeared to be the doubt about the participation of the PLD in the coming elections (e.g., presenting twice in the story references to this possibility by the same representative of the PLD). The other networks did not allude to this at all. The idea that the public would have if they watched only TV13 is that because the PLD saw a possibility of fraud by the party in power, it would not participate in the elections. At least doubt was created among some voters. TV13 also emphasized that Jiménez did not explain how the supposed fraud would be achieved, though in fact he did that at the press conference, as can be seen in what the other networks showed of the event.

Colorvisión's coverage of this story was particularly incomplete because it did not even mention the party that the PLD was denouncing—the PRSC—as the instigator of the fraud. In the way this story was presented—not only what is in the transcripts but also in the tone employed—there was a clear tendency to minimize the possibility of fraud.

The presentation of Teleantillas was more news-oriented. It did not present evaluative commentary, as Colorvisión and TV13 did: Jiménez "did not identify the presumed employee of the Electoral Junta" (Colorvisión) and "He did not explain how the supposed fraud would be achieved" (TV13). Neither did Teleantillas contrast the denunciation with another element within the same story that undermines it as Rahintel did: "the Electoral Junta is intensifying security measures as the election approaches" (Rahintel). Teleantillas concentrated on the proof the representative of the PLD was presenting (references to the origin of the seals and the envelopes containing the false electoral registration forms), which other networks did not mention. In doing so it conveyed, probably more than the other networks, the information that the PLD wanted to present.

Rahintel did not comment in an evaluative manner (as did Colorvisión and TV13), but there was an insistence in the story that the JCE was taking measures to avoid fraud. Rahintel inappropriately inserted remarks on the action of the Junta within the news story about the PLD's claim of fraud by the PRSC (it appeared that this newscast was reporting two stories in one).

The content of these different newscasts reflects a general tendency in the networks. This is also revealed by the amount of time allowed to each party. Behind an appearance of objectivity in form (they all presented this story) there is a difference among the networks concerning given parties, above all those perceived as in opposition to the economic group that controls a particular network. There is also a difference in how the staff (news directors, editors, and journalists) fulfill their job. It is clear that some are less professional than others, and some tend to follow the position of their employers or sponsors more than a supposed ethic of "objectivity."[13] Overall, the economic control of the network influences the general ways the news departments operate and the content of particular stories in the context of the electoral campaign.

FINANCIAL RESOURCES AND POWER OF COMMUNICATION

Money and politics have always had an intimate relationship, and it is intensified during a political campaign. Transmitting information to the voters requires that the candidates have not only an organization but also enough economic resources to produce political spots and to buy time on television, as well as goods and services. With the extensive use of television, huge sums are indispensable for political campaigns.

The money spent on television propaganda increased enormously between 1986 and 1990. In fact, television absorbs the largest part of the campaign cost. The production of a spot costs between U.S. $20,000 and U.S. $35,000, and its broadcast in prime time varied during the 1990 campaign from U.S. $300 to U.S. $500 each time.[14] It is necessary to broadcast these ads many times.

In other words, a large amount of money is spent by most political parties to win votes. It is very difficult to know exactly how much is spent, since the budget of the campaign, as well as the origin of the financing, is carefully concealed by each party. Based on interviews with several persons connected to the political propaganda industry, I estimate that in the Dominican Republic in the 1990 political campaign a major party spent between U.S. $12 and U.S. $17 million (the PRSC seems to be the one that spent the most). This includes the campaign for the presidency, Congress, and municipal offices. The campaign centers on the candidates for president (with a few exceptions the other candidates are elected by association with the party of the candidate for president).

The number of votes is not automatically proportional to the amount of money invested in propaganda (although there is a strong correlation between amount of money spent and being elected),[15] but spending money is fundamental to being elected. This is revealed by numerous and detailed studies in other countries (Alexander 1984; Johnston 1987; Ginsberg 1986), and it is acknowledged by most leaders of the political parties in the Dominican Republic. This implies that parties and candidates have to seek financial support.

Before starting the electoral campaign, the candidates have to find possible financial supporters. In this search for financial support, the candidates must present at least some general ideas of their intentions if elected, and these ideas must appear acceptable to those who possess the economic resources. In the Dominican Republic the economic support for a candidate can be goods or services (offices, cars, use of mass media at low cost, etc.) or direct contribution of money or provision of credit. This support is generally based on negotiated exchange of favors. The persons or companies that put resources at the disposal of politicians will ask for something in exchange; frequently, they want the candidates to include in their projects actions that protect, reproduce, or increase their resources. The financial supporters of a candidate consider the resources that they offer as an investment.

In other words, the financiers will choose which candidates and party they will support, and they expect that once in power, the party will help them protect their investments. To reduce the risk of the investment, at first the interest groups or individual capitalists usually support several candidates close to their political and economic concern who seem to be possible winners, and as the campaign progresses, the concentrate their resources on the candidate in line with their interest who has the greatest chance of winning. For this reason the polls and the perceptions that television and other media project to the population about who has a chance of winning are so important. The level of economic resources very often will increase or decrease for a given candidate as a function of his chances of winning according to the polls and media analysis. Therefore parties are constantly trying to be seen as a viable force with a tremendous chance of success. Even the most insignificant party claims to have a chance of winning the election.

Because the capital owners who can contribute a substantial amount of money are limited in number and because of their similar interpretation of the world, there is a tendency to standardize the intentions of the candidates, with a pronounced orientation to favor the largest enterprises and their interests. That is, most candidates with a real chance of winning the election will contribute to the reproduction of the existing social order or will not radically affect it.

For example, the moderate-left PLD was able to raise a fair amount of money among some capitalists,[16] probably because of its position as an alternative power but also because it became more and more moderate in its political goals. From a clearly leftist-Marxist orientation in 1982, the PLD presidential candidate moved to liberal views about some aspects of the economy (e.g., his proposal to sell the enterprises of the state to the private sector); his general propositions in the 1990 campaign were attempts to reform some aspects of the system rather than to make basic structural changes.

This did not, however, imply an abandonment of the most conservative parties by the capitalists. In general in the 1990 elections, the wealthiest citizens continued to give more support to the traditional conservative parties. All indications (interviews, visible money spent, newspaper analyses) show that Balaguer and his allies, as well as right-wing parties such as the PRI, had the confidence of most capitalists.

The most conservative parties advertised most often on television. In fact, the main consequence of the use of television in political campaigns has been to make the traditional financial advantages of the Right a more critical political factor. The political spots in the last two weeks of campaigning were largely dominated by the conservative political parties. During this period the PRSC broadcast twice as many political spots as the PLD. And including the right-wing parties Quisqueyan Democratic Party (PQD) and La Estructura (The Structure), which campaigned for the presidential candidate of the PRSC, Joaquín Balaguer, the number of political spots promoting this candidate outnumbered the political spots endorsing the candidate of the PLD, Juan Bosch, by four to one. Considering two and a half hours of prime time—between 8:30 P.M. and 11:00 P.M., Monday through Friday, on all five networks—analyzed in this research, during the last two weeks of the campaign (May 2 to May 14, 1990) the PRSC broadcast 25.8 percent of the total political spots I recorded, followed by the PRI with 14.1 percent, and the PQD with 13.0 percent—all right-wing parties. Next was the PLD with 12.8 percent, followed by the social-democrat PRD with 11.2 percent, the small right-center party PAC with 11.2 percent, another ally of the PRSC (The Structure) with 7.7 percent, the FNP with 2.0 percent, other small center and right-wing parties with 1.7 percent, and leftist movements 0.6 percent (see Figures 6.1 and 6.2).[17]

The four private networks I studied broadcast spots from most parties. The public network had very few spots, and all were from the conservative parties.

The networks on which the parties broadcast the bulk of their propaganda spots were those favored by the ratings: Colorvisión, Teleantillas, and Rahintel. Some parties concentrated on two networks: the PLD and

Figure 6.1
Percentage of Television Political Spots, by Party

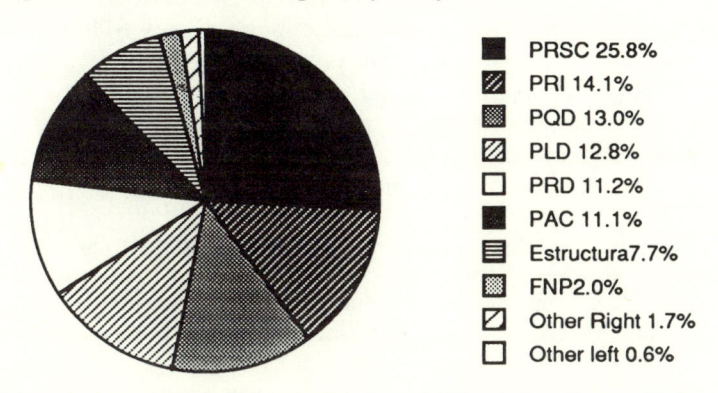

- PRSC 25.8%
- PRI 14.1%
- PQD 13.0%
- PLD 12.8%
- PRD 11.2%
- PAC 11.1%
- Estructura 7.7%
- FNP 2.0%
- Other Right 1.7%
- Other left 0.6%

Figure 6.2
Percentage of Television Political Spots, by Political Ideology

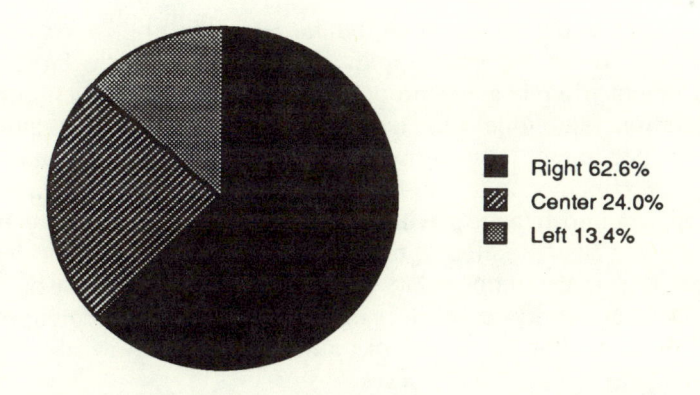

- Right 62.6%
- Center 24.0%
- Left 13.4%

the PRI, on Colorvisión and Teleantillas; the PRD, on Rahintel and Colorvisión.

This difference in the parties' presence on television through political spots is one more element which reveals that candidates or parties which cannot raise financial resources cannot compete on equal terms with those which have large economic resources. The few small parties on the Left that participated in elections—such as Capital City Integration and Unity Movement (MIUCA)—were almost absent from television. The superior organization of the parties on the Left cannot counterbalance the variety of resources available to parties on the Right. The difference between the Left and the Right in financial resources is evidenced by the fact that even very small right-wing parties such as the PAC, the FNP, La Estructura, and the PQD, with very few members and no chance to elect more than two or three representatives, could raise enough money to have a considerable presence on television through political spots.

The clear disparity in the financial resources available to the Left and to the Right exemplifies the partisan spirit in the confrontation of ideas and interests that the media generally drown within the haze of the consensus. As some leaders of the Left explain:

In the electoral period our party has not the same opportunity to be on television as other, more conventional political forces. However, there is some space that we have to win every day, giving opinions that could be interesting for the media to broadcast. In fact, we should be ready to fight in conditions of inequality. (Narciso Isa Conde, general secretary of the Communist Party)[18]

Television denaturalizes the electoral process because of the way it works right now. Those who monopolize the wealth have more access to promotion through television in order to obtain the political support of the population. (Rafael Taveras, president of the Socialist Party)

There is also inequality between the parties in the opposition and those in power. Control of the state apparatus opens the door to large means; the government will pay a vast proportion of the campaign spending of the party in power: telephone calls, transport, materials, facilities, and sometimes even personnel. The party in power can also make use of secret funds, assign public contracts to firms that will contribute during the electoral campaign, and arrange privileged information on some future financial operations. It is also possible to use the state resources, as President Balaguer did, to finance actions that can attract support—for instance, distributing food in the poorest sectors of the country. In fact, corruption and financial crimes tend to be an intrinsic, although not always visible, element of Dominican electoral democracy.

When all these inequalities are accumulated in favor of the conservative right wing, the PRSC and its allies, they have an advantage that is difficult to overcome. Even the tremendous crisis in the Dominican Republic during the elections did not cause a massive desertion by voters.[19] The PRSC won the election with about 2 percent more votes than the PLD.

The election process has two steps: getting financial support and getting votes. No candidate can succeed in the second step if he has not received enough economic support. In both steps the people choose between candidates to lead the country, but only the vote is official, regulated by the constitution, and subject to universal suffrage (one person, one vote). In the voting process a hypothetical egalitarian distribution of power takes place, whereas in economic electoral support, a very unequal and undemocratic distribution of power occurs, because it depends on the financial resources of parties and candidates' sponsors. Thus, contrary to the predominant ideology in which universal suffrage is presented as the basis of the legality or legitimacy in reality only those candidates who can accumulate enough economic support to mount a major promotional campaign on television and other media have a real possibility of being elected.

The true election does not involve the whole population. People in general do not elect the rich or the television decision makers; however, the economic elite are able to influence the elections in such a manner that most of the time they limit the political alternatives offered to the population. In other words, people will have the opportunity to choose only among those candidates who, once in power, will not attempt changes that will undermine the interests of the economic elite. As Domhof put it:

Class interests are served through the policy formation process, which is facilitated through the candidate selection process. The management of social consciousness proceeds through the ideology process, which involves the formation, dissemination and enforcement of the assumptions, beliefs and attitudes that permit the continued existence of policies and politicians favorable to the wealth, income, status and privileges of members of the ruling class. (1978, p. 38)

In this context, there is an extremely low probability that fundamental aspects of society, such as economic organization, political structure, or electoral system, will be substantially modified. This is true not only because of the possible violence that the power elite could inflict on the people but also because most people do not think about it. And they do not think about this type of modification of society because their basic system of ideas and social representations corresponds largely to shared dominant ideas, values, and social representations that have existed in society for a long time. And in the diffusion of these social representations in Dominican society, the mass media, of which the most important is television, have been playing a major role.

We have seen how the myths and conventions diffused by television reassure the people, encouraging political support of the prevailing institutions of authority. Television portrayals of elections constitute dramatized rituals that legitimize the prevailing power relations and help to sustain the myth of representative democracy, political equality, and collective self-determination. The political options presented most often on television and the information about these options do not allow people to question the basic organization of the society; on the contrary, they tend to lead the citizen to apathy and political resignation. Actually, the true struggle for power in this kind of society, as presented on television, occurs (and could only occur) between the different sectors of the ruling class. People vote not to participate in decisions but for legitimate leaders who are proposed to them by the power elite.

The 1990 election has left its mark on a society that, with great difficulty, seeks its way out of poverty and underdevelopment. The party that finally won is the one that allows priority to business, to immediate profit, and to those sectors of the society which sacrifice everything—including the culture and most social values necessary for the survival of any social organization—to obtain money and power. Television provides us with this spectacle of the politics of plenty. We see simultaneously spectacular edifices and avenues (the obsession of President Balaguer) and the havoc of great poverty, people nurtured by fortune and a profound social regression.[20]

NOTES

1. Elections are held in the Dominican Republic every four years. The president, senators, congressmen, mayors, and other officials are elected the same day. Until 1982 there was a single ballot form: A vote for a presidential candidate was a vote for every other candidate from his party. In 1986 a change was introduced; it was possible to split the vote in two: for president and mayor and for senator and congressmen. Citizens could vote for the president and mayor of one party and for senators and congressmen of a different party. And in 1990 the system was improved to allow people to split the vote in three: for president, for mayor, and for senator and congressmen.

2. In the 1982 election campaign the Partido de la Liberación Dominicana (PLD) used a little television, presenting some poorly produced spots a few times during the campaign. PLD strategists viewed television only as a complement to activities such as meetings and rallies. The attitude toward television within the Left is explained in the following terms by two eminent leftist leaders:

This has to do with the idea we had in the PLD that politics is to educate the people, politics is service, consciousness. All these instruments of promotion in the marketing style to attract people were seen as means of deceiving the people. However, we should understand now the importance of these instruments in modern politics. People respond to that kind of propaganda. And if we want to reach power, we need to use them. (member of the National Direction Committee of the PLD)

Most of the Left have been thinking for a long time in Leninist terms, believing that the newspaper which played the role of organizer in a small circle could still work today. For mass work it is necessary to use television. The newspaper within a given party plays more a role of internal cohesion than of diffusion of ideas to the population in general. I think that one of the most important elements which has contributed to the marginization of the left has to do with the incomprehension of this problem. (one of the leaders of the Marxist Left)

3. The party in power is the PRSC (right-wing); Joaquín Balaguer is the leader and the president of the Republic. The most important parties of the opposition are the PLD (moderate Left), whose leader is Juan Bosch; the PRD (center) affiliated with the Socialist International, whose leader is José Francisco Peña Gómez; and the right-wing Partido Revolucionario Independiente (PRI; Independent Revolutionary Party), whose leader is Jacobo Majluta. Half a dozen small parties compose the Left; the Partido Comunista Dominicano (PCD; Dominican Communist Party), whose leader is Narciso Isa Conde, and the Partido Socialista

(PS; Socialist Party), whose leader is Rafael Taveras, are the best-known of these parties. There are also several small parties on the right: Frente Nacional Progresista (FNP; National Progressive Front), whose leader is a well-known lawyer, Vincho Castillo; the Partido Quisquellano Demócrata (PQD; Quisqueyan Democratic Party), whose leader is Elias Wessin y Wessin (allied with the PRSC); La Estructura (The Structure), whose leader is Andrés Vanderhost (also allied with the PRSC); and a center Right party, the Partido de Acción Constitucional (PAC; Constitutional Action Party), whose leader is José Rafael Abinader.

4. The difficulties of collecting taxes in the Dominican Republic has been recognized by governments from various political parties. If the PRSC government wanted to reveal all the firms that owe money to the Dominican state as a result of unpaid tax, probably more than 80 percent of all firms would appear on that list, several of them with sums larger than the U.S. $9,000 that the vice presidential candidate of the PLD was supposed to owe. Among the debtors would probably be several leaders of the party in power.

5. Peña Gómez is a leader whose dramatic rhetoric is relatively effective on the radio but not on television. In the 1960s and up to the mid–1970s radio played the role that today is played by television. In 1962 Bosch used radio effectively, as did Peña Gómez, at that time Bosch's disciple. Peña Gómez came to be known through his position as radio announcer on the PRD program "Tribuna Democrática." His political leadership was consolidated to a great extent through the radio.

6. Saussez (1986) states that television communication is impressionistic; it appeals to emotions through anecdotes. Television communicates images and impressions better than facts and rational judgments. The viewers tend to forget the words, but the emotions and impressions stay in their minds. Several other researchers have supplied data to support this tendency, which is followed extensively in commercials and in political propaganda. For example, see Napolitan's (1972) findings on emotions.

7. Very often I heard Dominicans say that politicians are all demagogues and liars. I also ascertained in earlier research the lack of confidence in politicians among the young people (Menéndez 1987). Nevertheless, a large part of the population of the Dominican Republic still believes or wants to believe in the possibility of a savior.

8. Actually, Bosch never explicitly said that he would cancel the agreement with the Vatican; he only said that all religions would have the same rights and prerogatives. But this was enough for some reporters to deduce that he would end the agreement with the Vatican.

9. A political poll published in the newspaper *El Siglo*, April 21, 1990, showed that 86 percent of the population was familiar with Balaguer and his political positions, 83 percent with Bosch, 71 percent with Peña Gómez, and 64 percent with Majluta (*El Siglo*-Gallup 1990).

10. Juan Bosch was the absolute leader of the PRD until 1972, when he left that party after confrontations over political strategies with other leaders of the party, headed by José Francisco Peña Gómez. Bosch and a group of followers resigned from the PRD and decided to create a new party, the PLD. This party was for years a small leftist party that grew continually. In 1986 it started to break the traditional two-party system that had dominated the country. Bosch had been

elected president of the Republic in 1962 but was ousted from power by a military coup d'état backed by the United States seven months after he took office. The PRI of Jacobo Majluta split off from the PRD. Majluta, who was vice president during the second administration of the PRD (1978–82), confronted Peña Gómez about his candidacy for president of the Republic. And since he lost support within the party, he created another party in order to present his candidacy for president in 1990.

11. There were four more candidates who did not have any chance of being elected. Sixteen parties presented candidates for the presidency, Congress, and municipalities. Ten parties presented candidates for Congress and municipalities, and one only for municipalities. However, since half of the parties were allied with some of the most important parties, particularly the PRSC and the PRD, and thus presented common candidates for several positions, there were only eight candidates for president.

12. In the Dominican Republic certain political talk shows clearly favor a given political party or candidate. For example, the talk show "Cuarto Poder" has long been a forum for Majluta, leader of the PRI, and for Vincho Castillo, leader of the tiny party FNP. Likewise, "Aeromundo" was for a time pro-Balaguer (PRSC); when the producer changed his political affiliation, it became pro-Jorge Blanco (PRD), president of the Republic from 1982 to 1986. However, these are politicians in the system. If leaders of the revolutionary Left were interviewed so often, the program would have difficulties getting enough advertisements to survive. In the past, programs that interviewed leftist leaders on a regular basis never lasted very long.

13. By "objective" I mean the general agreement among Dominican journalists on presenting the facts without value judgments and allowing each party the same weight in the news.

14. In May 1990 the exchange rate was seven Dominican pesos to a dollar. By U.S. standards the price of an ad on television could be considered low. In a city like New York, thirty seconds of television costs around $30,000 (Berke 1988). The price of an ad in the Dominican Republic, although less expensive than in the United States, is still high, given the financial resources of most parties. (In 1990 the price of the ad corresponded to approximately two months' salary of a high-level employee in the television industry.)

15. The PRSC has traditionally had the largest financial support from the Dominican bourgeoisie, including use of the state resources, and has won six of the eight elections since the fall of Rafael Leonidas Trujillo. In the United States, according to data presented by Alexander (1984), from 1860 to 1980, twenty-three out of thirty-one presidents elected have been those who have spent more money on the campaign. That was also the case in the U.S. congressional elections of November 1990, according to data reported by the networks ABC and CBS. The same tendency was observed in the House and Senate elections of 1978 and 1980 by Ginsberg (1986).

16. According to an important member of the leadership of this party. That this party had considerable resources could also be deduced from the type of campaign it ran.

17. In order to count the number of political spots, the author watched one network every day for five days and at the same time recorded another. The other

three networks were covered (watching and recording) by an assistant on two other television sets and a second assistant in his home. Of course, this is a tendency registered during prime time. If we were considering the programming during an entire day, the data would change slightly but not radically.

18. The Communist Party did not have candidates in the 1990 elections.

19. Balaguer has dominated Dominican politics since he returned from exile and won the election of 1966 with the support of the United States. He also had been a puppet president under the dictatorship of Trujillo.

20. The impact of the economic crisis is profound. The level of unemployment in 1990 was 40 percent. The average personal income is at the poverty level—about $150. Corruption, bribery, lack of water, power failures, enormous price increases, and excessive profits constitute some of the basic ills of the country. The government, suffering from corruption at all levels and lack of initiative to develop productive investments, has been unable to act because of the low prices for sugar in the international market and the reduction of U.S. aid in the 1980s.

Chapter 7

Conclusion: Diversity and Pluralism

THE LOGIC OF THE MARKET AND DIVERSITY

The argument, common in Western societies, that diversity in television is achieved by competition between private networks is far from true in the Dominican Republic.

Although all but one of the seven Dominican television networks are privately owned, they are mirror images of each other, leaving viewers few genuine alternatives. Newton Minow, the former chairman of the U.S. Federal Communications Commission, said in 1961 that U.S. television programming was a "vast wasteland of violence, repetitive formulas, irritating commercials, and sheer boredom" (1964, p. 52). This is equally true of Dominican television in the 1990s.[1] At any given moment, all the networks (with the exception of Independencia, which mostly presents movies and music videos) are likely to be airing the same program or at least the same sort of show. Likewise, Dominican television newscasts concentrate on superficialities, stereotypes, and the spectacular rather than on a more conceptual content.

This limitation of diversity and emphasis on the superficial and spectacular is not endemic to the medium itself. What matters is not the medium as an immutable essence, as McLuhan and Fiore (1967), Postman (1985), and others have suggested, but how it is used. Television does not have a technological force of its own. Television encodes its shows only within the frame of reference of those who control and conceive the programs according to the goals of the industry. People who run the networks are the ones who influence and choose the manner of presenting the events within the constraints placed on them by owners and sponsors, who aim almost exclusively at making television a money producer.

Boorstin (1978) and others argue that since television needs to be marketable, network staffs produce shows which follow popular culture, with a view to attracting large audiences. However, the television industry reduces popular culture to whatever obtains the highest ratings, thereby producing mass culture. In the Dominican Republic this means that most programs cater to the tastes of the heavy viewers, who are typically of low socioeconomic status and poorly educated.

Thus, instead of contributing to the progress of Dominican society by stimulating its culture, television inhibits its progress. Indeed, by continually reproducing the same symbols and messages, Dominican television closes rather than opens the world to the people; nor does it reduce the cultural gap between the elite and the masses.

The culture of Dominican society is not just what is represented as the "greatest common denominator" of television viewers at a given moment. Culture, like the other aspects of life, is constantly changing; television could be a means of expressing the world and the nation in their diversity, instead of reproducing and reinforcing violence, sexism, and cultural mediocrity. We cannot say that all people like violence and reject educational programs and what are commonly categorized as "high culture" programs, although such a view is reflected in television most of the time. Even if this were true, television could give people the chance to evaluate, to see, to learn; it could give them the opportunity to choose. People with a low level of education learn from television; hence television networks could serve as a very important element of learning. Unfortunately, television network owners and sponsors rarely consider this dimension of the medium. Television programs are sometimes censored because of sex scenes, but never for their failure to promote education and/or provide general knowledge.

Members of the Dominican television industry (particularly network staffs) would agree in theory that television should encourage culture, enhance national values, preserve morality, and stimulate artistic creativity. But these ideas remain at the abstract level, rarely becoming a reality. The structure of private television makes this impossible, and the single state-owned television channel cannot do it because it serves those who control the state apparatus.

The message of Dominican television is above all a consumerist one. And the ideology of consumerism standardizes tastes and legitimizes both the products of the system and the system itself, representing the commodity-driven life-style as the best one. This is true not only of the private networks but also, to a large extent, of the state-owned network; the latter has the additional handicap of being forced to serve as a propaganda vehicle for those who control the government.

In sum, the competition among the networks in their quest for money and power does not generate substantial diversity; the differences created in the programming by their strategies to compete for audience are few. In fact, the uniform content of television programming is a result not of a passive and homogeneous mass audience, as apologists often claim, but of the logic of the industry itself. In its search for a common taste to determine programming content, the industry categorizes viewers in artificial clusters. The tyranny of ratings imposes a specific taste upon every television viewer. These mechanisms are not alien to the role that those who control television assign to it; indeed, they demonstrate that television's fundamental tendency to mesmerize and distract the public, as well as its specific influence on culture, is to a large extent the result of the economic forces and the power structure in which it is enmeshed.

THE PARAMETERS OF PLURALISTIC INFORMATION

We have seen that a large amount of capital is necessary to provide the networks with modern communication technology. A dozen families, owners of large firms, comprise the corporate boards of the networks. These people are partly in competition and partly in association. Many general directors of the networks are also partners of banks, import-export companies, insurance companies, and so on. Beyond the apparent competition between the networks, then, there is in fact a concentration and some alliance between the large economic groups, a kind of unwritten nonaggression pact.

Also, and most important for pluralism, even if television network owners and sponsors compete at the economic level, their basic ideas and philosophy uphold the same model of social organization. These persons tend to consider the present arrangement of Dominican society, in which they are privileged, as the best for their immediate interests. Therefore, they would like to preserve the fundamental aspects of that society: the present structures of production, organization, and business regulations that allow them unlimited possibility for profits. And this is more or less reflected in television content. Although this influence of the dominant groups over the ideological content of television is largely indirect, the propositions of television programming in general tend to be in agreement with the kind of social views and structures these people favor.

This does not imply that there is a unified and coherent discourse within the subculture of the dominant classes about all economic and social issues. On many issues the firms and persons who control television represent different points of view and are more or less open to various artistic expressions and to divergent political ideas, within a range that goes from the center Left to the extreme Right. As Chapters 5 and 6 have shown, there are often contrasts in the ways a story is covered by the different networks.

Furthermore, television is not excluded from the contradictions that exist in society. In order for newscasts and other shows to be popular, they must present some contradictions of society and traces of the different subcultures and ideological currents that form the patchwork of Dominican society. To ensure their profitability (by keeping high ratings), occasionally the economic groups that control the television industry allow the presentation of ideas contrary to their interests, giving access to individuals who hold opposite political views—for example, the leaders of the Marxist parties.

The scattered presence of shows and stories with critical content enables advocates of the present organization of television to affirm that there is freedom of information and absolute pluralism. "We even invite leaders of the extreme Left to talk on some of our programs," said an administrator of a network, as proof of that network's open-mindedness.

That is, to operate efficiently, television networks must have credibility; they must obtain a certain amount of confidence from the public. To win that credibility, television discourse should appear to be reliable and unbiased. Newscasts in particular must give the appearance of objectivity. If owners were to show openly that their networks are instruments for their own interests, they would undermine the networks' credibility. This is reflected in the internal functioning of the networks, particularly the private ones; owners avoid exercising too overt a control over the news content. Network bosses oversee the news production process from afar and from time to time intervene with suggestions, but rarely with direct and explicit commands. To avoid being seen as censors, they grant the network staff some degree of independence, even making concessions now and then.

This attitude is part of a conscious strategy of power relationships. The authority of those in power is always more solid when it is not evident, and it is more convincing when it is derived from an appearance of mutual consent. As Schiller writes, "For manipulation to be most effective, evidence of its presence should be nonexistent.... It is essential, therefore, that people who are manipulated believe in the neutrality of their key social institutions" (1971, p. 11).[2] The undemocratic side of television, like the other business-dominated institutions of society, is covered by an impartial and pluralistic appearance. Owners know that if the appearance of newscasts' autonomy were transgressed too often and too conspicuously, it could have serious repercussions. This is precisely the problem with the state-owned television network, RTVD, since superiors and the government often intervene more directly in the functioning of the network than do those who control the private networks. This is reflected in the ratings of this network, and in the public's opinion of it. Very few people, unless they are fanatic followers of the political party that controls the government, believe in the neutrality of RTVD. On the other hand, quite a large number impute fairness and objectivity to the private networks.[3]

In addition, the primary concern of the networks' stockholders tends to be ensuring that their own business activities are not criticized, and that the network remains profitable, rather than promoting their political ideology. Ordinarily, commercial television is fundamentally oriented to accelerate the consumption of merchandise, and to sell itself to audiences. Yet in some circumstances the political message of television will be more explicit. For example, if the political situation of the country causes people to propose the modification of some aspects of the traditional structure of the market, or the introduction of changes that affect the dominant classes, then television networks become very specific and partisan voices of those who own and control them.

However, in both private and state-owned networks the ideological domination exercised by those who control them is far more insidious now than under the dictatorship of Trujillo. The difference in the control exerted over the private networks and the state-owned network is more of degree than of a clear opposition. It is not a situation where the state-owned network is subject to permanent and absolute censorship while there is absolute freedom of speech on the private networks. Even in the state-owned network, control is not exerted blatantly.

Networks owners and the government rely on hiring, promotion, and dismissal, as well as indirect controls such as unwritten guidelines and allowable boundaries, to exert maximum influence with minimum direct mediation.[4] These mechanisms are relatively effective, since reporters, editors, and producers often implement self-censorship, as most of those whom I interviewed admitted. In fact, the problem of staff (journalists, programmers, etc.) independence in television is often viewed as a question of a relationship between the employee and the enterprise. As a news director from a private network said, "Can we be independent in front of the enterprise for which we work and therefore to which we ought to be loyal?"

Still, there is some danger for the controlling elite in claiming that the network newscasts are free and independent. Information professionals do not always practice self-censorship and, based on this premise of independence, they sometimes produce news stories inconvenient to the ruling interests, such as coverage of the Central American crisis relatively in opposition to most owners' ideas. This confirms Parenti's assertion that "The idea of a free press is more a myth than a reality, but myths can have an effect on things and can serve as a resource of power. The power of a legitimating myth rests on its ability to be believed and not exposed as a sham" (1986, p. 236).

As a matter of fact, the specific arrangement of Dominican television allows a certain degree of pluralism. Particularly in comparison with other countries of Latin America or even the United States, Dominican television appears more pluralistic regarding political views presented in the news or in prime-time talk shows. There are very few other countries in Latin America where leaders of the opposition Marxist parties could be interviewed for half an hour at any time of the day, or could give an opinion on a social issue in a newscast (even granting that this does not happen on a regular basis on Dominican television).

The networks' messages are created within a fabric of contradictions. Television networks (private and state owned) are traversed by vertical and horizontal power relations, and even if their structure presents an arrangement with predominant vertical relations of power, the control is never total. As in other social institutions, there is an element of struggle and indeterminacy within the networks. Consequently, while the overall content of television is amply influenced by owners and sponsors, some stories are more marked by the reporters' personal prejudices and predispositions. Therefore, newscasts occasionally produce stories that irritate members of the economic and political elite. And in some cases these groups exert repressive measures against members of the network staff.

In other words, although television networks do not always follow the premises of the business community, they are not self-governing and independent of the corporate class that comprises owners and sponsors. Most newscast staff—from news directors to reporters—I interviewed stated that some coercive controls were exerted over them by owners, sponsors, and the management.

In sum, the mechanisms of control within Dominican television are different today from the more direct censorship exerted during the Trujillo dictatorship. And in the private networks the mechanisms of control are less visible and monolithic than in the government-controlled RTVD, although they are clearly hierarchical. Networks' owners and sponsors, as well as the government officials who manage the state network, try to minimize their use of coercion, but they do not contemplate leaving television totally unrestricted to dissident opinions. They consciously pursue their self-interest and try to use television to promote and safeguard their wealth and political interests, even if they rarely express it in these terms and if their control over television can never be total. Indeed, television networks are not utterly exempt from other pressure groups, such as political parties, unions, and popular organizations, as well as some form of dissent within their own staff.

The existence of varying opinions in the networks depends on priorities and on specific situations, but this difference is always within given limits. The different currents existing in society are not presented in a balanced manner. Dissenting voices are overwhelmed by voices that do not question the present organization of society. Television news stories are largely dominated by the economic and governmental elite.

Newscasts occasionally show some negative aspects of the present society, but the stories are presented in such a way that the basic organization and functioning of the society are rarely challenged. Television networks are not proponents of societal change. They do not look for new ways of structuring the economy or particular institutions, and generally offer a relatively narrow perspective, taking particular care to avoid messages that could be perceived as anti-business. Most radical criticism and in-depth deconstruction of the consumption system is excluded from commentaries and editorials. In fact, most ideas disseminated through Dominican television tend to reinforce values and norms that reproduce the system.[5] The discourse of television, in information programs as well as in fiction shows, sometimes implicitly and sometimes explicitly conveys the idea that the only possible and valid society is a predominantly business-oriented one. This general message is fundamental to a consumption society. For instance, the way democracy is depicted in television projects the impression that the consumption society is the ultimate form of democracy.

COMMON POOL OF VALUES AND NEWS DISTORTION

News stories that tend to reproduce the status quo are not solely a result of economic and political pressure. Nor is a general set of opinions that pervades Dominican television a result of the diabolical machinations of a conspiratory elite sitting around a table debating the best way to manipulate the audience. As has been pointed out in previous chapters, however, in some cases particular care is taken to project a given idea by planning the manner in which it is presented and the aspects that are emphasized.

Among newscast staff, there is a routine acceptance of ways of presenting the news that contribute to perpetuating the status quo. News people are not outside the dominant culture, and some of them take the basic ideas and beliefs of the dominant culture as given. Mainstream ideology often plays the psychological role of an emotional tranquilizer. Some news people go along with most things simply because they do not want to lose their jobs; others sincerely share the political view of the power elite and thus consider the news they produce to be "objective." Therefore, a good number of television journalists consider that even with the limits imposed by the power elite who control television, most news on Dominican television responds to and reflects public opinion.

This stems from the assumption that there is a common pool of ideas and values constituting public opinion. However, it is not at all evident that the (unconsciously or consciously) shared dominant themes constantly broadcast on television genuinely are the views of the people. Most of the public, including the news staff, does not share a common view about various aspects of Dominican society, such as official economic or cultural policies. What actually happens is that in the long run what is represented as public opinion becomes the universal point of reference. What is most often represented as public opinion is an established viewpoint that is constantly shown on television and in other media. On television the entire Dominican culture is reduced to a battery of accumulated habits and practices fashioned over time. Ideas and beliefs do not automatically reproduce and nurture themselves; they are diffused over a long period of time. And, as Parenti points out, "with time yesterday's propaganda becomes today's shared cultural values and beliefs" (1986, p. 242).

Hence, news distortion on Dominican television is both an unintentional product of shared cultural values and a deliberate product of acts of disinformation.

POLITICAL SHOW AND MONEY

The contribution of television to the Dominican political process has been quite important. Since its inauguration in 1952, television has been highly involved in the legitimation of authority both under the Trujillo dictatorship and under the electoral democracy. Its political functions include being largely responsible for determining which political views are aired and which are relatively silenced.

Research evidence suggests that, contrary to the "minimal effects" theory, television is significantly (although not absolutely) able to establish the boundaries of public discourse, to guide the perception of the public on certain issues, and to frame opinions.[6] It may not directly mold opinion, but it certainly creates opinion visibility, giving legitimacy to certain views and not to others. For instance, during elections, television exposure is a vital attractor of votes, though certainly not the only one. It considerably affects politicians' chances of obtaining support. Indeed, at the beginning of a political campaign, a large proportion of the voters do not have a definite opinion about the candidates they will vote for. Electoral choices are not made independently of the efforts of contending forces to mobilize mass support. In fact, the choices of voters are more the results than the causes of successful electoral campaigns.

Dominican television fulfills this political function without really enlightening the electorate. Rather, as it is used in elections, it contributes enormously toward causing people to vote for something fictitious. The television coverage of the election process is so personalized—emphasizing supposed personal characteristics of the candidates and anecdotes about their lives—that the most important issue becomes the created image of each candidate rather than the candidate's ability to deal with fundamental problems confronting society or to carry out a substantial and concrete political program. The substitution of personality for politics is objectionable enough; but even worse, the people do not vote for the true personality of the candidate but for an artificial image created to please them. As in most electoral democracies, show business is applied to politics.

Furthermore, there are vast inequalities in the abilities of different groups to control the flow of information on television. Political views supported by money easily obtain television exposure, while those opposed to the interests of the economic elite wither and remain invisible, either for lack of the funds needed for television propaganda or because of limitations imposed by network owners, sponsors, or management. The right-wing and conservative parties receive the greatest financial support from the business and industrial sectors.[7] Therefore, they have the resources to conduct a huge television campaign. Moreover, right-wing political parties are more linked to the television networks than are those on the Left. They are usually tied to the network owners via personal and business relations, and thus obtain network support for their parties' goals and policies.

The electorate's power to choose is restricted by the alternatives offered. Their options are mostly determined by the interest groups. The electoral process today, then, is a ceremony in which members of the power elite are acknowledged by the people as the masters of society, a sociodrama in the staging of which television plays a fundamental part. Television thereby contributes heavily to preserving the interests of the economic elite and protecting political options that do not seek significant societal transformations.

FREEDOM OF SPEECH AND FREEDOM OF ENTERPRISE

The question of pluralism and freedom of speech has very often been debated in the Dominican Republic in terms of the number of voices heard, often in connection with freedom of enterprise. However, the problem of pluralism depends not on the number of networks but on the ways television is used. Although television discourse projects an appearance of neutrality and independence, in reality it is used as an agency to preserve and expand the business society. Television is an integral part of the economic and political power structure. The power elite ultimately shapes television's outlook and receives reciprocal reinforcement from television networks.

I am not implying that economic power and the concentration of ownership explain everything about television content. That would be a simplistic reductionism. Influence on television content depends not only on the owners or sponsors but also on the cultural structure in which television is immersed and on the staff. Those who create the programs and those who decide what programs to broadcast play an important role in determining television content. However, the empirical data suggest that ultimately the owners and sponsors establish the limits within which the network staff can act. The economic and political control of television does not automatically convert into an absolute mastery over television messages, but it facilitates this mastery considerably.

Neither is pluralism in television a question of private versus state ownership. The existence of private commercial television does not really ensure pluralism, since private networks depend on publicity and other subsidies to subsist, just as the state-owned television network depends on the government subsidy. The economic power structure has a fundamental influence upon the information and ideas broadcast by television networks, whether public or private, even though only the public network is primarily supervised by the government.

Private Dominican television allows more pluralism than the state-owned network does, but only within boundaries. Television content is strongly mediated through the perspective of those who control the industry. As long as the predominant socioeconomic system allows so many rights to the owners, the extent of pluralism depends on who owns the networks. The same can be said of the state-owned television. Historically this network has had periods with more or less pluralism and diversity in its content, depending on the latitude permitted by the government and on the predilections of the incumbent general director. Furthermore, in the long run there is no real and absolute divergence in Dominican society between the actions of the state bureaucracy and those of the economic elite.

An additional example that supports these findings is offered by the television organization in most European countries. Until a few years ago the European television system was largely dependent on the state, yet pluralism was as extended as, if not more than, it is today in countries where privately owned television has always been predominant (e.g., the United States).[8]

In sum, the tendencies of television in the Dominican Republic to act as a mesmeric distraction, to promote the standardization of culture, and to favor the existing organization of society are the results of three factors: (1) the economic forces that shape television, (2) the patterns of television ownership and control, and (3) the distribution of social power in the culture. Television (particularly the private networks, but also to a certain extent the state-owned network)[9] is not only a medium for the transmission of ideas or values but also a means of production, and as such it is integrated into a complex economic system. The economic goals of the networks curtail the possibilities of diversity in programming and of a truly pluralistic pool of information.

The primary role of commercial television is to develop the circulation of goods and services and to produce benefits for its owners in a market economy. There is no separate and different cultural message that goes beyond this basic function of making the audience consumers, of developing the consumption of sign merchandise and of merchandise symbols. The cultural action television fulfills in the first instance is to serve the needs of a business society: to stimulate new consumption and create new markets. The ideological message it conveys is more a result of this logic, of this need, than of any explicit and organized intention to control all the messages it broadcasts. As business ventures, private television networks have to respond to the law of the marketplace; as ideological products of a commercial society, they defend the ideological interests of capitalist enterprises. Thus, a simple equivalence between freedom of speech and freedom of enterprise cannot be affirmed without reservation. Indeed, very often the two can be antagonistic.

NOTES

1. With the exception that today cable TV is an alternative for those who can afford it: a small group of high-income households.

2. The opposite happens in countries where a dictatorship predominates and the government controls television and other media—for instance, during the government of Trujillo, the government of Franco in Spain, or even in the socialist countries of eastern Europe, few people believed their official media.

3. When we asked several questions concerning this issue, almost all viewers identified RTVD as backing the government, but more than half considered the private networks as presenting different views in their programming and as being balanced. Opinions on whether the information on the news was balanced were as follows: TV13, 49 percent; Rahintel, 52 percent; Colorvisión, 66 percent; Teleantillas, 62 percent; RTVD, 12 percent.

4. Most of the staff of RTVD are members or sympathizers of the party in power.

5. This seems to be a general tendency of the media. Numerous other studies in Latin America, the United States, and Europe agree in considering the mass media as tending to reproduce dominant ideas and beliefs (Martín del Campo and Rebeil Corella 1986; Mattelart 1979a; Hall 1986; Gerbner 1984; Golding 1974).

6. Several studies in the United States also point in that direction (Iyengar et al. 1984).

7. The fact that as a form of insurance Dominican businessmen give money to the parties of the moderate Left—especially if there are possibilities that these parties will have candidates elected—does not invalidate this appraisal.

8. In most representative democracies of Europe (Spain, France, Great Britain, Sweden, etc.), until 1987 television networks were largely financed and controlled by the state, and newspapers relied on the state for a large portion of their revenues. Nevertheless, it cannot be said that in these countries there was less television pluralism (in information, in politics, and in entertainment) than in the United States, where private ownership of television stations has long prevailed. Contrary to the belief of numerous scholars, it is far from evident that state-controlled stations are less free than private stations; for example, Eisendrath (1982) argues that cases such as the coverage of Watergate or the critical reports about the Vietnam war would not be possible in a country like France. This appraisal is absolutely wrong; cases where a part of the media (including television) strongly criticizes the government are fairly common in France: the reporting on the war in Algeria in the 1950s; the Greenpeace affair in 1985; the killings of the "canaques" in New Caledonia by French police in 1987. It is true that there are some constraints, such as criminal sanctions for defamation, but there are also valuable rules for ensuring the independence of the press. For example, all newspapers with a certain minimum circulation receive some economic support from the state; without this support,

such prestigious liberal newspapers as *Le Monde* and *Libération* would probably be out of business, or at least would not have the current content of ideas presented in their pages. At the beginning of the 1980s *Le Monde* experienced a sharp drop in its advertisements because it was considered leftist, and for the same reason *Libération* has never had much commercial advertising. Further, no journalist can be fired because of his or her ideas. And even a cursory observation of television news in France would show that the journalists there are far more controversial than in the United States. This does not mean that everything is perfect there, but as an example of the European state television system as it was, it does dismiss the idea that a free press is possible only if the state does not intervene in the media industry. Actually, as Chomsky (1986) points out, the tradition of a free press in the market economy paradoxically produces media rather docile toward those in power. It would be interesting to investigate what is happening now in the countries of Europe that have been developing a private television system.

9. Two elements shape the state-owned network: economic needs and political control. Generally, political control predominates over commercial requirements.

Appendix A

Procedure

The study population was the seven Dominican television networks, with emphasis on five of them that were selected for the interviews, field observation, and content analysis by convenience sample[1] (c.f. Wimmer and Dominick 1987). This sample was drawn to include the public network and private networks controlled by various economic groups.

In order to keep the analysis as close as possible to reality and, as Geertz (1973) suggests, to organize it in such a way that the connections between theoretical formulations and descriptive interpretations will not be lost, multiple techniques were used. I compiled different sources of evidence, operating at different levels of the television environment, and relied upon the use of four techniques of data collection: field observation, individual in-depth interviews, document analysis, and content analysis.

Field observation is a relatively new technique in mass media research; Lowry (1979) revealed that before 1979 only 2–3 percent of articles reporting social research had employed this technique. I followed the format of nonparticipant observation. This technique had several unique advantages for my purpose, even though it lacks control and quantifiable measures. It allowed me to study the everyday interaction of people involved in television programming (journalists, anchormen, producers, etc.) in their natural setting. In this manner it was possible to make careful examinations and collect data rich in details and subtlety. The observation focused on the attitudes and relationships the television production staff members display in their everyday interactions, how the work is done, and what elements of this situation affect television content (e.g., the decision-making process). I was also a participant observer in five homes in order to evaluate the reactions and comments of viewers regarding television shows, particularly U.S. serials and Latin American soap operas.

Personal in-depth interviews gave me extensive information about the ideas, perceptions, and considerations of the people who work in the broadcasting industry, as well as those of the audience. The interviews allowed me to establish a connection between their ideas, values, and beliefs, and the resulting message.

To select interviewees, I used a combination of key informants and stratified quota sampling. In order to avoid overweighting data from particular informants, the interviewees were diversified at different levels of the television industry, and those informants who were most representative of the studied phenomenon were selected. I interviewed members of the administrative staff, directors of marketing departments, producers of entertainment, directors of news programs, chief editors, national and international editors, reporters, and anchors—and advertisers. A total of fifty-two persons within the television industry were interviewed. Fourteen leading figures of the six principal political parties and grass-roots organizations were interviewed.

Finally a sample of sixty televiewers was interviewed. This sample was drawn by using a quota technique based on age, sex, and neighborhood. The aim was to gather a socioeconomically stratified sample. I selected people to interview in six neighborhoods (two neighborhoods of each of the three socioeconomic statuses) following the Padco Borrell et al. (1980) neighborhood classification of the city of Santo Domingo; ten people from eighteen to sixty-five years old were interviewed in each neighborhood (five females and five males). The socioeconomic status was established as a function of income per family,[2] level of formal education, economic activity of family members, place of residence, and condition of housing (number of rooms, quality of furniture, etc.).

Interviewers used a semistructured questionnaire. Each respondent was interviewed for about an hour, with mostly open-ended questions. All the interviews of the television staff, advertisers, politicians, and leaders of grass-roots organizations were tape-recorded. The interviews of the audience were recorded on paper.

Interviews were oriented differently for each group, though some general aspects—such as ideological orientations, the meaning of television broadcasting, and how they see their role in society—were common to all interviews of people involved in broadcasting.

The interviews of the top directors and producers specifically focused on how the programming is done: what problems or obstacles they encounter, whether owners or sponsors interfere, the participation of staff members in the programming, what situations are considered controversial, and whether there is control of expression. The interviews also focused on the kinds of relationships these persons have to programming, what they consider most important in the television business, what their relationships with sponsors are like, and so on. These questions allowed me to infer the managerial assumptions that affected television content. For the journalists, besides most of the previous questions, the interviews emphasized hierarchical relations and the possibilities of free circulation of ideas.

The interviews of the television viewers consisted of an evaluation of television programming, including perceptions of television as a whole, and the importance viewers attach to news programs. These data allowed me to form an interpretative critique and establish a general categorization of the viewers. The interviews were conducted in the respondents' homes, where we could see and discuss the organization of the space as a function of television.

Except for general statements made by public figures, such as leading politicians, no identification of the speakers is provided, in order to maintain confidentiality.

Document analysis was useful for (1) obtaining data about the registration of television network owners with the Ministry of Industry and the Chamber of Commerce; (2) analyzing norms, rules, and records within the television networks; (3) analyzing publications related to the problem studied; and (4) studying trends in the networks' operation.

Several studies from the United States provided insights for the content analysis procedures, particularly Dominick, Wortzel, and Lometti's (1975) studies of the characteristics of broadcast news; Altheide (1985) on news content; Gitlin (1980) on news coverage of protest movements; Greenberg and Atkin's (1983) work on the behavior shown on television; and DeFleur's (1964) research on U.S. census data and the image of the work environment shown on television.

The term "content analysis" is used here in a broad sense. The technique applied in this research is not solely quantitative interpretation as Berelson (1952) defines it; and it is not exclusively semantics and hermeneutics, as in Lindkvist's (1981) restricted conceptualization. Both of these approaches, however, are part of my interpretation.

The content analysis focused exclusively on news programs. Both implicit and explicit message content was analyzed, as well as specific items of information and how the same information was broadcast by different stations.

For the specific purpose of this research, the following technique was used. First, in relation to the message per se, at least two sensitive pieces of information with national and international political and economic implications were chosen; each piece constituted a unit of analysis. The news broadcasts were videorecorded during prime time, between 7:30 P.M. and 11:00 P.M. (see Appendix B for more detailed information) on the selected networks. The evening newscasts are those with a greater audience.

Broadcast news on the five networks were videotaped for analysis from June 19 to June 23, 1989 (while the country was experiencing a general strike on June 19 and 20); June 28 and 29, 1989; on September 29 and 30, 1989 (no particular events occurred then); and from April 30 to May 15, 1990 (the general election took place on May 16, 1990). This procedure, besides allowing analysis of television content in different particular situations, offered some possibilities for longitudinal analysis.

By recording the news it was possible not only to analyze broadcasts simultaneously but also to make a careful analysis of all the aspects of information in which I was interested. The verbal coverage of the events and the visual components of television news were examined. The interpretation of the videotapes focused particularly on the following categories: (1) shot duration (time allowed for oral presentation and time allowed for the image); (2) position in the newscast (lead story, second story, etc.); (3) aspects stressed in the piece (fair, unfair, etc.); (4) type of presentation of information (commentary, anchor, report, interview); (5) shot selection (what images are shown); and (6) camera angle. The analysis of visuals (shot selection and camera angle) is based on meanings that correspond to the dominant cultural expressions in the Western world, particularly the semiological analysis propositions of Berger (1987). That is, the content analysis of visuals was performed according to the following assumptions:

Type of Shot

Signifier	Definition	Signified (meaning)
Close-up	face only	intimacy
Medium shot	most of body	personal relationship
Long shot	setting and characters	context, scope, public distance
Full shot	full body of person	social relationship

Camera Work and Editing

Signifier	Definition	Signified (meaning)
Pan down	camera looks down	smallness, weakness
Pan up	camera looks up	power, authority
Zoom in	camera moves in	observation, focus
Fade in	image appears on blank screen	beginning
Fade out	image screen goes blank	ending
Cut	switch from one image to another	simultaneity, excitement
Wipe	image wiped off screen	imposed conclusion

The fieldwork was conducted in two steps. The first began in June 1989 and was completed by the beginning of October 1989; the second was performed from mid-April to the end of May 1990.

NOTES

1. Cable television networks were not considered in this study because this system is still limited, and therefore has little impact on Dominican society in general.

2. Low income was 25,000 Dominican pesos a year (about U.S. $4,000) or less; middle income, between 25,001 and 80,000 pesos (about U.S. $4,001–11,000); high income, more than 80,000 pesos. This classification corresponds to the economic situation of the Dominican Republic at the time the field research began, in June 1989. There has been a great change since then. Due to rising inflation, the range of middle income was much more limited in 1991; for example, less than 40,000 pesos a year was a low income. In 1989 the exchange rate was approximately 6.4 Dominican pesos for 1 U.S. dollar. At the end of 1991 it was around 14 pesos for 1 U.S. dollar.

Appendix B

Programming on Four Private Networks

Appendix B

Monday through Friday

Time	Colorvisión	Rahintel	Teleantillas	TV13
5:00 A.M.		Teleradionoticias (news)		
5:55			Un Mensaje a la conciencia (religious message)	
6:00			Uno+Uno –Teleperiódico (general information program)	
6:15				Reflexiones Cristianas (religious message)
6:25				El Hermano Pablo (religious message)
6:30	Hoy Mismo (general information program)			Noticentro (news)
7:00		El Telematutino Buenos Días (general information program)		
8:00				Para Todos (variety show)
9:00			El Evangelio es Noticia (religious show)	Viva un Poco Más (health show)
9:30			Club 700 (variety show)	Mañana Musical (musical show)
10:00			Sección Dos (talk show)	
11:00			Como en Botica (talk show)	
11:30	El Show del Mediodía (variety musical show)		Escuadrón Especial (U.S. serial)	Super Éxitos (Musical show)
12:00 P.M.		Teleradionoticias (news)		
12:30			Noticiario Teleantillas (news)	El Almuerzo de TV13 (interviews show)

Appendix B

1:00			Síntesis (talk show)	
1:30		Punto por Punto (talk show)		Noticiario TV13 (news)
2:00	El Chavo (Mexican sitcom)	Día a Día (talk show)	Gente Común (talk show)	18-50 (talk show)
2:30	Nociario Mundovision (news)		Porky Pig (cartoons)	Muñequitos (cartoons)
3:00	Variedades (songs, video, shopping info.)	Club Tobogan (cartoons)	Iron Man (cartoons)	Chiqui Alegría (children show)
3:30			El Mago de Oz (cartoons)	
4:00		Mujer 2000 (cooking show)	El Inspector Gadget (cartoons)	Viva un Poco Más (health show)
4:30			Arbegas (cartoons)	Actualidad Hípica (horse race info.)
5:00		Rahintel en las Noticias (news)	Cristal (soap opera)	Muppets (cartoons)
5:30	Chiquilladas (children's show)			Noticiario TV13 (News)
6:00	Chespirito (children's sitcom)	Notiarte (news about art)	Primavera (soap opera)	Radio TV (variety show)
6:30	Carrusel (soap opera)	San Tropel (soap opera)		
7:00	Luz y Sombra (soap opera)	Caballo Viejo (soap opera)	Alma Mía (soap opera)	
7:30				Tres Patines (sitcom)
8:00	La Casa (soap opera)	Niña Moza (soap opera)	Matt Houston (U.S. serial)	Avance Deportivo (sports news)
8:30	Lo Blanco y lo Negro (soap opera)			Bloque de Programas (different show each day)
9:00	Noticiario Mundovision (news)	Roque Santeiro (soap opera)	Noticiario Teleantillas (news)	Buenas Noches (talk show)
9:30	Punto Final (sitcom and variety show)			
10:00		Rahintel en las Noticias (news)	Selva de Cemento (soap opera)	Noticiario TV13 (news)

10:35			Mercado y Libertad (talk show on economics)
10:45	Rahintel en los Deportes (sports news)		Deportes en la Cumbre (sports news and commentary)
11:00	Última Tanda (U.S. movie)	El Show de la Noche (varieties Show)	
12:00			
12:30	Mensaje Duerme Tranquilo (short religious message)		Reflexiones Cristianas en el Camino (short religious message)

Saturday

	Colorvisión	Rahintel	Teleantillas	TV13
7:00		Cine Infantil (children's movie)		
8:00	Carrusel (children's show)	Documental (documentary)		Mundo de Amor (children's show)
8:25			Un Mensaje a la Conciencia (religious message)	
8:30			Angulo Abierto (talk show)	
9:00		Los Niños Pueden (children's show)		Religioso (Religious show)
9:30	500 Años de Historia (educational show)		Realidades Dominicanas (talk show)	Pantalla 10 (talk show)
10:00			Educación Cívica (educational show)	Actualizando mi País (educational show)
10:30	El Show de Manny Mota (cartoons)		Actividades Financieras (business show)	Capitan Power (cartoons)
11:00		Musical (popular musical show)		Aqui Juventud (variety musical show)
11:30	Personajes (variety show)			

Appendix B

12:00	Lucha Libre (wrestling)	El Sabado Grande (marathon one-man variety show)		El Pueblo Cuestiona (talk show)
1:00			Con el Consumidor (information talk show)	Trialogo (talk show)
1:30	TV Todo (variety show)		Mi Mensaje (talk show)	
2:00			El Comercio al Día (talk show)	The Muppets (cartoons)
2:30			Figuras del Deporte (sports talk show)	
3:00			Beisbol de Grandes Ligas (sports)	TV-Informatica (business show)
4:00				Radar Deportivo (Sports show)
5:00				Auto Revista en TV (car race show)
6:00			Memorias del Padre José (religious show)	Fantasía (variety show)
7:00		Musical (music video show)	Compu-Análisis (business show)	Crónica de los Cronistas (talk show)
7:30	Turi Enlace (talk show)	Merengue Show (popular music show)		
8:00	El Show de Charytin (variety show)	Cien Grados (variety show)	Aunque Usted no lo Crea (U.S. variety show)	Lo Mejor de Radio-TV (variety show)
9:00	Nuria en el 9 (variety show)		Hotel (U. S. serial)	
9:30		Rahintel en las Noticias (news)		
10:00	Esta Misma Semana (information review)	Ciudadano Cine (U.S. movie)	Planeta 3 (talk show)	Fuego Cruzado (talk show)
11:00	Cuarto Poder (talk show)		Pilar de Fuego (U. S. serial)	Entre Puntos (talk show)
12:00	Mensaje Duerme Tranquilo (short religious message)			

Appendix B

Sunday

	Colorvisión	Rahintel	Teleantillas	TV13
7:00				The Muppets (U.S. children's show)
7:30	El Ministerio de Earl Paulk (U.S. TV evangelist show)		Club 700 (religious show)	El Camino (religious show)
8:00		Cine Infantil (children's movie)	Arriba el Softball (sports show)	
8:30		Enfoque Semanal (weekly news commentary)		Vida Nueva 2,000 (talk show)
9:00			Tú Puedes (children's show)	Hechos y Opiniones (talk show)
9:30	Puntos de Vista (talk show)	Miras del Progreso (talk show)		
10:00		Resumen de Telenovelas (weekly review of soap operas)	De Buena Fuente (educational show)	Economía al Día (talk show)
10:30	Prisma (talk show)		Integramente Ramón Leonardo. (musical-religious show)	
10:45		El Patio de Medrano (sitcom)		
11:00				Teleofertas (business show)
11:30	Aeromundo (Talk show)			
12:00	El Gordo de Semana (marathon one-man variety show)		Padre Murphy (U.S. serial)	Debate Económico (talk show)
12:30		Con Cuquín (marathon one-man variety show)		Soluciones (talk show)
1:00			Síntesis (talk show)	
1:30				Deportes en la Cumbre (sports show)
2:00			Video Moda (fashion show)	

Time				
3:00			Fantasía Deportiva (sports show)	
3:30				Fútbol Solo Fútbol (sports show)
4:00				
5:00			Si Usted Fuera Presidente (talk show)	
6:00			Estefanía (U.S serial)	Televentas (business show)
7:30				Sin Límites (U.S. serial)
8:00	El Show de Luisito y Anthony (variety show)	Cecilia en Facetas (variety show)	El Show de Charytín (variety show)	
8:30				Cine del Ayer (movie)
9:00	Cine Continuo 1ra parte (U.S movie, 1st part)			
10:00		Ciudadano Cine (U.S. movie)		
10:30				Las Gatitas de Marcel (sitcom)
11:00	Cine Continuo 2da parte (U.S. movie, 2nd part)		Especial del Domingo (variety show)	
11:30				Película (U.S movie)
12:00	Mensaje Duerme Tranquilo (religious message)		Crucero del Amor (U. S. serial)	

Appendix C

Television Networks' Share of Audience

Monday through Friday

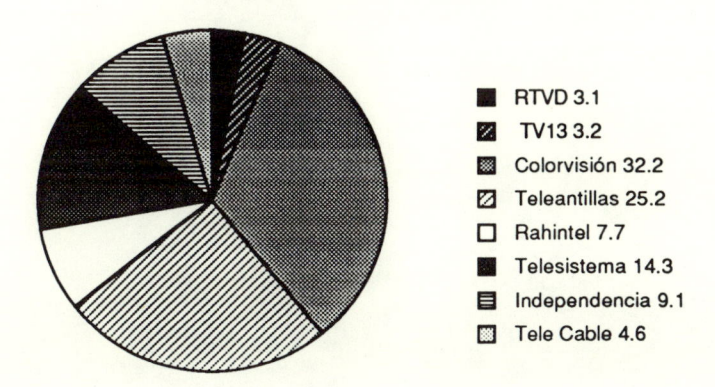

- RTVD 3.1
- TV13 3.2
- Colorvisión 32.2
- Teleantillas 25.2
- Rahintel 7.7
- Telesistema 14.3
- Independencia 9.1
- Tele Cable 4.6

Saturday and Sunday

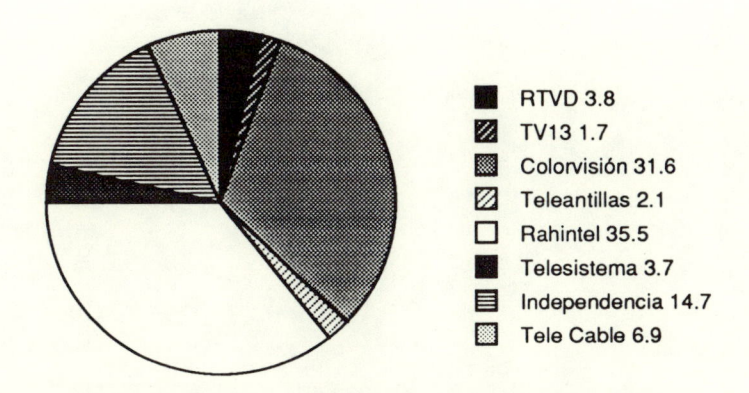

- RTVD 3.8
- TV13 1.7
- Colorvisión 31.6
- Teleantillas 2.1
- Rahintel 35.5
- Telesistema 3.7
- Independencia 14.7
- Tele Cable 6.9

Source: Orientación Mercadológica S.A., Report no. 2, April 1990.

Appendix D

Typical Editorial of RTVD Newscast

The secretary of state for public infrastructures and communications, Mario A. Subero, has just delivered in the Dominican Chamber of Construction an important speech in which, with very precise details, he described the nature, amplitude, and magnitude of the government's... public investment. The high state official and ... engineering professional... demonstrated that public investment currently represents the most... effective instrument of our present and future development. Secretary Subero proved that President Balaguer invests in what is needed and for what is needed. Through his analysis of the areas of investment he... showed that this government is working for the present and above all for the future of the Dominican nation, with the sole objective of consolidating the basis of a harmonious, primary, and efficient development of our agricultural, industrial, and tourist potential.

As such, a government is defended, and as such the force of truth is defended. That is why we say... that the speech of the secretary of state of public infrastructures,... Mario Subero, should be followed and imitated by other officials of similar rank in order to remind the people that what each person is seeing as separated actions are in reality part of the whole, eminently patriotic effort of this government.

This has been... the editorial of "The World Today."

Appendix E

International News on Dominican Television: Average of All Networks

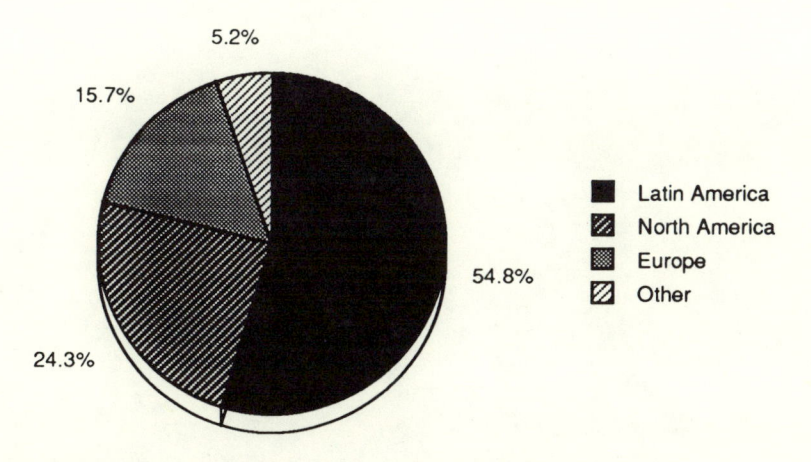

- Latin America: 54.8%
- North America: 24.3%
- Europe: 15.7%
- Other: 5.2%

Note: North America refers to the United States and Canada.
Source: Author's data.

Bibliography

Adorno, T. 1957. "Television and the Patterns of Mass Culture." In B. Rosenberg and D. Manning White, eds., *Mass Culture: The Popular Arts in America*. Glencoe, IL: Free Press.
———. 1982. *Prism*. Cambridge, MA: MIT Press.
Advertising Age. 1989. July 24, p. 45.
Alexander, H. E. 1984. *Financing Politics: Money, Elections, and Political Reform*. Washington, DC: Congressional Quarterly Press.
Allen, R. 1985. *Speaking of Soap Operas*. Chapel Hill: University of North Carolina Press.
Allman, W. F. 1989. "Science 1, Advertisers 0: Studies on Efficacity of TV Ads." *U.S. News and World Report* 106 (May 1): 60–61.
Almánzar, R. 1972. "Usos de los Medios de Comunicación en la República Dominicana." *Revista Ciencia* (Universidad Autónoma de Santo Domingo).
Altheide, D. 1985. *Media Power*. Beverly Hills, CA: Sage.
Althusser, L. 1984. *Essays on Ideology*. London: Verso.
Argumedo, A. 1982. "Comunicación y Democracia: Una Perspectiva Tercer-Mundista." In *Comunicación y Democracia en América Latina*, pp. 265–81. Lima: Desco.
Asa Berger, A. 1987. "Semiological Analysis." In O. Boyd-Barrett and P. Braham, eds., *Media, Knowledge and Power*, pp. 132–54. London: Croom Helm/Open University.
Baudrillard, J. 1974. *La Société de Consommation: Ses Mythes, ses Structures*. Paris: Gallimard.
Beals, C. 1961. "Gunboat Diplomacy and the Dominican Crisis." *National Guardian* 14 (December 11): 1, 4.
Berke, L. R. 1988. "Rivals Will Be Big Spenders for the Battle of New York." *New York Times*, April 7, p. 15.
Belson, W. A. 1967. *The Impact of Television*. London: Crosby Lockwood.

Beltran, R. L., and Fox de Cardona, E. 1980. *Comunicación Dominada*. Mexico: Instituto Latinoamericano de Estudios Transnacionales/Nueva Imagen.
Berelson, B. 1952. *Content Analysis in Communication Research*. New York: Free Press.
Bisbal, M. 1988. "Predominio de los enlatados." *Nueva Sociedad*, no. 95 (May–June): 135–43.
Blumler, J., and Ewbank, A. 1969. "Trade Unionists, the Mass Media and Unofficial Strikes." *British Journal of Industrial Relations* 8, no. 1 (March 10): 32–54.
Bogart, L. 1972. *The Age of Television*. New York: Frederick Ungar.
Boorstin, D. J. 1978. *The Republic of Technology*. New York: Harper & Row.
Bosch, J. 1961. *Trujillo: Causas de una Tiranía sin Ejemplo*. Caracas.
Bourdieu, P. 1979. *La Distinction*. Paris: Editions de Minuit.
Boyd-Barrett, O., and Palmer, M. 1981. *Le Trafic des Nouvelles*. Paris: Alain Moreau.
Brea, R. 1975. "Análisis de la Programación Diaria de Radio Guarachita." *Revista Ciencia* 2, no. 2 (April–June).
Buffle, J. C. 1986. *Dossier N . . . Comme Nestlé*. Paris: Alain Moreau.
Cantor, M. G. 1980. *Prime Time Television*. Beverly Hills, CA: Sage.
Caroit, J. M. 1990. "Menaces de Ciclone sur les Caraïbes." *Le Monde Diplomatique*, September, pp. 6–7.
Castillo, J. del, et al. 1975. "La Ideología en los Medios de Comunicación de Masas." *Revista Ciencia* 2, no. 2 (April–June).
Cathelat, B. 1976. *Publicité et Société*. Paris: Payot.
Cazeneuve, J. 1972. *La Société de l'Ubiquité*. Paris: Denoël.
Chadwick, B., Bahr, H., and Albrecht, S. 1984. *Social Science Research Methods*. Englewood Cliffs, NJ: Prentice-Hall.
Debord, G. 1977. *Society of the Spectacle*. Detroit: Black & Red.
DeFleur, M. L. 1964. "Occupational Roles as Portrayed on Television." *Public Opinion Quarterly*, no. 28 (Spring): 57–74.
Deighton, J., Henderson, C., and Neslin, S. 1989. "The Last Word: Scanners and the Framing Effect." *Marketing and Media Decisions* 24 (October): 112.
Domhof, W. G. 1978. *The Powers That Be: Processes of Ruling-Class Domination in America*. New York: Random House.
Dominick, J., Wortzel, S., and Lometti, G. 1975. "Television Journalism vs. Show Business: A Content Analysis of Eyewitness News." *Journalism Quarterly* 52, no. 2 (Summer): 213–18.
Dorfman, A., and Mattelart, A. 1975. *How to Read Donald Duck*. New York: International General.
Dunn, R. G. 1986. "Mass Media and Society: The Legacy of T. W. Adorno and the Frankfurt School." *California Sociologist* 9, no. 1–2 (Winter/Summer): 109–43.
Durkheim, E. 1970. *Rules of Sociological Method*. New York: Free Press.
Eisendrath, C. R. 1982. "Press Freedom in France: Private Ownership and State Controls." In J. L. Curry and J. R. Dassin, eds., *Press Control Around the World*, pp. 62–81. New York: Praeger.
Elliot, P. 1973. "Uses and Gratifications: A Critique and a Sociological Alterna-

tive." Centre for Mass Communications Research, University of Leicester. (Mimeo.)
El Siglo–Gallup. 1990. "Informe Sobre las Preferencias Electorales." *El Siglo* (Santo Domingo), April 21, pp. 1–2.
Epstein, E. J. 1973. *News from Nowhere: Television and the News.* New York: Random House.
Espaillat, A. 1963. *Trujillo: The Last Caesar.* Chicago: Henry Regnery.
Eudes, Y. 1988. "Vers un Marché Mondial de l'Information Télévisée." *Le Monde Diplomatique*, June, p. 11.
Europa World Year Book. 1990. London: Europa Publications.
Fejes, F. 1986. *Imperialism, Media, and the Good Neighbor.* Norwood, NJ: Ablex.
Fiske, J. 1987. *Television Culture.* London: Methuen.
Foucault, M. 1980. *Power, Knowledge: Selected Interviews and Other Writings, 1972–1977.* New York: Pantheon Books.
Fox de Cardona, E. 1975. "Multinational Television." *Journal of Communication* 25, no. 2 (Spring): 122–27.
Friedrich, O. 1987. "What Really Mattered." *Time*, October 12, p. 94.
Gallo, M. 1989. "La Sarabande des Media." *Le Monde Diplomatique*, December, p. 32.
Gandy, O. H. 1982. *Beyond Agenda Setting.* Norwood, NJ: Ablex.
Gans, H. J. 1979. *Deciding What's News: A Study of CBS Evening News, NBC Nightly News, Newsweek and Time.* New York: Pantheon.
Garfinkel, H. 1967. *Studies in Ethnomethodology.* Englewood Cliffs, NJ: Prentice-Hall.
Garnham, N. 1986. "Contribution to a Political Economy of Mass Communication." In R. Collins, J. Curran, N. Garnham, P. Scannell, P. Schlesinger, and C. Sparks, eds., *Media, Culture and Society: A Critical Reader*, pp. 9–32. London: Sage.
Geertz, C. 1973. *The Interpretation of Cultures.* New York: Basic Books.
Gerbner, G. 1964. "Ideological Perspectives and Political Tendencies in News Reporting." *Journalism Quarterly* 41, no. 4 (Autumn): 494–508.
———. 1968. "On Content Analysis and Critical Research in Mass Communication." In L. A. Dexter and D. M. White, eds., *People Society and Mass Communication*, pp. 477–500. New York: Free Press.
———. 1970. "Cultural Indicators: The Case of Violence in Television Drama." *Annals of the American Association of Political and Social Science* 338 (Autumn): 69–81.
———. 1984. "Charting the Mainstream: Television's Contributions to Political Orientations." In D. Graber, ed., *Media Power in Politics*, pp. 118–30. Washington, DC: Congressional Quarterly Press.
Gerbner, G., Gross, L., Signorelli, N., Morgan, M., and Jackson-Beek, M. 1979. "The Demonstration of Power: Violence Profile, No. 10." *Journal of Communication* 29, no. 3 (Summer): 177–96.
Giddens, A. 1976. *New Rules of Sociological Method.* London: Hutchinson.
Ginsberg, B. 1986. *The Captive Public: How Mass Opinion Promotes State Power.* New York: Basic Books.
Gitlin, T. 1980. *The Whole World Is Watching.* Los Angeles: University of California Press.

———. 1983. *Inside Prime Time*. New York: Pantheon.
Golding, P. 1974. *The Mass Media*. London: Longman.
———. 1980. "The Missing Dimensions—News Media and the Management of Social Change." In E. Kantz and T. Szecskö, eds., *Mass Media and Social Change*, pp. 63–81. London: Sage.
Gómez, L. 1979. *Relaciones de Producción Dominantes en la Sociedad Dominicana 1875–1975*. Santo Domingo: Alfa y Omega.
Graber, D. 1984. *Media Power in Politics*. Washington, DC: Congressional Quarterly Press.
Gramsci, A. 1977. *Pasado y Presente*. Mexico City: Juan Pablos Editora.
Green, J. 1982. *Morrow's International Dictionary of Contemporary Quotations*. New York: William Morrow and Company.
Greenberg, B., and Atkin, C. 1983. "The Portrayal of Driving on Television." *Journal of Communication* 33, no. 2 (Spring): 41–65.
Greenfield, P. M. 1984. *Mind and Media: The Effects of Television, Video Games, and Computers*. Cambridge, MA: Harvard University Press.
Gurevitch, M., and Blumler, J. G. 1979. "Linkages Between the Mass Media and Politics." In J. Curran, M. Gurevitch, and J. Woollacott, eds., *Mass Communication and Society*. London: Edward Arnold.
Hall, S. 1973. "Encoding and Decoding the TV Message." CCCS mimeo, University of Birmingham. Quoted in Morley, D. 1980. *The Nationwide Audience: Structure and Decoding*. London: British Film Institute.
———. 1979. "Culture, the Media, and the 'Ideological Effect.'" In J. Curran, M. Gurevitch, and J. Woollacott, eds., *Mass Communication and Society*. London: Edward Arnold.
———. 1986. *Politics and Ideology: A Reader*. Philadelphia: Open University Press/Milton Keynes.
Halloran, J. 1970. *The Effects of Television*. London: Panther.
Head, S., and Sterling, C. H. 1987. *Broadcasting in America: A Survey of Television, Radio, and New Technology*. Boston: Houghton Mifflin.
Herman, E. S., and Chomsky, N. 1988. *Manufacturing Consent: The Political Economy of the Mass Media*. New York: Pantheon Books.
Hirsch, P. M. 1975. "Occupational, Organizational and Institutional Models in Mass Media Research." In P. M. Hirsch, P. V. Miller, and F. G. Kline, eds., *Strategies for Communication Research*. Beverly Hills, CA: Sage.
Horkheimer, M., and Adorno, T. 1972. *Dialectic of Enlightenment*. New York: Herder and Herder.
Hoskins, C., and Mirus, R. 1988. "Reasons for the U.S. Dominance of the International Trade in Television Programs." *Media, Culture, and Society* 10 (October): 499–515.
Iyengar, S., Peters, M. D., and Kinder, D. R. 1984. "Experimental Demonstrations of the 'Not-So-Minimal' Consequences of Television News Programs." In D. A. Graber, ed., *Media Power in Politics*, pp. 54–60. Washington, DC: Congressional Quarterly Press.
Johnston, R. J. 1987. *Money and Votes*. London: Croom Helm.
Katz, E., and Lazarsfeld, P. F. 1955. *Personal Influence*. Glencoe, IL: Free Press.
Kellner, D. 1988. "T.V. and Postmodern Theory: Some Critical Reflections on Watching Television." Paper presented at annual convention of the Amer-

ican Culture Association/Popular Culture Association, New Orleans, March 23-26.
Klapper, J. T. 1960. *The Effects of Mass Communication.* New York: Free Press.
Lazarsfeld, P., and Menzel, H. 1963. "Mass Media and Personal Influence." In W. Schramm, ed., *The Science of Human Communication,* pp. 94-115. New York: Basic Books.
Leo, J. 1984. "Not by Issues Alone. Psychologists Explore What Makes Voters Decide." *Time,* November 12, pp. 124-37.
Lindkvist, K. 1981. "Approaches to Textual Analysis." In K. E. Rosengren, ed., *Advances in Content Analysis,* pp. 23-42. Beverly Hills, CA: Sage.
Lippmann, W. 1950. *Public Opinion.* New York: Macmillan.
Lora Medrano, L. 1984. *La Voz Dominicana, Su Gente y Sus Cosas.* Santo Domingo: Editora Tele 3.
Lowry, D. T. 1979. "An Evaluation of Empirical Studies Reported in Seven Journals in the '70s." *Journalism Quarterly* 56, no. 2 (Summer): 262-68.
Lull, J. 1985. "Ethnographic Studies of Broadcast Media Audiences." In J. Dominick and J. Fletcher, eds., *Broadcasting Research Methods.* Boston: Allyn & Bacon.
Luzón, H. 1989. "TV Dominicana Reconoce Difunde Pasiones, Violencia." *Listin Diario,* July 10, pp. 1, 21.
Marcuse, H. 1964. *One Dimensional Man.* London: Routledge and Kegan Paul.
Martín del Campo, A. M., and Rebeil Corella, M. A. 1986. "Commercial Television as an Educational and Political Institution: A Case Study of Its Impact on the Students of Telesecundaria." In R. Atwood and E. G. McAvary, eds., *Communication and Latin American Society,* pp. 143-64. Madison: University of Wisconsin Press.
Mattelart, A. 1979a. "Communication Ideology and Class Practice." In A. Mattelart and S. Sieglaub, eds., *Communication and Class Struggle,* vol. 1, pp. 115-23. New York: International General; Bagnolet, France: International Mass Media Research Center.
———. 1979b. *Multinational Corporations and the Control of Culture: The Ideological Apparatuses of Imperialism.* Sussex, UK: Harvester Press.
McBride Report, International Commission for the Study of Communications Problems. 1980. *Many Voices, One World: Toward a New, More Just and More Efficient World Information and Communication Order.* Paris: UNESCO.
McKuen, M. B., and Coombs, S. L. 1981. *More than News: Two Studies in Media Power.* Beverly Hills, CA: Sage.
McLuhan, M., and Fiore, Q. 1967. *The Medium Is the Message.* New York: Random House.
McQuail, D. 1979. *Sociología de los Medios Masivos de Comunicación.* Buenos Aires: Editora Paidos.
Menéndez, A. 1984. "Estudio Sociocultural en Relación con la Escuela." Santo Domingo: United States Agency for International Development/Secretaria de Estado de Educacion Bellas Artes y Cultos (AID/SEEBAC). (Mimeo.)
———. 1987. *El Universitario Dominicano.* Santo Domingo: Intec.
Meyer, D. J., and Exoo, C. F. 1988. "News Coverage of Political Ethics: The Muzzled Watchdog." Paper presented at annual meeting of the American

Culture Association/Popular Culture Association. New Orleans, March 23–26.
Miles, M. B., and Huberman, M. 1984. *Qualitative Data Analysis: A Sourcebook of New Methods*. Beverly Hills, CA: Sage.
Mills, C. Wright. 1956. *The Power Elite*. New York: Oxford University Press.
Minow, N. 1964. *Equal Time: The Private Broadcaster and the Public Interest*. New York: Atheneum.
Morley, D. 1980. *The Nationwide Audience: Structure and Decoding*. London: British Film Institute.
Murdock, G., and Golding, P. 1987. "Theories of Communication and Theories of Society." *Communication Research* 5, no. 3 (July): 339–56.
La Nación. 1942. May 3, p. 3 (Santo Domingo).
———. 1952. August 2, p. 8 (Santo Domingo).
Napolitan, J. 1972. *The Election Game and How to Win It*. New York: Doubleday.
O.N.E. 1987. *Oficina Nacional de Estadísticas. Boletín Anual*. Santo Domingo: Secretariado Técnico de la Presidencia.
Padco Borrell, A. 1980. "Distribución espacial por características socioeconómicas." Santo Domingo. (Mimeo.)
Paletz, D. L, and Entman, R. M. 1981. *Media Power Politics*. New York: Free Press.
———. 1984. "Accepting the System." In Doris A. Graber, ed., *Media Power and Politics*, pp. 149–54. Washington, DC: Congressional Quarterly Press.
Parenti, M. 1986. *Inventing Reality: The Politics of the Mass Media*. New York: St. Martin's Press.
Pascuali, A. 1977. *Comunicación y Cultura de Masas*. Caracas: Monte Ávila.
Postman, N. 1985. *Amusing Ourselves to Death*. New York: Viking.
Quiterio Cedeño, M. 1975. "Una Semana de Prensa en la República Dominicana: Análisis Cuantitativo y Estudio de Prensa Comparado." *Revista Ciencia* 2, no. 2 (April–June).
Real, M. R. 1977. *Mass Mediated Culture*. Englewood Cliffs, NJ: Prentice-Hall.
Rivera, T. 1986. *Relaciones de los Bienes e Inversiones de Rafael Leonidas Trujillo Molina, Esposa e Hijos al Día 5 de Julio de 1961*. Santo Domingo: Ediciones Taller.
Roncagliolo, R. 1988. "Políticas de Televisión: Una Necesidad." *Nueva Sociedad*, no. 95 (May–June): 135–43.
Ryan, J. K. 1969. "Is It Too Soon to Put a Tiger in Every Tank?" *Columbia Journal of World Business* (March–April): 69–75.
Salvaggio, J. 1980. *A Theory of Film Language*. New York: Arno Press.
Saussez, T. 1986. *Politique de Séduction. Comment les Hommes Politiques Reussissent a Vous Plaire*. Poitiers: J. C. Lattes.
Schiller, H. I. 1971. *Mass Communications and American Empire*. Boston: Beacon Press.
Schlesinger, P. 1987. "On National Identity: Some Conceptions and Misconceptions Criticized." *Social Science Information* 26, no. 2 (June): 219–64.
Schramm, W. 1964. *Mass Media and National Development*. Stanford, CA: Stanford University Press.
Schutz, A. 1962. *Collected Papers*, vol. 1, *The Problems of Social Reality*. The Hague: Martinus Nijhoff.

Schwartz, F. 1988. "La Maquinaria de un Candidato." *El País*, September 20, pp. 2, 15.
Straubhaar, J. D., and Viscasillas, G. M. 1991. "Class, Genre, and the Regionalization of Television Programming in the Dominican Republic." *Journal of Communication* 41, no. 1 (Winter): 53–69.
Szulc, T. 1968. *The Winds of Revolution: Latin America Today and Tomorrow*. New York: Praeger.
Tellis, G. 1988. "Advertising Exposure, Loyalty, and Brand Purchase: A Two-Stage Model of Choice." *Journal of Marketing Research* 25 (May): 134–44.
Thorburn, D. 1982. "Television Melodrama." In H. Newcomb, ed., *Television: The Critical View*, pp. 529–46. New York: Oxford University Press.
Tuchman, G., ed. 1974. *The T.V. Establishment. Programming for Power and Profit*. Englewood Cliffs, NJ: Prentice-Hall.
———, ed. 1978. *Making News*. New York: Free Press.
Varis, T. 1985. *The International Flow of Television Programmes*. Reports and Papers on Mass Communication no. 100. Paris: UNESCO.
Villalba, R. 1975. "Usos de Comunicación Colectiva en Santo Domingo." *Revista Ciencia* 2, no. 2 (April–June).
Villaverde, A. 1975. "La Investigación de la Comunicación Social." *Revista Ciencia* 2, no. 2 (April–June).
UNESCO. 1959. *Faits et chiffres*. International Statistics Relative to Education, Culture and Mass Communication Series. Paris: UNESCO.
———. 1976a. *Statistical Reports and Studies*. Paris: UNESCO.
———. 1976b. *Statistics of Radio and Television*. Paris: UNESCO.
———. 1983–1987. *Statistical Yearbook*. Paris: UNESCO.
United Nations. 1960. *Statistical Yearbook*. New York: United Nations Statistical Office.
University of California–Los Angeles. 1960–1975. *Statistical Abstract of Latin America*, vols. 18–27. Los Angeles: UCLA.
Weiner, R. 1990. *Webster's New World Dictionary of Media and Communications*. New York: Webster's New World/Prentice-Hall.
Wheen, F. 1985. *Television*. London: Century Publishing.
Wiarda, H. J. 1968. *Dictatorship and Development: The Methods of Control in Trujillo's Dominican Republic*. Gainesville: University of Florida Press.
Wilkie, W. J., and Ochoa, E., eds. 1989. *Statistical Abstract of Latin America*, vol. 27. Los Angeles: UCLA Latin American Center Publications.
Williams, R. 1974. *Television: Technology and Cultural Form*. London: Fontana.
Wilson, C., and Gutiérrez, F. 1985. *Minorities and Media: Diversity and the End of Mass Communication*. Beverly Hills, CA: Sage.
Wimmer, R. D., and Dominick, J. R. 1987. *Mass Media Research*. Belmont, CA: Wadsworth.
Winick, C. 1959. *Taste and the Censor in Television*. New York: Fund for the Republic.
Wober, J. M., and Gunter, B. 1988. *Television and Social Control*. New York: St. Martin's Press.

Index

ABC, 72, 109–10
Adorno, Theodor, 7
Advertising: agencies, 9, 27, 36–37, 44, 50, 66–69; effects, 10, 29; effects on culture, 66–67; income, 37, 39–40; industry, 124–26; participatory, 36; subliminal, 124
Aesthetics, 70, 87
Africa, 12
Agence France Presse, 108–9
Agenda setting, 120–21
Alexander, Herbert, 150
Allen, Robert, on soap operas, 60
Altheide, David, on news content, 8
Althusser, Louis, 51
Argentina, 17
Argumedo, Alberto, 5
Asesores Asociados S. A., 41
Audience: impact, 65; interest, 88–89; taste, 7, 38–39, 47, 54
Authoritarianism, 17, 98, 122

Balaguer, Joaquin, 32, 100, 102–5, 107, 129, 144
Barceló rum, 70
Baudrillard, Jean, 27
Beals, Carleton, 30
Beltrán, Ramiro, 28

Bermúdez family, 24
Bias in the media, 83, 88, 110, 111, 156
Bisbal, Marcellino, 51
Blumler, Jay, 7
Bogart, Leo, 31
Bolivia, 12
Bonetti family, 25
Bonilla, Pedro, 23
Boorstin, Daniel, 49, 154
Bosch, Juan, 17, 83, 119, 123, 127, 128, 131, 132
Bourdieu, Pierre, 8
Boyd-Barrett, Oliver, 110
Brazil, 17
Brugal rum, 52
"Buenos Dias," 95–97
Buffle, Jean Claude, 77
Bureaucratic structure, 81
Burnett, Leo, 77
Business: culture, 50, 69–71, 95–96; ideology, 65, 73–74, 113, 159; and television, 11, 24–29, 35–38, 62, 95, 103, 163

Canada, 17
Cantor, Muriel, 53, 64
Caribbean, 129

Caroit, Jean François, 114
Cathelat, Bernard, 68, 70
Catholic church, 16; voters, 127
Cazeneuve, Jean, 4
Censorship, 5, 9, 16, 50, 86–88, 98, 155–58
CEPAL, 21
Chomsky, Noam, 8, 164
CNN, 109–10
Coca-Cola, 69
Colombia, 16
Colorvisión, 24, 39–40, 83, 99, 108, 112, 141–42
Comision Nacional de Espectáculos Públicos, 71
Commercial: arrangements, 71–72; pressures, 35; requirements, 5, 50, 80, 96, 111, 131; role of television, 11; television system, 23, 28–29, 46, 73, 158, 162
Common denominator, in determining programming, 39, 49, 72, 154
Communicative structure, 7
Communist Party, 130
Congress, 99
Consumer ideology, 66, 69
Consumption: mass, 27, 38; society and, 70, 159; and television, 6, 11, 28–29, 74–75, 79, 157, 162
Control, mechanisms of, 158
Controbersial content, 5, 50, 60, 73, 85, 95, 123, 126
Corporan de los Santos, Rafael, 31
Corriere della Sera, 110
Corripio, José Luis, 24
Cultural symbols, 39, 154
Cultural values, 10, 50, 60–62, 75, 89, 97, 159–60
Culture: with fun, 57; national, 27, 55, 65; popular, 49–50, 70, 154; television as generator of, 55–56

Dalí, Salvador, 44
"Dallas," 62
Debord, Guy, 8
Decision makers, 106
Demagogic technology, 128
Democracy, and television, 7, 11

Developing countries, 9
Development, 5, 27
Dictatorship, 10–16, 23, 27, 105, 127, 158, 160
Differentiated audience, 47–48
Disney, Walt, 64
Dissent, 11, 90, 95, 105, 112, 158
Distributors, 73
Diversity, in television content, 7, 46, 50, 62–63, 71–73, 153–62
Documentaries, 45
Domhof, William, 147
Dominican Republic, 4, 5, 6; flag, 18
Dorfman, Ariel, 64
DPA, 108–9
Dramatic potential, 81–82
Dunn, Robert, 89
Durkheim, Emile, 12

ECO, 109
Economic dependency, 11, 50
Economic elite, 4, 11, 28, 75, 87–92, 97, 130, 161–62
Economic imperatives, 46
Economic organization, 28, 147
Economic power, 11, 60, 87, 95, 161–62
Ecuador, 12
Editorial line, 25
Educational programs, 44–45
Efe, 108–9
El Caribe newspaper, 25
Elections: campaign and television, 11, 118–25, 146–48; electoral democracy, 105, 144, 146, 160; electoral market, 123; electoral system, 146–47
"El Gordo de la Semana," 57, 58
Elliot, Philip, 4, 49
El País, 110
"El Show de la Noche," 46
"El Show del Mediodia," 53
Entertainment programs, 57
Entman, Robert, 8
Environment, 70
Espaillat, Arturo, 30
Ethics, 97
Eudes, Yves, 116

Europa World Year Book, 21
Europe, 3
Everyday life and television, 4
Exoo, Calvin, 96

Fabric of symbols, 49
Fairness, 88, 156
Fatt, Arthur C., 69
Ferquido fertilizer, ads, 68
Field research, 80
Financial resources, 108, 142–43, 145–46
Fiore, Quentin, 153
First World, 8
Fiske, John, 7, 63, 69
Flag, of Dominican Republic, 18
Foote, Cone, and Belding, 77
Foreign productions, 42–43, 71
Foucault, Michel, 95
Fox de Cardona, Elizabeth, 28
Framework of reference, 81
France, 13
Frankfurt School, 7, 8
Free society, 71
Free speech, 23, 86–88, 94–95, 105, 157, 161–63
French television, 8, 163
Fuerza Nacional Progresista, 123

Gallo, Max, 65
Game shows, 40
Gandy, Oscar, 106
Gans, Herbert, 105
Garham, Nicholas, 28
Gerbner, George, 63, 73, 88
Germany, 30
Giddens, Anthony, 6
Gitlin, Todd, 64
Golding, Philip, 8, 114
Gomez Díaz family, 25
Government: influence on television, 24, 50, 88, 95, 156–57, 162; repression, 19; and television coverage, 17, 23, 84, 98, 103–5, 107, 118
Gramsci, Antonio, 27
Great Britain, 13, 30

Hall, Leonard, 123
Hall, Stuart, 7, 8, 72
Hegemony, 65, 74
High culture programs, 44, 154
Hollywood, 62
Homogenization, 73
Homosexuality, 60
Horkheimer, Max, 7
Human rights, 71

Ideology: conditioning, 85; dominant, 5, 9, 63–64, 79, 147; political, 36; and television, 8, 36, 58, 65, 73, 126, 145, 159
Imported model, 65
Independencia network, 53
Independent producers, 36–37, 42, 50
Information: and elite, 91–92; flow of, 10, 26, 56–57, 71, 80, 86–87, 160; freedom of, 11, 16, 21, 79, 113, 156; international, 11, 96, 108–11; objectivity of, 81, 88, 95–98, 131, 141–42, 147, 160; source of, 80–81, 85; subsidies, 105–7. *See also* Newscasts
International agencies, 110–11
International editors, 110
International Social-Christian Party, 124
International specialists, 124
International television, 66, 110–11
Interracial marriage, 60
Isa Conde, Narciso, 130, 146
Issues, 121, 124, 155
Iyengar, Shanto, 5, 73

Japan, 27
Jimenez, Léon, 25
Jorge Blanco, Salvador, 24
Journalists' code, 115

Kellner, Douglas, 8
Klapper, Joseph, 7

Latin America, 3, 4, 8
Latin American Savings Association, 104
"La Voz del Yuna," 16, 17
"La Voz Dominicana," 16, 17

Lazarsfeld, Paul, 7
Leacock, Stephen, 66
Learning resource, television as, 57–58
Leftist movements, 144
Le Monde, 110
Lippmann, Walter, 5
Lora Medrano, Luis, 21
Luzón, Hector, 78

Mainstream conventions, 61
Majluta, Jacobo, 123
Marathon shows, 58–59
Marcuse, Herbert, 7
Market: considerations, 25, 46, 47, 49–50, 62, 66, 75; rules, 89, 111, 153, 162; structure, 45, 113, 157, 162
Marketplace, 5, 79, 80, 162
Marlboro, 69
Marriage and the family, 60
Martin del Campo, Alberto, 8
Mass communication, 2, 4, 8, 9, 27–29
Mass culture, 8, 10, 49, 58, 154
Mass media, 2, 4, 7, 28, 73, 75, 147
Mattelart, Armand, 4, 8, 63, 64
McBride Report, 79, 113
McCann-Ericson, 77
McLuhan, Marshall, 7, 153
McQuail, Dennis, 4
Media analysis, 143
Media technologies, 8
Medium of production, 35
Mejia, Juan B., 130
Messiah, leader as, 127
Mexico, 17
Meyer, Diane, 96
"Miami Vice," 62–63
Minow, Newton, 153
MIUCA, 145
Moral teachings, of television, 64
Morley, David, 7
Murdock, George, 8
Musical shows, 39, 59
Myths, 147

National identity, 71
Nationalism, 18

National news, 104, 106, 110. *See also* Newscasts
National realities, 8
NBC, 30, 109–10
Network: control, 17–18, 22–25, 108, 121; rivalry, 37
Newscasts: bias, 111; control, 106; and elite, 158; and ethics, 111; general content, 11, 80–87, 99–103, 108; independence, 156–57; and politics, 121–23; and polls, 107, 128–29; programming, 95–97, 131; and social issues, 158, 159; and spectacle, 121–23; and stereotypes, 153. *See also* Information
Newspapers, 19, 25, 80, 98, 110, 118
New York Times, 109
News production, 5, 81, 84–85, 156
Novelty, 81–82
Nuñez del Risco, Jacky, 31

O.N.E. (Oficina Nacional de Estadisticas), 26
Opinion research firms, 117
Opinion visibility, 160
Oral tradition, 62
Organización Revolucionaria de los Trabajadores, 130
Organizational needs, 107–8
Organizational routines, 111
Organization of American States (OAS), 31
Organization of society, 65
Orientación Mercadológica, S. A., 51
Ornes family, 25
Orwell, George, 10
Ownership: control, 86, 154–62; interests, 27, 158; patterns of television, 5, 162

Paletz, David, 8
Palmer, Michael, 110
Parenti, Michael, 157, 160
Participant observation, 76
Partido Acción Constitucional, 123, 144

Partido de la Liberación Dominicana (PLD), 83, 91, 117–20, 122, 130, 141, 144
Partido Reformista Social Cristiano (PRSC), 24, 117, 119, 120, 122–24, 144
Partido Revolucionario Dominicano (PRD), 32, 91, 117, 122–24, 130, 131, 144
Partido Revolucionario Independiente (PRI), 123
Pascuali, Alberto, 4, 8
Peña Gomes, José Francisco, 32, 119, 123, 124
Pepsi, 69
Personalities, emphasis on, 83–86
Peru, 12
Peynado, Jacinto, 115
Pluralism, 11, 54, 113, 129, 155–56
Political actions, 118, 128
Political campaign, and television, 5, 106, 117, 148
Political consequences, on use of television in politics, 5
Political democratization, 65
Political interests, 143, 158
Political opinion, 47, 119
Political opposition, 15, 19, 22, 126, 141, 146, 157
Political parties, 91, 106–7, 117, 122–23, 126, 143, 161
Political power, 6, 11, 27, 91, 106, 108, 116, 118. See also Power, elite
Political projects, 126, 160
Political spots, 123–25
Political structure, 147
Polls, 107–9
Polysemy, 7, 72
Popular leaders, 103
Postman, Neil, 7
Power: of communication, 142; elite, 5–15, 27, 87, 97, 119, 147, 159–61; relationships, 88, 156–58; of television, 2. See also Economic power; Political power
Pravda, 110

Prerecorded events, 106
Press releases, 106
Profits, and television, 36, 46, 148
Programming, 3, 10, 36–37
Propaganda, 17–18, 105–6, 124
Public agenda, 110–11
Public discourse, 160
Public education, 80
Publicity, 107
Public network, 44, 87, 104–6, 144, 162. See also State-owned network
Public opinion, 88, 159
Public relations, 106
Puerto Rico, 53
"Punto Final," 46

Racial prejudice, 70
Radial observers, 21–22
Radio, 16
Radio Free Europe, 116
Radio Martí, 116
Radio Televisión Dominicana (RTVD), 23, 29, 103–4, 113, 121, 156, 158
Rahintel, 22, 103, 108, 113, 137, 141–42
Ratings, 10–11, 38–43, 155–56
RCA, 30
Real, Michael, 64
Rebeil Corella, María, 8
Representation of life, 70
Reuters, 108–9
Right-wing parties, 144
Roman Catholic. See Catholic church
Roncagliolo, Rafael, 12
Roper organization, 38
Rothschild, Michael, 76
Rules, of television industry, 47–48
Ruling classes, and television control, 8. See also Power, elite
Rural life, 70
Ryan, John, 69

Saatchi and Saatchi, 77
Saliency, of news, 81
Sandinistas, 111

Santo Domingo, 19, 59
Saussez, Thierry, 125
Schiller, Herbert, 8, 156
Schlesinger, Philip, 73
Schramm, Wilbur, 32
Schutz, Alfred, 6
Self-imitating artifacts, 70
Senate, 107
Sexual liberation, 69
Sexual symbols, 60–62, 69–70
Show business, 96–97, 160
Sitcoms, 51
Social class, 10, 47, 130
Social control, and television, 26
Social equality, 95
Social groups, 80
Social identity, 79
Socialist Party, 146
Social mobility, 60
Social organization, 148
Social power, 162
Social processes and television, 3, 4, 88
Social representations, 147
Social structure, and television, 27
Social trends, 80
Social values, 50, 148
Societal change, 158
South Korea, 27
Soviet Union, 30
Sponsors, 10–12, 50–51
Staff independence, 156–57
Staging, 124
Standardization, 7, 47
State apparatus, 146
State enterprises, 127
State-owned network, 29, 59, 91, 103, 107, 121
State ownership, 50
State resources, 146
Stockholders, influence on television content, 33
Structures of power, 5
Subculture, 63, 73
Szulc, Tad, 30

Taiwan, 27
Taveras, Rafael, 119, 130, 146

Teleantillas, 24, 25, 103, 108–9, 113, 137, 141–42
Teleinde, 24
Telemarketing, 122
Telenovelas, 37, 61–62
Telepolitics, 121
Telesistema Dominicano, 24
Televisa, 31
Television: effects, 2–5, 7–8, 114, 159, 160; exposure, 160; as object of ritual, 57; owners, 10, 11; political role, 59; producers, 39, 72; as social agent, 10; sociological significance, 2; technology, 5, 7
Tellis, Gerard, 76
Third World, 8
Thorburn, David, 60
Thorson, Esther, 67
Transnational companies, 10
Trujillo, José Aristides, 16, 17
Trujillo Molina, Rafael Leonidas, 10, 15, 16, 20, 65, 105, 110, 127
Tuchman, Gaye, 8, 112
TV13, 103, 107, 112, 132, 141–42

UNESCO, 21
Uniformity, 47, 155
Union actions, 61
United Nations, 16
United Press International, 108–9
United States, 2, 3, 4, 8
Universal suffrage, 146
University of Santo Domingo, 82
Univisón, 109
"Uno+Uno," 93, 95–97
U.S. manufacturers, 77
U.S. productions, 58
U.S. serials, 39, 58, 62–65, 71

Variety shows, 66, 91
Varis, Tapio, 51
Vatican, 127
Venezuela, 12
Ventura, Johnny, 59
Veras Goico, Freddy, 31, 59

Vicini-Cabral group, 25
Video clips, 73
Villeya–San Miguel, 25
Visuals, 80, 82
Voters, 117, 124. *See also* Elections
Voyeuristic pleasure, 62

Western societies, 77, 153
Wheen, Francis, 31
White House, 116

Wiarda, Howard, 15
Williams, Raymond, 8
Wilson, Charles, 7
Winston cigarettes, 69
Wire agencies, 108
World Health Organization, 68
World War II, 3
Wright Mills, Charles, 9

Young & Rubicam Damaris, 77

About the Author

ANTONIO V. MENÉNDEZ ALARCÓN is scholar at the Kellogg Institute for International Studies. He has been professor of sociology at Indiana University, South Bend; Instituto Tecnológico de Santo Domingo; and Universidad Autónoma de Santo Domingo and has published several books and articles in Spanish. He holds a doctorate from the University of Notre Dame, Indiana, and he earned his bachelor's and master's degrees from the Université de Paris.